THE SPANISH ARMADAS

WINSTON GRAHAM was born in the north of England but has lived most of his life in Cornwall and Sussex. He has been a full-time novelist since he was twenty-three, and his work has ranged from historical novels such as THE GROVE OF EAGLES, which is set in the period of the Spanish armadas, to stories of character and suspense such as MARNIE, and novels in the most contemporary style like ANGELL, PEARL AND LITTLE GOD. His work has been translated into sixteen languages and has been outstandingly successful in the United States, where eight of his books have been major book-club choices. Six of his novels have been filmed, and a sixteen-part serial of his Poldark novels has just been produced on BBC television.

The
Spanish Armadas

Winston Graham

FONTANA/COLLINS

First published in Great Britain in an illustrated edition
by William Collins Sons & Co. Ltd, Glasgow, 1972
This edition first published in Fontana 1976

Copyright © Winston Graham 1972

Set in 9 pt Linotype Pilgrim
Made and printed in Great Britain
by William Collins Sons & Co. Ltd, Glasgow

To Luxton Arnold

Contents

Courses of the
First & Third
Armadas

Shetland

Fair Isle

NORTH
SEA

Edinburgh

August
1588

ATLANTIC
OCEAN

SPLIT BY STORM
September
1588

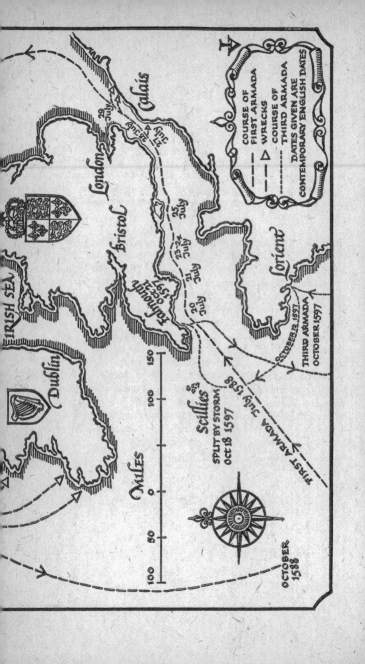

AUTHOR'S NOTE. I would like to thank Miss Ann Hoffman for her invaluable research assistance, my wife for much vital encouragement, Dr A. L. Rowse for helpful criticism and advice, Mr Wilfred Granville and Mr Robert Clark for generously reading the typescript, and Mr Lothar Mendes for some Spanish quotations. I would also thank Frances Partridge and Constable & Co. Ltd for kind permission to use extracts from her translation of Captain de Cuellar's narrative, and Albert J. Loomie and the editor of *The Mariner's Mirror* for equally kind permission to use extracts from his translation of an Armada pilot's survey.

In 1582 Pope Gregory XIII introduced a new calendar, advancing the year by ten days. Continental Europe adopted it, but England for long clung to the old style. A historian of the sixteenth century may advance his dates – as Europe did – when the new calendar came in, and apply it to England. By doing this he alters all the dates which traditionally have been given to events in England by English historians. Or he may, as some English historians do, retain the old Julian calendar throughout, thereby distorting European dates. The only other method is to quote his dates with O.S. (Old System) or N.S. (New System) after each one to indicate his varying choice, a cumbersome and unattractive procedure. Readers of this book are therefore asked to assume that after 1582, where an event refers to the continent of Europe, the new calendar is used; where England, or a continental adventure seen through English eyes, the old. Fortunately the days of the week did not change. The Battle of Gravelines took place on a Monday both in English and Spanish eyes.

W.G.

1

The Peaceful Invasion

Late on Wednesday afternoon on the 18th July 1554, a Flemish squadron cruising in the English Channel off Portland Bill caught sight of a Spanish fleet moving east under full sail in a favourable breeze towards the Solent. The fleet consisted of about a hundred and thirty ships, some hundred of them substantial vessels, well equipped with bronze pieces, and carrying, aside from their crews, over eight thousand Spanish soldiers. A light rain was falling at the time, but the fleet as it approached land was in process of being dressed and beflagged; so the Flemish squadron dipped its flags in salute and fell in as escort. Near the Needles a dozen English naval sloops joined them, and by the morning of the 19th the whole armada was proceeding up the estuary of Southampton Water. It was four in the afternoon before all had dropped anchor under the eye of the castle.

The port of Southampton was flagged too and crowded for the occasion. Hardly one of its three hundred houses was not decorated, hardly one did not shelter some members of the English court, brilliant in velvet, gold chains and medals. Every hovel swarmed with servants, every stable and byre steamed with horses; carts and baggage jammed the greasy cobbled streets. For England, the southern part of a moderate-sized island on the periphery of Europe, was waiting to welcome the greatest prince in Christendom.

It was not difficult to pick out the Prince's ship among the newly arrived fleet, a Biscayan of nine hundred tons, the *Espiritu Santo*, because of the carved and gilded decorations on forecastle and poop. As soon as she came to anchor the bulwarks of this ship had been hung with heavy scarlet cloth; silk pennons fluttered in the damp, sultry breeze and two royal standards, each ninety feet long, of crimson damask with the Prince's arms painted on them, hung from the mainmast and the mizzen. Three hundred sailors in crimson lined the decks.

Soon an ornamented barge left the quayside with a party of gaudy young English noblemen who had been chosen for their looks and their distinction to welcome the Prince. Suspicious eyes from a hundred windows watched them go. Householders, lackeys, sailors, ostlers, rich merchants and fishwives, urchins and beggars, all strained anxiously – and suspiciously – from vantage points to catch a first glimpse of visiting royalty. For he was a Spaniard, his name was Philip, and he had come to marry their Queen.

It had not been a good time, these last twenty years, for the people of England. The autumnal tyrannies of the Great King, his divorces, his quarrels with Rome, his suppression of the monasteries, his persecutions, clouded in people's minds the popularity and goodness of his earlier years. But the decade since Henry's death had been far worse than anything that had gone before. Ever higher prices, the infirmity of central government, the infiltration of the new order everywhere, the enclosure of common land, the raising of rents and the turning out of long-rooted tenants, the disregard for public rights, the neglect of the fleet, and corruption and profiteering on a scale hitherto unknown even in sixteenth-century England, had led all men, or almost all men, to welcome the Queen when cold young Edward died. For years she had been neglected by her father, she had been persecuted by Anne Boleyn, she had been under constant pressure to change her religion, and she had been denied access to her mother, even when her mother lay dying; yet through it all she had retained the quiet loyalty of English people, who saw her the only true heir and swiftly swept aside the pretensions of the Dudleys and Lady Jane Grey.

So, although she was the first queen the English had accepted for four hundred years, she had been crowned with great acclaim, and her early conduct and decrees had seemed conciliatory and clement and reasonable. She had even spared most of those who had conspired against her.

But now, within a year – exactly within a year of Edward's death – she was preparing to marry this foreign prince. The English have always been hypercritical and morbidly suspicious of foreign royalty who presume to marry their queens. They mistrust every gesture of friendship, analyse every public and private utterance he makes for signs of criticism or condescension, and see a plot for foreign domination under every secretary's cloak. It was her marriage to Geoffrey Plantagenet which made Matilda unacceptable in the twelfth century and finally lost her the throne. Mary's betrothal to Prince Philip had nearly done the same for her. Wyatt's formidable rebellion had stopped only at the gates of London.

So Lady Jane Grey had finally gone to the block, but Mary had been unshaken in her resolve to pursue her marriage plans. Half Spanish herself, she saw nothing but good in a union with the future king of Spain. Spain and England had a long tradition of friendship. Henry's divorce of Catherine and England's subsequent apostasy had put some strain on that friendship, but now that England was returning to Catholicism such a union could only help to repair what had been damaged. It was true that Mary was now a virgin of thirty-eight and her husband a young widower of twenty-seven; it was true that they had never met or even corresponded, that all the courtship had been done on behalf of his son by Charles, Philip's father; it was true that Spain was at war with France and that an Anglo-Spanish marriage might drag England into the same war; but the advantages to Mary seemed far to outweigh all these objections.

Indeed, she might have argued – the later example of her half-sister not being available to her – what was a queen to do? Whomsoever she married she would offend someone. And it was essential for the continuance of the Tudor dynasty and the preservation of the Catholic faith that there should be an heir. Who more suitable to father one than a man who was heir to the Holy Roman Empire and who furthermore was a direct descendant of Edward III of England?

The watchers in the windows of all the little houses were not to see their new king that afternoon. Philip remained closely within the confines of his staterooms aboard the *Espiritu Santo* and slept aboard. It was not until the morning of the 20th that he stepped on to the splendid barge awaiting him and was rowed ashore surrounded by English and Spanish noblemen. On the barge the Earl of Arundel invested him with the Garter, and was in return presented with the wand of Chamberlain. The rain had temporarily eased when Prince Philip stepped ashore, so he was able to listen in more comfort to the Latin speech of welcome delivered by the enormous Sir Anthony Browne and to receive the gift of the white charger which the Queen had sent to him to greet him on arrival. The Prince said he would walk to the house prepared for him, but at this Sir Anthony demurred and 'took him up in his arms and put him on the saddle'. Thereupon, preceded by all the English and Spanish courtiers and nobles, he passed through the curious and mistrustful and largely silent crowd to the Church of the Holy Rood to return thanks for his safe arrival.

What sort of man did the English see? An impressive figure, despite his medium height and slight build, for he was in black and silver, hung with gold chains and glittering with jewels on coat and bonnet and breast. A quiet dignified young man – looking younger than his years – with a gracious manner and a charming, diffident smile. Titan's portrait of him, painted about this time and now in the museum in Naples, shows him to have a high forehead, strong up-growing rather short-cropped blond hair, firm winged eyebrows over heavy-lidded eyes, full lips, and a trace of a moustache and blond beard partly hiding the Hapsburg jaw. Not a young man, one would think, to whom women would be indifferent. Mary, when she met him, was not indifferent.

He had inherited considerable charm from his mother Isabella of Portugal, and he chose to exercise it upon the English. In the next weeks he was to need it all, not only to soften the distrust of the English but to allay the resentments of his own nobility who were to find themselves everywhere brusquely treated, and cheated and robbed at the slightest excuse. Of all the eight-thousand-odd Spanish soldiers, not one was allowed to land. The fleet was sent off to Portsmouth to revictual and the troops dispatched to the Netherlands. The Spanish guard were kept in frustrated idleness on board one of the few ships remaining in Southampton Water, and attendance on the Prince was confined to Englishmen only. The noble Spanish watched in disgust at the – to their eyes – unrefined attempts of the English to wait on their new master.

And it rained: how it rained! The weather in that century was nearly always on the side of the English, and now it weighed in with a commentary to suit the mood of the most convinced Lutheran. For all of the three days Prince Philip remained in Southampton it rained so hard that the Spanish prince had to borrow a cape and hat to cross the street from his lodging to the church. When he eventually rode to Winchester for the wedding with an escort of three thousand nobles and retainers, halberdiers, archers and light horse, the weather was so bad that he was compelled to stop a mile from the city in the shelter of a recently dispossessed monastery to change his finery before entering the city.

Thereafter followed his welcome at the doors of the great cathedral by a sonority of mitred bishops, a procession to the high altar, sung Mass, and all the ceremonial by which God's anointed was greeted in a foreign but friendly land. This was Monday, and the wedding was not until Wednesday, but in the evening of Monday Queen Mary, unable longer to restrain her curiosity, sent secretly from the bishop's palace, saying she wished to meet him informally at ten o'clock that night and to bring only a select few of his retinue.

The events of their first meeting, as described by the Spaniards who accompanied the Prince, are in strange contrast with the reputation that Philip has been given by English, French and American historians of later centuries. It is hard to reconcile his behaviour with the picture of the monster many of them draw : the persecutor of the Netherlands, the bigot, the fanatic, the cold-blooded despot. Yet perhaps it is all – or nearly all – true. Perhaps age and authority changes men. Who, seeing Mary's father as the golden-haired boy coming to his throne and winning the hearts of his people at eighteen, could have foreseen the dangerous and unpredictable tyrant of his last years?

Prince Philip accepted the invitation of his future wife, but the 'select few' of his entourage amounted to more than twenty noblemen. On this point he was taking no risks. The party entered the bishop's palace by way of a back door and mounted a spiral stone staircase to the room where the Queen was waiting, attended only by Gardiner – the all-powerful Lord Chancellor and Bishop of Winchester, who had spent five years in the Tower for his religious principles – and by some dozen elderly noblemen and noblewomen. All women of her own age or younger Mary had excluded.

Tonight she was wearing a high-cut black velvet gown, a petticoat of frosted silver, a black velvet gold-trimmed wimple covering the head and sides of the face, and some of the finest diamonds at throat and waist that the English crown possessed. Mary at thirty-eight was a slim, rather small woman whose fair hair had become mousy in colour, and she seldom wore it about her face. Her eyes were grey and unwavering under sandy lashes and scarcely existent eyebrows. Her complexion, though naturally pale, was good and still youthful. She had a strong, rather deep voice and a warmth and sincerity of manner that was not leavened by self-criticism or a sense of humour.

Philip at once bowed and went towards her, first accepting her hand and then kissing her full on the lips in what he said was 'the English manner'. It was a greeting that she clearly did not find distasteful; and she led him by the hand to two chairs placed under a brocade canopy where they sat talking in private for a long time. Presently the Prince asked if he might meet the Queen's ladies-in-waiting, and reluctantly she took him into the next room where they were all assembled, many of these being young and pretty girls. Philip kissed the lot. Again he claimed it was the English custom and no one denied him.

Afterwards Mary led him back into her private room and they chatted together for a further half hour. She was captivated. It was now well after midnight and Philip rose to go, but said that he must first return to the ante-chamber to wish the ladies-in-waiting good night. How did one say this in English? The Queen taught him, and he started for the door, only to return laughing to say that he had forgotten already. Playfully she coached him again, and, repeating 'God ni hit' half under his breath, he returned to the ladies to salute them once more.

'Fickle Philip' he was sometimes called by his friends. It all seems a long way from 'the Spider of the Escorial'.

The wedding took place on the Wednesday, still in the pouring rain. Not for nothing had the cathedral been dedicated to St Swithin. But in its five hundred years of history there could never have been a more brilliant scene than this. Philip wore a white satin suit and a mantle of cloth of gold embroidered with jewels. The Queen again wore black velvet, but was so ablaze with precious stones that she seemed on fire. Her fifty ladies, according to the Spanish, 'looked more like celestial angels than mortal creatures'. The long ritual completed and the Mass done, the King of the Heralds, preceded by a blast of silver trumpets, proclaimed the titles of their majesties: 'Philip and Mary, by the grace of God King and Queen of England, France, Naples, Jerusalem and Ireland, Defenders of the Faith, Princes of Spain and Sicily, Archdukes of Austria, Dukes of Milan, Burgundy and Brabant, Counts of Hapsburg, Flanders and Tyrol.' It was a formidable list.

When the wedding was at last over, the King and Queen

walked side by side to the palace through the crowd, which behaved with notable restraint. At the palace was a banquet for one hundred and fifty-eight, with four services of meat and fish, each service comprising thirty dishes, and endless toasts and more ceremonial, swords of state and ritual staffs, and loving cups. The Spaniards noted that Mary was served on gold plate, Philip on silver; she, too, had the higher chair, was given precedence in everything. The English were leaving them in no doubt as to how they saw the future. Only one Spaniard was allowed to serve the King at table, elsewhere ever since he landed his attendants had been English, the Spanish pushed out.

The meal lasted until six, then dancing until nine. Here there was difficulty, as the Spanish gentlemen and the English ladies did not know the same steps. Philip and Mary solved the problem by dancing in the German style. As night fell candles and torches lit the brilliant scene, but soon the King and Queen retired, not surprisingly after the fatigues and tensions of the arduous day. Mary's mother, so steadfast in her loyalty to the country of her birth and the faith of her ancestors, would have been happy to have seen that night. It looked as if friendship with Spain was restored and re-cemented and a permanent return to the Old Faith guaranteed.

What went wrong? Clearly Mary's inability to produce a child. Had a son been born it seems certain that the English, however much they hated the union which produced him, would have accepted him as their king. He would have been a male Tudor in direct descent from the two Henrys who had founded the line. The only other possible claimants were women.

The idea of Philip and Mary's union had originated with Philip's father, the Emperor Charles V, and had it succeeded it would have been a stroke of political statecraft of the first magnitude. In order to appreciate it one has to look at Philip's ancestry and at the map of Europe.

Philip's grandfather, Philip the Handsome, had married Joanna, daughter of Ferdinand of Aragon and Isabella of Castile, so combining the powerful houses of Hapsburg and Burgundy with the Spanish royal dynasty. Philip the Handsome died when Charles, Philip's father, was only six, and a succession of other deaths and misfortunes so struck the families with which he was connected that Charles before he was nineteen became master of a domain greater than Charlemagne's. To his possessions in the Low Countries and Spain were added Mexico, Peru, the Isthmus, the Caribbean Islands, Aragon, Catalonia, the Balearics, Naples and Sicily, Austria, Styria, Tyrol, Carinthia and Germany.

So the boy Charles became Charles V, Holy Roman Emperor. Born in 1500 in Ghent, Charles soon showed himself to be an able and autocratic ruler. A strong-willed, lusty and vigorous man, ever indulging his appetites, ever travelling about his domains, down-to-earth, practical, astute, gluttonous, he was both the savage persecutor of heretics and the brave defender of Christendom from the Turks. But the strain of kingship and the arduous life he lived wore down even his iron constitution, and by the time he was fifty-four he was an exhausted and sickly man. In 1540 he had created his son Duke of Milan, and, on his marriage to Mary of England, made over to him the Kingdom of Naples. With rare wisdom Charles had become convinced that the empire he had inherited was too unwieldy ever to be successfully governed by one man, and already he had given his brother Ferdinand his Austrian possessions. For the rest, he planned that Philip's son by his first wife, the infant Don Carlos, should succeed in Spain and that the child of Philip and Mary should inherit not only England but the Netherlands, thus taking the Low Countries away from Spain and giving them a strength and protection from across the Channel. One empire would become three kingdoms, each independent of the others, but all in friendly and fraternal alliance.

If Don Carlos died, Mary's child was to be King of Spain and of all Spain's vast possessions in the New World too. It is not surprising that Mary had so much to hope for.

And in those first weeks, despite the sullen looks of the English, all seemed well. It was true that the Duchess of Alva was highly offended at missing the wedding. She arrived from Southampton three days late, and even Mary's reception of her did not assuage her injured dignity. When she was presented, with splendid ceremonial, the Queen came to meet her and kissed her and, there being only one chair in the room, would not take precedence over her by sitting on it so suggested that they should both sit together on the floor. Not to be outdone in courtesy, the Duchess insisted that *she* only would sit on the floor. Mary therefore sent for two stools, and the comedy continued with first one on a stool and then both on the floor and then the other up and the first down, until at last they were seated side by side and talking amicably about something other than precedence. (The Duchess was offended all over again when the Earl of Derby tried to kiss *her* on the mouth. No one had had the impertinence to attempt such a thing ever before, and even though she was able to turn her cheek to him she could not contain her annoyance.)

The new and as yet uncrowned King of England used every grace and charm to engage the affections of his new subjects. He distributed gifts of silver to all the lords of the council and to many others besides. He promised pensions of thirty thousand ducats annually. He cancelled a debt of two and a quarter million ducats that his new wife owed him. He treated everyone he met with the utmost courtesy, and scrupulously avoided any hint of interference in the affairs of the kingdom. Writing home to Spain a month after the wedding, one of his stewards, Don Pedro Enriquez, a nephew of the Duke of Alva, says:

> Their majesties are the happiest couple in the world, and are more in love with each other than I can say here. He never leaves her, and on the road is always by her side, lifting her into the saddle and helping her to dismount. He dines with her publicly sometimes, and they go to mass together on feast days.

By this date they were at Richmond on their way to Hampton Court. The great gatherings at Winchester and Southampton had dispersed. Those of the English who were not in actual attendance on their majesties had galloped off home to their baronial estates. The Spanish were in less happy case. The Admiral of Spain was on his way back with part of his fleet to Coruña; the rest had convoyed the troops to Flanders. There still remained some hundred noblemen with their servants, who had accompanied the Prince and who now in desultory fashion followed him to London.

Among them discontent at their early treatment had been succeeded by profound disillusion. The English were crude and ungentlemanly. And very unfriendly. There was no attempt on *their* part to hide their feelings. It was a barbaric country, full of heretics and renegades. The Spaniards found themselves jeered at in the streets, overcharged wherever they went, and actually attacked by vagabonds if they strayed far afield. Don Juan de Pacheco was robbed of a large sum of money and all his jewellery. The monks had to keep out of sight for fear of being set upon. Even such grandees as the Duke of Alva were given inferior lodgings on the way. When they reached London it was little better. There were constant quarrellings, and one week three English and one Spaniard were hanged for brawling. Two of the most distinguished of Philip's knights were set on in the streets by a raucous crowd who had taken offence at their costume and tried to strip it off their backs. What was worse, the political outcome of the marriage seemed likely to be far from what they had hoped. The Queen was surrounded by a group of powerful and suspicious councillors who would block as far as they could any Spanish influence over her decisions.

Soon the Spanish noblemen were craving their Prince's leave to go, and by late September all had slipped away except for Alva and four others and their personal servants. Thankfully the dukes and marquises, the counts and the knights took ship for home, bearing with them a memory of a land of uncivil and unpolished barbarians. But also a land of richness and plenty, the halls of the nobles doubly resplendent with the loot of the despoiled monasteries; a land of beautiful open harbours, of green fields and abundant flowers, of great flocks of sheep, of splendid palaces and churches and populous and prosperous villages and towns. They were memories that would linger long in the minds of the visitors. They had come to conquer in friendship. But they had received no friendship. The first Spanish invasion of England was nearly over.

Philip stayed a little over a year. During that time Mary fell completely in love with him, and she adored him for the rest of her short life.

In November Cardinal Pole returned from Rome to be made Archbishop of Canterbury, and was greeted with great joy by both Mary and Philip. On the 30th Pole solemnly absolved the Lords and Commons and the whole country from their apostasy and accepted England back into the Roman Catholic Church. At the end of the year the old heresy laws were revived, and the first Protestant was burned at the stake on the 4th February 1555.

It is difficult to apportion the blame for the reign of terror that spread through England, mainly in the south and east, for the next three and a half years. Pole certainly was the instrument of Rome; yet during his fourteen years of exile in Viterbo his rule was firm but mild: no record of the persecution of heretics. Gardiner was a controversial figure, deeply involved in many of the heresy trials; yet in his own diocese no victim suffered the fire until after his death. Bonner, Bishop of London, bears the stigma of the largest number of victims condemned in any diocese; but he was several times taken to task by the Privy Council for not being severe enough.

At the time, of course, the odium fell on Philip. The young man whose father had striven to root out heresy in his own kingdom wherever he found it and had burned the first Lutheran martyrs in Brussels in 1523, the young man who a few years later when attending a royal *Auto-da-fé* at Valladolid stated that 'if my own son was a heretic, I would carry wood to burn him myself', the young man who as he grew older grew steadily more fanatical in his hatred of Calvinism, would seem the natural instigator of the fires of Smithfield. Yet the evidence shows that he constantly urged moderation and clemency on his wife and her ministers. This may have been a piece of political calculation undertaken to endear him to his enemies. If so it failed. But if it were so it showed a degree of statecraft that would have served him well in later life. One can only conclude that at this date Mary was the more rigid sectarian, and that her charity towards her enemies – which she showed even to those who had tried to rob her of her throne – did not extend towards the enemies of her Catholic faith.

Of course some of the Protestants who burned did make things difficult for themselves. What could one do, for instance, with a preacher who on New Year's Eve 1555 offered up prayers from his pulpit for the Queen's death?

In November 1554 Mary announced that she was with child, and thanksgiving services were held in London churches. In March 1555 there were joustings, and the King and Queen spent Easter at Hampton Court. By May it became clear that Mary had been mistaken. In August Philip received word of his father's decision to abdicate in his favour, and on the 3rd September he left Dover to cross to Calais and ride to Brussels, where in the Hall of the Golden Fleece he formally accepted the sovereignty of the Netherlands. Early in the following year he became King of Spain.

Affairs of state, which were all-demanding, kept him away from England and his wife for eighteen months. When he returned in March 1557 and was reunited with Mary, it was to urge that England should honour her alliance with Spain and declare war on France. Easter they spent at Greenwich, together with the Duchess of Alva and the Duchess of Lorraine. But he was restive and unsettled and cold towards Mary. There are accounts of banquets and Garter processions and noble stag-hunts at Hampton Court in company with members of the Privy Council. On the 7th June England entered into a war for which she was completely unprepared, and soon after Philip announced his departure. On the 3rd July he and his Queen set out for Dover, spending a night at Sittingbourne. Mary was weak and ailing, and grieved at the thought of another separation. When he left her on the 5th July neither of them was to know that it was their last meeting. In sixteen months she was dead. Philip was never to visit England again. One other event of great consequence occurred during Philip's visits to England. He met the tall, pale, slim, auburn-haired girl of twenty-one who was to succeed Mary and who was to be his adversary all his life.

At the end of April 1555 the Queen, still convinced that she was pregnant, went to Hampton Court to await her confinement, and, this being perhaps the happiest time in her joyless life, with Philip still beside her and the expectation of bearing his child, her feelings softened towards her half-sister. She had never forgotten the ignominy and humiliation thrust upon her and her mother by this girl's mother; yet although Elizabeth was kept in close confinement, Mary had been unable or unwilling to have her put to death, as she was often urged to do. Now in the warmth and burgeoning of her life (a fruitful marriage to a man she loved, a heart-warming return of England to the Old Faith) reconciliation and forgiveness were in the air. A modest forgiveness, anyhow. Elizabeth was summoned from Woodstock, but was allowed to bring only five servants and she rode under heavy guard. The journey took four days, and she entered Hampton Court by a back gate and was lodged in rooms recently vacated by the Duke of Alva.

This meant she was near the King, and it gives a ring of truth to the account given by Antoine de Noailles, the French Ambassador, and confirmed by Giovanni Michieli, the Venetian Ambassador, that Philip visited Elizabeth secretly, before his formal introduction to her in the presence of Mary. It would not be surprising if he were curious to meet this young woman, still a heretic, but known to be witty and popular wherever she went, the issue of that scandalous and adulterous union between Henry VIII and his so-called second wife. Recently suspected of complicity in plots to dethrone Mary, walking a tight-rope to save her life, living in a world where every innocent word had to be watched lest it smell of treason, yet firmly named by her father as the next successor to the throne – as if no question of her legitimacy had ever crossed his mind – Elizabeth was very clearly a person of the greatest interest to Mary's husband.

Later, when Mary at last consented to see Elizabeth and taxed her angrily with plotting against her throne, there is the well-known story that Philip hid behind the arras and listened – so far as he could follow it – to what was being said. Another account states that after the first formal meeting Mary sent Philip for a private conversation with Elizabeth to try to persuade her to confess her errors and throw herself on the mercy of the Queen.

In any event it is unquestionable that Philip and Elizabeth got on well together. Philip, at least until his middle years, always had an eye for a pretty girl, and Elizabeth, if not exactly pretty, had grace and vitality and charm and the in- effable glamour of youth – a very different person from the intent, plain, spinster-like, delicate woman who was his wife. As for Elizabeth, all her life she was susceptible, and Philip was not quite twenty-eight. He was a prince, had a charming courtesy of manner, and he was a potential ally. And she was most certainly a maiden in distress. More than ever in her life before or after, at that moment, she sorely needed an ally. Michieli, reporting later to Venice, wrote : 'At the time of the Queen's pregnancy Lady Elizabeth contrived so to ingratiate herself with all the Spaniards and especially the King, that ever since no one has favoured her more than he does', and that 'the King had some particular design towards her.'

No doubt their friendship was politic on either side, but it was a genuine attraction too. Mary became jealous – it was the last emotion that Elizabeth would have wished to arouse – and Philip saw little more of her. But she was *preserved*. Philip pressed Mary to promise this before he left England. He also pressed it on various members of the Council and received an assurance from them. After being kept in close confinement at a house a few miles from Hampton Court, Elizabeth was permitted to see Philip off at Greenwich on his way to Dover at the end of August, though she was not allowed to take part in the state procession.

It is improbable that Philip saw Elizabeth on his second visit, for she was at Hatfield. There he sent the Duchess of Parma and the Duchess of Lorraine to press Elizabeth into a marriage with Emmanuel Philibert, Duke of Savoy. This would have meant that, if Mary died, the new Prince Consort would have been a devoted friend of Spain and an enemy of France. But Elizabeth, with that genius for dissimulation and delay she was to show so often, succeeded in putting off a decision until the crisis was past.

So Mary, after hoping a second time, though less publicly, that she was with child, slowly slid into her last illness and died, as sad a woman as she had lived, at the age of forty-two. When he knew of her grave illness King Philip pleaded pressure of business and sent Count de Feria to represent him. When Mary died de Feria made it known to the Privy Council that the King of Spain would support Elizabeth's claim to the throne.

Shortly after Elizabeth was crowned Count de Feria craved a private audience of the new Queen and there presented to her Philip's formal proposal of marriage. The proposal was couched in warmly diplomatic terms; but, being a Spanish prince, Philip forbade his ambassador to remind Elizabeth of any favour that she might owe him. It appears, however, that de Feria disobeyed his royal master, for Elizabeth's reply is documented in a manuscript still lying in the Spanish archives in Simancas. 'It is the *people* who have placed me in the position I at present hold as the declared successor to the Crown.'

2

Philip and Elizabeth

When in 1514 Louis XII of France lost his Queen, Anne of
Brittany, Henry VIII of England proposed a marriage between
Louis and his youngest sister Mary. Louis, who was fifty-two,
agreed to the match. Mary was eighteen and passionately in
love with the rich and charming Charles Brandon, later Duke
of Suffolk. She stormed and raged and wept at her brother's
decision, but finally had to surrender to it. When at last she
sailed to meet her French husband in October of that year a
splendid retinue accompanied her; among them a pretty little
maid of honour called, in the *Cottonian MSS.*, Madamoyselle
Boleyn.

The following January the narrow-shouldered and sickly
Louis died – they said that his English wife danced him to
death – and the young Queen contrived after some vicissitudes
to marry her charming duke and retire to Suffolk, where in
the due course of time she became the grandmother of Lady
Jane Grey. Madamoyselle Boleyn, however, stayed on at the
French court until 1522 when she returned to England, with
consequences that we all know.

Madamoyselle Boleyn's daughter ascended the English throne
in 1558. She had the disadvantage, like Mary, of being a
woman, with the added drawback of being, in the eyes of
many of her subjects, illegitimate. All Henry's thunderings
and contrivings failed to convince the people that his true wife
was not alive in the person of Catherine of Aragon when he
married Anne Boleyn; and when Elizabeth was born some of
the junketings and bonfires held throughout England were
privately to celebrate that the child was but a girl and Henry
had only got his just deserts.

Yet twenty-five years later England – which throughout its
history had refused, often to its cost, to consider talented and
brave royal bastards as having any claim to the throne at all

— accepted this girl without hesitation, indeed with great rejoicing.

The reasons are numerous and quite clear. Henry VIII's will still counted for something in people's minds. And there was no alternative male of the Tudor line. The only alternative, and legitimate, female was married to the Dauphin of France, which put her right out of the running. The majority of the country, although preferring the old forms of worship, did not like being under the tutelage of Rome. The new rich, although confirmed in some of their spoils by Mary, felt safer with a Protestant ruler. Everybody — except a crust of rigid fanatics — was disgusted and revolted by Mary's reign of terror. And Protestantism under persecution had increased rapidly through the country. These reasons, and a last personal one: Elizabeth was already popular and a convincing figure among those who knew her, and the word had spread.

Yet it was a sorely tried young woman who came to the throne. When one thinks of the abnormalities that psychiatrists today blame upon the relatively minor traumas of youth, Elizabeth's level head, emotional stability and unwavering judgment are qualities to be wondered at. No king's daughter of those days could have a simple and placid childhood, constantly, as they were, in the spotlight of court interest and an inevitable pawn in the matrimonial game of European power politics. But Elizabeth's mother had been beheaded for adultery when Elizabeth was two years and eight months old. Thereafter she was taught that her mother was an evil woman and that she was herself a bastard. When she was eight her stepmother and cousin, Katherine Howard, was executed for similar reasons. Fawned upon or ignored according to the whim of her father, she had endured the sexual attentions of one Seymour and the suspicions of another, had been the inevitable focus of plotting Protestantism under Mary and had been sent to the Tower, from which few royal personages ever safely emerged. Now at an age when most young women were happy to spend their time choosing a dress or a husband, she found herself on the lonely eminence of a throne, surrounded by advisers whose integrity she could only assess by her own fallible judgment, without a near relative on whom she could safely lean; and Queen of a country that was torn by religious bigotry, almost bankrupt, in the grip of inflation, the army defeated and the navy neglected, and at war with the French — who now had one foot in Calais and the other in Scotland.

24

It was a daunting prospect.

One of the most daunting features of it was the emergence from their holes in Germany and Switzerland of all those Protestant exiles and Calvinist fanatics who had fled the country during the Marian persecutions and who were now returning post-haste to exact their revenge and to scour out the kingdom and cleanse it of the last vile vestiges of Popery. And, only two weeks after Elizabeth's accession, news reached her that when the announcement of Mary's death reached France the King had proclaimed his daughter-in-law to be the true Queen of England; and from that time Mary Queen of Scots and her husband the Dauphin of France began to quarter the royal arms of England with their own.

In these conditions Count de Feria waited upon the young Queen and brought her news of Philip's proposal of marriage. She thanked him and said she would consider the matter.

It is quite possible that she did consider the matter. They had met and been attracted to each other. They were of suitable age – he only six years the elder. His attempts while in England to moderate Mary's persecution of the Protestants suggested that at heart he put politics above religion, as Elizabeth proposed to do. Further confirmation of this, as she would certainly see with her acute mind, lay in his preserving her and supporting her accession to the throne; for, apart from her desirability as a woman, he had no doubt concluded that it was better to have an independent Protestant on the English throne than a Catholic bound to France. Also Elizabeth knew of the inheritance promised to a child of Mary's marriage, and therefore one could assume the same for any child of hers if Philip were the father. It was not to be lightly dismissed.

Probably she toyed with it for a while, knowing in her heart that the bitterness which Mary had created in England towards Rome and Spain would make such a marriage virtually unworkable. A Catholic Elizabeth? They would not tolerate it. A Protestant Elizabeth with a Catholic husband? Balance and counterpoise. How better to preserve the country from the worst excesses of religious bigotry? It was just worth considering.

She was still considering some months later when she learned that Philip, despairing of an answer, had married the French princess, Elizabeth of Valois, instead. She said in annoyance to de Feria: 'Your master must have been *much* in love with me not to be able to wait four months!' Yet she continued to keep his portrait in her private cabinet all through the long years ahead, while friendly rivalry gave way to hostility and hostility at last to war.

The disruptive forces of the sixteenth century were too strong for all but the wisest and most cautious of rulers. Charles V, Philip's father, the last and one of the greatest of the Holy Roman Emperors, abdicated from his throne and his responsibilities and retired a broken man to the monastery of Yuste where he died in 1558, conscious that most of his ideals had come to nothing and that all his strivings and battles to preserve Christian unity had foundered. For they had come into conflict with intolerances worse than his own.

He was foredoomed to fail, as Philip failed after him. When Charles was born, Martin Luther was a chorister of seventeen waiting to read law at the university of Erfurt. Twenty-two years later, a noble and formerly dissolute Spaniard of thirty-one, Ignatius of Loyola, fasting in his cell in a Dominican convent and spending seven hours a day on his knees, began to have visions of the Virgin and her Blessed Son which led to the foundation of the Society of Jesus. At about the same date a Swiss boy, John Calvin by name, was sent by his parents to Paris to avoid the plague, and it was not many years before he too had a vision which convinced him that he alone was the chosen voice of God. In 1480 the Inquisition had been instituted, primarily then as an anti-Jewish measure, by the chaplain to Queen Isabella, a Dominican friar called Tomas de Torquemada, and had spread throughout Spain. So the forces for Reformation and Counter-Reformation were poised. An emperor who sought to reconcile these forces, whether by reason or by arms, was trying to subdue an earthquake.

Because of this religious conflict, the sixteenth became the bloodiest, bitterest century in Europe until the ignoble twentieth dawned. For, in whatever mood the Reformation was conceived, by the middle of the century its tolerance was as narrow, as cruel and as bigoted as the Catholic opposition. As John Buchan once said, there is no such disruptive force as a common creed held with a difference. Looking at the picture of devastation and persecution, particularly in France and the Low Countries, it is hard to believe that both sides could so completely have lost sight of the principles of the founder of their faith and of the tenets of tolerance, charity, loving kindness, humility and brotherly love that he preached. At least in the twentieth century some of the cleavages, some of the issues, seem to have been real. One believes that even when viewed from the perspective of four hundred years they may still appear to have been real. But in the sixteenth, both sides committed the atrocities they did carrying the same New Testament in their hands.

Yet as it happens most of the rulers of the day, excepting Philip, were humanists. Catherine de' Medici, although she bears the terrible stigma of the massacre of St Bartholomew, was no religious fanatic, and, so long as it ministered to the well-being of her house and children, she was all for moderation. William of Orange, though in a sense a willing prisoner of the Reformed Church, since it alone provided the dynamic of revolt, was personally a believer in freedom of conscience and worship for everyone. Henry of Navarre changed his religion twice – once to save his life and once to gain his kingdom. The rule of Mary Queen of Scots was perhaps too brief and stormy to assess, but her son James would certainly not have allowed a mere sectarianism to obstruct his view of the main chance, and it was he who shrewdly observed that 'one Puritan presbiter equals one Papist priest'.

The most successful of all these rulers was the one most successful in balancing the disruptive forces which threatened her kingdom, first from within and then from without. Elizabeth was fortunate in that the great mass of the people of her kingdom shared her views: they wanted the Anglicanism of Henry, not the fanatical Çalvinism of Edward's time nor the savage Catholicism of Mary. They were fortunate in that they found in her the perfect expression of their will. Early in her reign she remarked that there was only one Jesus Christ and one faith, the rest was dispute over trifles.

In the destruction of the monasteries the bones of St Frideswide of Oxford, a holy woman who died in 735 after founding a nunnery on the site of the cathedral there, were cast out upon a dung heap, and the body of the wife of a Canon of Christ Church, a distinguished Protestant divine, was buried in their place. When Mary succeeded, the remains of the newly dead lady were thrown out too. On Elizabeth's accession a dispute arose among the Canons as to who should be reinterred in the place of honour in the cathedral. Elizabeth's reply was terse and to the point, and with great ceremony the bones of the two women were reburied together.

It was a portent of the new reign; and only the cold winds of bigotry from outside England, the revolt in the Netherlands, the bloody massacres in France, the anathemas of Rome, the claims of Mary of Scotland and the threat of invasion from Spain, forced Elizabeth and her Council into the narrowing restrictive measures of the 1580s.

Elizabeth and Philip corresponded from time to time in the early years of their reigns. Indeed both were assiduous correspondents and devoted workers at the tasks to which God had called them. Elizabeth, who spoke French and Italian fluently by the time she was eleven and could write to her brother in Latin at thirteen, dealt with visiting potentates without needing an interpreter and treated her Council early to the quality of her mind and tongue. Perhaps the most English of monarchs since Harold, she never left the country even to visit her grandfather's Wales.

Philip, although his mother was Portuguese and his father born in Ghent of Burgundian blood, was as true a Spaniard at heart as Elizabeth was English. After his return from England he travelled little and was only happy in Spain. And unlike his father, who was a big clumsy man of enormous appetites and popular appeal, Philip was reserved, dignified, quiet-mannered, proud, the perfect Spanish grandee. He became as well loved in Spain as Elizabeth did in England and gave expression to the Spanish will as truly as she did to the English.

The period following his marriage to Elizabeth of Valois was the happiest of his life. He fell in love with the fourteen-year-old princess, who was fresh and charming and appeared untouched by the corrupt French court in which she had been brought up. She bore him two daughters, who were always his favourite children, and died when she was twenty-three – almost inevitably – in childbirth. By this time Philip was forty-one and had shouldered the responsibilities of kingship for thirteen years. It had aged him, made him more cautious, more exacting, more set in his religious convictions and more prone to withdraw from court society. More than ever he sought not compromises but solutions to every problem. (Elizabeth of England, on the contrary, had realized that solutions are rare in politics; if one shelves a problem often enough it may in the end disappear. At least it is likely to be superseded by another more urgent!)

By this time Philip had just begun his life's monument by laying the foundation stone for his great palace-monastery of El Escorial, dedicated to St Lawrence the Martyr, whose convent in St Quentin had been burned by Spanish troops when taking the town from the French in 1557. Ever since, Philip, who had a special devotion to this saint, had been looking for a suitable site to build a commemorative monastery near his new capital of Madrid. From 1563 until 1584 the great project was in process of building, employing three thousand workmen for over twenty-one years and costing in all over three and a half million ducats. Whenever he could spare the time in those early years Philip would go to a seat quarried out of rock at the foot of the mountains called the Hermits to watch the work in progress. The building was designed to the shape of an upturned gridiron, the instrument on which St Lawrence was put to death, and four great towers one hundred and eighty feet high represented the feet of the gridiron. The whole giant sombre building is six hundred and eighty-two feet long and five hundred and eighty-one feet deep, and is settled on the south-western slopes of the Guadarramas, with the gaunt and gloomy mountains rising behind. Without shelter and exposed as it is to the searing heat of summer and the blighting winds of winter, it has a loneliness and a harshness and a dignity peculiarly in keeping with the nature of the King who conceived it. Built of dark grey almost greenish granite, it has seven towers, fifteen gateways and twelve thousand windows and doors, almost all of them small, and within the building the great monastery church resembles St Peter's, Rome.

Yet, despite its forbidding appearance, the interior of the Escorial when it was completed showed the rich garnerings of an Empire. White and coloured marbles from the Apennines, green and black jaspers from Granada, wrought bronze from Flanders, veined and spotted alabaster from Tuscany, rose-coloured coral from Sardinia, delicate ironwork from Aragon, all contributed to the magnificence. The new woods of the Indies had been brought to combine with fine brocades from Florence, crystal chandeliers from Venice and the silk damasks of Seville. Artists and sculptors had worked for two decades decorating the walls and ceilings with carvings and frescoes, statuary and paintings.

Even so, it is still more the pantheon than the palace, and

here in due time Philip brought many of his relatives to be reburied, including his father and mother, Charles and Isabella; his aunts, Queen Leonore of Portugal and Queen Mary of Hungary; his first wife Maria; his two brothers, Don Fernando and Don Juan, who had died in infancy; his son Don Carlos; his half-brother Don John of Austria; and his grandmother Joanna, who had been insane for thirty-nine years before she died. Picturing this slightly-built, humourless, deeply religious, self-contained man sitting with his cloak wrapped round him to protect him from the winds of the Sierras, watching the slow growth of his own monastery and his own tomb, one thinks of the fourth dynasty Egyptians building their great pyramids at Giza. Perhaps no one since the Pharaohs has been so preoccupied with death. Perhaps no one since the Pharaohs has so closely intermarried as did the Hapsburgs of Philip's time. The result was a strain of insanity running through the family, together with hyperaesthesia and melancholia.

At the time of the death of Elizabeth of Valois, Philip's son, Don Carlos, also died, after being imprisoned in his rooms for six months hopelessly insane. Six years earlier he had seriously injured his head in a fall and had almost died; and some blame this fall for the deterioration which followed. But the Venetian Ambassador, writing soon after the accident, says that for three years Don Carlos had 'suffered an alienation of the mind'. It was the dread hereditary weakness claiming another victim.

These deaths left Philip without a wife and without a male heir, but there is no record of his having approached Elizabeth again. In the ten years since she came to the throne the two countries had drifted too far apart on the tides of religious conflict. A political system in Europe which had endured since the last decades of the fifteenth century was dissolving, and no man knew how – or if ever – it would solidify again.

3

The Widening Chasm

For some seventy years the pattern of alignment in Europe had been relatively unchanged. On the one side was the Holy Roman Empire, a loosely associated group of nations and states, consisting of Spain, Germany, Italy and the Netherlands, to which, ever since Henry VII had concluded an alliance with Spain, England and the Tudors had adhered. Confronting this group, almost surrounded by it, and relatively smaller, but powerful, homogeneous and militant, was France, to which Scotland under the Stuarts was allied.

Now the explosion of the religious dynamic shattered these easily drawn frontiers. The revolt in the Netherlands gradually drew English sympathy towards the struggling co-religionists of the Low Countries and away altogether from Spain; and the rapid spread of Calvinism in Scotland meant an inevitable strain on her relations with a still Catholic France. And in countries unlike Spain (where Protestantism was early rooted out by the Inquisition), in countries where people of both creeds sought to live in peace, the demand by the fanatics was that religious loyalties should cut across national loyalty.

In its early days Calvinism was the religion of the opposition. Catholicism represented the older monarchies and the aristocratic and propertied families of the Middle Ages; Protestantism, though led by aristocrats, the thrusting new middle classes. The Protestant faith, by going back to the poverty and simplicity of the early Church, more closely resembled Christianity in its first days. But in the sixteenth century it was disfigured, as both extreme wings of religious belief were equally disfigured, by what D. M. Loades calls 'criminals whose anti-social neuroses were driven into religious channels by the atmosphere of the time'.

When Philip married his Elizabeth of Valois he was, apart from marrying a young girl whom he fancied, attempting a change of policy which would lead to Spanish friendship with

France and would also, he hoped, help to combat the rise of Lutheranism there. But wedding celebrations in France that century had a way of going wrong. (It was another such event which sparked off the massacre of St Bartholomew.) On this occasion Elizabeth's father, Henry of France, a robust and vigorous man of forty who loved violent exercise, took part in the tournament celebrations, and·after several passages at arms, wanted to break another lance before retiring and so commanded that the Count de Montgomery should be his opponent. Montgomery pleaded to be excused. The Queen told Henry that he was tired and should ride no more. Henry would have none of it and so the two men galloped towards each other and broke their lances after the approved style. But Montgomery forgot to release the broken end of the lance from his gloved fingers, and the splintered end entered the King's visor and pierced his eye. The King fell forward on the neck of his horse, which carried him with slowing pace to the end of the enclosure. In ten days he was dead.

The King had been one of the most fanatical Catholics of his day, and as Henri Martin, the French historian, says: 'All Protestant Europe hailed the arm of the Almighty in this thunderbolt which had struck down the persecuting king in the midst of his impious festivities.'

Whether the reformers were right or wrong Henry's death, in the height of his vigour and authority, was a profound calamity for France and for his family, for it ushered in thirty years of bloody anarchy which saw towards its end the final disappearance of the house of Valois. At his bedside through his last days and when he died were two of the most famous women of the century. His young daughter-in-law, the Queen elect, was Mary, Queen of Scotland and the Isles. His wife was Catherine de' Medici.

It is generally overlooked that Mary Queen of Scots, although a Stuart by name, was by blood just as much a Tudor as a Stuart. Her grandparents were James Stewart, Margaret Tudor, Claude of Guise and Antoinette of Bourbon. Elizabeth was the granddaughter of Henry VII. Mary was his great-granddaughter.

Although her childhood was not as traumatic as Elizabeth's, it contained more than its share of tension, shock and high drama. She was born in December 1542, nine years later than her English cousin, and her father, James V of Scotland, died a week after her birth, at the age of thirty. She was not expected to live but she was crowned Queen when she was nine months old, and her mother, the French Mary of Lorraine, became Queen Regent. She did live, and, there being no question of her legitimacy, was quickly put on the marriage market as a political pawn of great importance. Before she was sixteen she married the Dauphin of France, and while she was yet sixteen she became Queen of France.

After her shaky start in life Mary grew to be a tall girl, and a very attractive one, but her husband, the first of Catherine de' Medici's three sons to reign, was thin and undeveloped, small in stature and of low intelligence. During the short time that she was on the throne, Mary surrounded herself with courtiers, artists, musicians and poets, and gave herself over to the pleasure of being young and sought-after and gracious and charming; the affairs of the nation were left to her uncles, the Cardinal of Lorraine and Francis, Duke of Guise. It would have been virtually impossible for her to have done otherwise. Her husband was not yet sixteen, and of retarded development. Behind her two uncles, though not yet the formidable figure of later years, was her mother-in-law.

Mary might have developed into a considerable political force in France as she grew older and Francis grew older, for she already had almost complete dominance over him; but she was not given the chance. Francis reigned only sixteen months and then died from an abscess in the ear. Mary was left a beautiful young widow with no future at the French court. Her mother-in-law disliked her and was jealous of her, and schemed to take over the regency on behalf of the next of her sons, Charles, who was only ten. Mary hesitated for a while, surveying the European scene, and then proposed that she should next marry Don Carlos, the heir to the Spanish throne.

This proposition, coming from a glamorous, high-spirited girl in her teens, casts an interesting light on her character. Don Carlos was about the same age as herself, but was one of the most unprepossessing young men in Europe. Apologists of Mary have always argued that she eventually brought about her own ruin by allowing her heart to rule her head. Whatever happened later, on this occasion there was no sign of such a failing.

But the proposal was vetoed by Catherine de' Medici, who feared for her own daughter Elizabeth's precedence in Spain, and opposed by the other Elizabeth, who saw danger for England in such a marriage; so nothing came of it. In August 1561 Mary accepted an invitation from the Scottish parliament to return to take up her crown, and arrived on the 19th of that month at Leith.

It could hardly have been a more unpropitious time, for religious war had only ceased the year before on the death of her mother, and in the interval the Scottish Protestants had embraced the doctrines of Calvin in their most extreme form. Mary was greeted apparently in expectation that she would instantly give up her Catholic faith, dropping it as it were overboard like an unwanted valise before she landed, and when she did not the fury of her parliament and council knew no bounds.

Nevertheless, in spite of her precarious hold on the country, she imported courtiers, musicians and furnishings from France, gave balls, dinners and receptions of considerable taste, and, as a side issue, dispatched an envoy to the court of Elizabeth requesting that Elizabeth should recognize her as the next successor to the English throne. Elizabeth, while expressing the warmest sentiments, politely refused. 'Would you,' she asked, 'require me in my own life to set my winding sheet before my eyes? Princes cannot like their own children, those that should succeed them. How then shall I like my cousin being declared the Heir Apparent? I know the inconstancy of the people of England, how they ever mislike the present Government and have their eyes fixed upon that person that is next to succeed.'

Elizabeth at this stage, and all through the long quarter century ahead, was far more favourably disposed towards Mary than the English Privy Council or general public opinion. They would have had her blood long before. Mary indeed tried to arrange a meeting with Elizabeth, hoping not unreasonably that her charm would work towards a closer understanding of her rights of succession; but one crisis after another supervened and it never took place.

Mary had still not abandoned the hope of marrying Don Carlos, and her envoy in England constantly treated with the Spanish Ambassador to this end. Perhaps to take Mary's mind off the more formidable power politics in which she was engaged, the young Lord Darnley was permitted to travel up to Scotland. Elizabeth 'allowed' it, rather in the way she allowed Drake and others to sail on their expeditions to the Spanish

Main. Permission by absence of prohibition, while officially looking the other way, was a technique she brought to perfection in her long reign.

Mary met the handsome young man, for the first time in four years, at Wemyss Castle on the rocky coast of Fife, and this time instantly fell in love with him. In spite of 'official' opposition from England, they quickly married. Darnley was another great-grandchild of Henry VII, but his Tudor blood, like Mary's, was diluted with more feckless strains. Although their son eventually was the means of unifying England and Scotland, the marriage was an unmitigated disaster for both parents. Within four years Darnley had been found strangled in the garden of Kirk o' Field House, Mary had married Bothwell, who in the revolt which followed was forced to fly the country to save his life, and Mary, to save hers, had entered English territory and asked Elizabeth for sanctuary.

So began the long imprisonment – though imprisonment is a harsh word to describe a confinement in which Mary was throughout allowed an entourage of forty, and was permitted to hunt and to visit the local spa to take the waters. During it she never ceased to intrigue – or listen to intrigues – against Elizabeth's life and throne. This situation, which was dangerous to Elizabeth and frustrating and exasperating for Mary, persisted through two generations before it ended on a cold grey February morning in the great hall of Fotheringhay.

Elizabeth was no killer, especially not of another Queen, especially not one of Tudor blood. She resisted her Council to the very last, and then at the very last sought to evade the responsibility. Mary was not a compulsive martyr, not like Thomas à Becket, or her own grandson, Charles I. But, for all her many other qualities, she was a compulsive schemer and, in the context of the time, the outcome was bound in the end to be the same.

During these two decades, geographically between Spain, which remained rigidly Catholic in the iron grasp of the Inquisition, and England, which, first from choice and then for self-preservation, became steadily more Protestant, religious war ravaged Europe. In the Netherlands, with Calvinism providing the explosive force, this became increasingly a nationalistic war to free the Low Countries from Spanish occupation. In France, under a succession of weak kings, it was always a dynastic conflict – at least at the top – with great Catholic families striving against great Protestant families to control the country.

The mother of the kings, Catherine de' Medici, was constantly struggling, scheming, working to preserve the Valois dynasty into which she had married. Despised by the French nobility, neglected during her husband's lifetime for his mistress Diane de Poitiers, without Elizabeth's intellect or royal blood, and lacking the charm of Mary Queen of Scots, she yet contrived to remain a power behind the throne and to perform an intricate *pas de deux* with each of her sons in turn, while she played off against one another the three great families of France: the Guises, the Bourbons and the Montmorencys.

The resultant civil war was not the consequence of her intrigues but the consequence of their failure. Time and again she conspired with one side or the other in an attempt to bring peace to France – while Huguenots stormed Catholic monasteries and compelled the monks to hang each other, while Catholics tore Huguenots to pieces and threw the pieces into the sewer, while whole villages and towns were put to the sword indiscriminately by either side.

The wedding of Henry of Navarre, a Protestant and a Bourbon, with the King's sister Marguerite, a Catholic and a Valois, was planned with a political reconciliation in mind – rather as Henry Tudor, a Lancastrian, had married Elizabeth of York. But Catherine de' Medici and her younger son the Duke of Anjou had long found Admiral Coligny's brusque influence over the King intolerable, and planned to have this leader of the Huguenots assassinated. The attempt failed and the twenty-two-year-old King Charles IX of France was then persuaded, after hours of resistance, to sanction a massacre in order, as he was told, to save his throne from the avenging Protestants.

So from the morning of the 24th August, with hysterical savagery the slaughter began, running its course for four days, spreading to the provinces, and not finally expending itself until mid-September, when the Protestant dead are likely to have numbered about thirty thousand men, women and children.

Such was the religious tolerance of the time that, when the news reached the Pope, he ordered that fireworks should be set off and bonfires lit for three nights to celebrate the deed and a commemorative medal struck. Pope Gregory further said that news of this slaughter was a hundred times more welcome than the news of the great naval battle of Lepanto in which the Christian navies had defeated the Turks. *Te Deums* were sung and a great number of little children danced in the streets 'blessing God and praising Our Lord who had inspired King Charles IX to so happy and holy an undertaking'. Some recent historians have sought to excuse the Catholic reaction by explaining that all these rejoicings were instituted as a thanksgiving that Charles had escaped a supposed attempt at assassination; but a study of the records of the time shows this to be completely untrue. It is an apologia dreamed up in more sensitive centuries.

In Madrid Philip was startled out of his customary melancholy dignity. When the news reached him he 'began to laugh' and demonstrated his extreme pleasure and content. Even his closest intimates were astounded at the extent of his joy. He wrote to Catherine congratulating her on possessing such a son and to Charles on possessing such a mother. But of course Philip, as was not unusual with him, was able to associate religious fervour with political gain.

In England news of the massacre and the arrival of a few terrified survivors brought a shock of dismay, an intense hardening of feeling against Rome and a cold war which expressed itself as always through its Queen. A treaty had just been concluded with France and a marriage between Elizabeth and Catherine's favourite son, the Duke of Anjou, was in the air. (Never more than 'in the air' with Elizabeth, but now it was definitely out of the air.) For some days the Queen would not see La Mothe-Fénelon, the French Ambassador. When at length he was summoned to Richmond, he passed in utter silence through a court in which everyone was dressed in black, until he reached the person of the Queen. There he was told in undiplomatic language that this was 'a most horrible crime' . . . 'a deed of unexampled infamy'. Sir Thomas Smith wrote to Walsingham: 'Grant even that the Admiral and his friends were guilty of such a plot against the King's life, what did the innocent men, women and children at Lyons? What did the suckling children and their mothers at Rouen and Caen and elsewhere? Will God sleep?'

The Protestants all over Europe were determined that God must not be allowed to sleep.

Philip's satisfaction was understandable, for at a stroke Charles of France had not only destroyed the heretics but had made himself a prisoner of the Catholics at his court. Furthermore

Admiral Coligny had been pressing Charles IX to furnish an army to go to the support of William of Orange; now the risk of Alva's Spanish army being trapped between two enemies was removed for good. Thirdly, the murder of so many of France's leading soldiers meant a weakening of her military strength for years to come.

Little wonder it was a happy day for him.

Now married, for the fourth time, to his niece Anne of Austria, he was finding his days increasingly preoccupied with the problems of his Netherlands possessions. The Duke of Alva, sent there to subjugate by terror, had succeeded only in setting all the provinces aflame. And it was not a matter of small concern, for, apart from the high cost of the war, this loose federation of small disparate states was the most densely populated trading centre in Europe; and the revenue from the taxes levied upon them was vital to the prosperity of Spain. No amount of treasure from the gold and silver mines of the New World was sufficient to make up for this loss. As fast as a victory against the rebels promised an end of the war, a new wave of revolt would break out. Massacring whole townships and burning the buildings to the ground so that nothing was left only served to harden the resistance and provoke reprisals. Even the Duke of Alva, who was now well into his sixties, was discouraged and suffering from ill-health and exposure to the cold and damp of campaigning.

What also galled Philip was the part his sister-in-law was playing: troops in France not so long ago to aid the Protestants in the civil war there; a flow of volunteers in the Netherlands – whole regiments, in fact; discreet loans where most needed; protection for the rebel navies. During the years he had watched her somewhat shaky progress in her efforts to keep the English crown and the English religion on an even keel. He had seen her besieged by suitors – up to ten at one time – as quite the most eligible match in Christendom; but while she appeared to enjoy the courtship she did not seem able to surrender her person to a foreign prince. In a poem she wrote herself she said:

> When I was fair and young, and favour graced me,
> Of many was I sought, their mistress for to be;
> But I did scorn them all, and answered them therefore,
> Go, go, go seek some otherwhere,
> Importune me no more!

As for the English suitors, they too were numerous; yet none of the successive Spanish ambassadors, who had their own spies close to the Queen, could find proof to confirm the rumours. Even the Venetians, who sometimes leavened their perceptions with imagination, could not produce the evidence for which all the Catholic world waited.

It may of course be that Elizabeth was not highly sexed. A. L. Rowse has pointed out that all the Lancastrian kings, Henrys IV, V, VI, and VII, were singularly moral, being men of affairs rather than womanizers, and that Henry VIII took after his grandfather, the Yorkist Edward IV. Most historians have argued that a daughter of Henry VIII could not fail to be highly sexed; but it is very possible that in this respect she took after her Lancastrian forbears, and particularly her grandfather. Certainly she did not fall into the same traps as Mary Queen of Scots when she married Bothwell. Yet, only thirty-nine in the year of St Bartholomew, Elizabeth was still capable of marrying someone and bearing an heir to the throne; and she was under great pressure from her ministers and from Parliament to do so. If she died or was deposed, Catholic Mary was still the obvious successor, and a plot directed at marrying Mary to the Duke of Norfolk and putting them on the throne together had been formulated only the previous year by a Florentine banker called Ridolfi. The plot had collapsed, but it had received Spanish support, and as a consequence de Spes the Spanish Ambassador had been told to leave the country.

For fifteen years Philip had cautiously favoured Elizabeth's occupancy of the throne in preference to a queen of his own beliefs who had such close ties with France. Now he was gradually coming round to the view that, with France so riven by civil war and with England steadily gaining in strength and confidence, it was better to have a friend of the Valois on the throne of England than a friend of William of Orange.

Cumulatively, events were pushing Philip and Elizabeth into opposition. But neither yet contemplated outright conflict. Elizabeth hated war: she felt that it seldom solved anything, and it *was* so expensive. Her incursions into France to help the Protestants had met with little success – or indeed thanks – and had cost her heavily in both money and men. Philip resented the slights and the insults put upon his countrymen from time to time, but he had his hands full in Europe and a vast empire to consider. Time would tell. He bided his time.

But other events apart from those in Europe were rubbing at the edges of patience and prudence. A new generation of English seamen was progressively challenging Spanish power wherever it was met. English ships, under new and ever more venturesome captains, were exploring the oceans for discovery, for trade, for plunder. Where one of their objectives failed they chose another, and since Spain and Portugal were the two great colonial powers, it was their property that usually came back to England in the holds of the little 60- to 100-ton barques and enriched the investors who sent them.

They went out too in a spirit of Evangelical fervour. To them the Scarlet Woman of Rome – who was indistinguishable anyhow from the imperial house of Spain – was the anti-Christ to be set upon and destroyed; and naturally if there was profit in the destruction who were they to complain? It is improbable that Elizabeth with her tolerant and humanist eye at all understood this fervour, or approved of it. Although there were notable exceptions, when she took the initiative, for the most part she was pulled along, following in the wake of her aggressively Protestant and self-reliant people, ever nearer to the abyss of war.

And of course Elizabeth could seldom resist the opportunity of making a little money. So she began to invest in the expeditions which were launched exactly like joint-stock companies, with partners investing so much money and sharing proportionately in the dividends. Therefore as time went on it became increasingly difficult for the Queen to disown her famous sea captains. The best she could say to a protesting Spanish ambassador was that So-and-so had grossly exceeded his warrant and would be suitably punished. This really deceived no one, since the Queen pocketed her profit and the captain was rarely disciplined. And the depredations became steadily more daring and more successful.

On the 4th July, three years before St Bartholomew, the most successful of the captains, Francis Drake, was married to a girl called Mary Newman at St Budeaux church in south Devon. In the year of St Bartholomew, and in the month of the massacre, Drake landed on the isthmus of Panama near where the mule-trains carried their loads of precious metal across the narrow neck of land dividing the Pacific from the Caribbean. There with a total of seventy-three men he captured Nombre de Dios, a town the size of his native Plymouth. Seriously wounded, he failed this time in his objective, but the following year, having lurked in the vicinity during the intervening months, he attacked and took a mule-train and returned presently to Plymouth with £40,000 value in gold and silver booty.

It was this sort of activity, which went so far beyond the casual privateering raid, that Elizabeth found so difficult to explain away. It was this sort of activity which was earning England the reputation of being 'a nation of pirates'.

But of course the provocation was not on one side alone. English seamen were everywhere considered and treated as heretics when they happened by design or misfortune to land at Catholic ports. As early as 1561 a Bristol merchant had sailed to Cadiz and travelled overland from there to Malaga to buy wines. While he was absent, representatives of the Inquisition boarded his ship and searched it and, finding there books printed in English, assumed them to be blasphemous and arrested him on his return. He was flung into prison and three times racked and his ship and cargo and money seized. This was not an exceptional case.

Drake and Hawkins would ever bear with them the memory of San Juan de Ulua when the tiny English flotilla was set upon by the Spanish warships of the Flota, after having exchanged mutual guarantees of neutrality and safe conduct. While they barely escaped with their lives, many were killed and, of the seamen captured, four were burned at the stake and most of the others spent years in Spanish gaols. For this outrage Elizabeth seized Spanish gold on its way up the Channel to pay the army in the Netherlands.

Yet still both monarchs continued patiently to work for an avoidance of outright war. In 1573 indeed there was a *détente*, and Drake, arriving back with his booty from Nombre de Dios, was an embarrassment to the scene. He dutifully disappeared, and little was then heard of him until he undertook the voyage in the *Golden Hind* which ended in his circumnavigation of the world and earned him an immortality beyond the summits of war. By the time he returned to Plymouth it was September 1580; and by this time Philip, though he continued intermittently to work for peace with England, was toying with the idea of its possible destruction. He had also considered for some time the advantages which would accrue to him from Elizabeth's assassination.

4

Plans for War

The morale of political murder must be seen in its sixteenth-century context. In our century the assassination of kings or heads of state is usually left to the criminally unbalanced who hatch out their paranoiac hate-fantasies in private, or at most in concert with a few like-minded psychopaths. Four hundred years ago the deliberate assassination of a leader of an opposing faction was an act of power politics earning only one-sided opprobrium.

As early as 1570 the Papal Bull issued by Pius V declared all Elizabeth's subjects absolved from their oath of fealty, and was widely interpreted as meaning that her assassination would be considered lawful in the eyes of the church. When Gregory XIII succeeded him, the Cardinal Secretary at the Vatican informed two enquiring Englishmen that 'there is no doubt whatsoever that who sends that guilty woman of England out of the world with the pious intention of doing God's service, not only does not sin but gains merit.' Cardinal Allen writing a decade later urged all Englishmen to purge their souls by seeing to the death of Elizabeth.

The names of some of those who suffered assassination in this brief middle period of the century will show how often these attempts were successful; Francis, Duc de Guise, in 1563, by a Protestant; Lord Darnley, King of Scotland, in 1567, with the tacit connivance of his wife; the Earl of Moray, Regent of Scotland and half-brother of Mary Stuart, in 1570, by a Catholic Hamilton; the Earl of Lennox, another Regent of Scotland and Mary Stuart's father-in-law, in 1571, also probably by the Hamiltons; Admiral Coligny, in 1572, by order and in the presence of Henry Duc de Guise; William of Orange, after several previous attempts, in 1584 by a Catholic, under assignment from Philip II; Henry Duc de Guise in 1588 by order and in the presence of Henry III of France; Henry III of France in 1589 by a young Dominican monk.

This list is not exhaustive, but it suggests that in this respect the Protestants were more sinned against than sinning.

It is not to be wondered at, therefore, that as Elizabeth passed out of the child-bearing age and so could not perpetuate her line, her Council and Parliament should be in ever greater concern to perpetuate her life. Mary remained in confinement, the continuing nucleus for Catholic discontent. It was true that her son James, whom she had not seen since he was ten months old, had been brought up a strict Protestant in Scotland and might eventually be a more suitable successor, but in 1580 he was only fourteen, and a backward, shambling, spavin-shanked fourteen at that.

So in England, as one assassination plot followed another, pressure grew to remove Mary, and tighter and stricter laws were introduced to compel Catholics to conform to the new religion. Walsingham, whose spies constantly preserved Elizabeth from death, was given greater liberty to enforce his secret decrees, and the 1580s became the decade of the dungeon and the rack. Elizabeth's great Summer Progresses through the land, which were often attended by a court and train of five hundred persons, were curtailed, and she seldom moved far from her palaces around London. Not that she took care for her own person. By her lack of simple safety precautions, by her confidence in the loyalty and good sense of her own people, she was a constant anxiety to her ministers and friends.

In 1577 Mary Queen of Scots made a will whereby she left all her rights in the English throne to Philip II of Spain. It was an open invitation to him to come and free her. The English Privy Council, and particularly the triumvirate of Cecil, Leicester and Walsingham, saw Mary's existence as the greatest single danger to the freedom and continued independence of England. Not only was she the magnet which lay at the source of all plots of assassination and invasion; she was also the stumbling-block to any *rapprochement* with France. There could hardly be an understanding between the two countries while an ex-Queen of France was held captive in England. Once she was gone, the sore place would heal.

But Elizabeth still would have none of it. Others could go to the block: not Mary, not a royal person.

Lest it appear that Elizabeth was morally elevated above the other monarchs of the day, it should be mentioned that for two years before the St Bartholomew massacre, and in the year after, Sir Henry Killigrew, that cousin of the wild and lawless Cornish Killigrews but himself one of Elizabeth's most trusted and confidential servants, was up and down to Scotland with various secret and disreputable propositions to discuss with a succession of Regents: Moray, Lennox and Mar. The concept was that the English should release Mary and allow her to return to Scotland on condition that the Scots would guarantee to execute her as soon as she arrived. It was not at all a new idea to the Scots. Each of the Regents in turn was entirely agreeable to the proposal, indeed had assisted in its initiation, but each in turn, while haggling over the financial details of his reward, was overtaken by death.

After St Bartholomew feeling ran high in Scotland. Knox, in the last year of his vehement life, thundered at the French Ambassador: 'Go tell your King that God's vengeance shall never depart from him nor from his house, and that his name shall remain an execration to posterity.' Many Scots blamed Mary for her French blood and more than ever would have been glad to see her disposed of; but Morton, succeeding to the regency in October 1572, though no more principled than his predecessors, was, in the words of a contemporary, 'too old a cat to draw such a straw as that after him'. He continued to negotiate with Killigrew but without any intention of concluding the sordid pact. If the English wanted to be rid of Mary, then let them bear the odium of the deed.

In 1580 Philip annexed Portugal. King Sebastian of Portugal, when only twenty-four, had been killed while fighting a religious crusade against the Moors, and he died without issue. Philip's mother had been sister to King João III, Sebastian's grandfather, and Philip's first wife had been sister to the Crown Prince João, Sebastian's father. The legitimacy of Philip's claim to the throne was supported by thirty thousand of the best soldiers in Europe, and the ill-organized resistance was brief. Don Antonio, the natural son of João III's brother, fled abroad; and in a stroke Philip had gained for himself a huge overseas empire second only to the Spanish, and an ocean-going fleet, a little run down but potentially as good as or better than his own. Additionally he had unified the Iberian Peninsula and had acquired in Lisbon and Oporto two fine ports on the Atlantic coast to match Cadiz.

As Elizabeth continued obdurately to hold out, to survive the secret infiltration of Jesuit priests, and to oppose him apologetically on all fronts, the idea of an open invasion of the island became more clearly the one ultimate sanction left. Pope Gregory had for some time been urging Philip to land in Ireland and build up a powerful force there before launching his attack on England. Don John of Austria, Philip's half-brother, had proposed to the Pope that he personally should lead an invasion across the narrow seas from the Netherlands. But Philip was slow to move. It was his nature. Also he knew England and knew Elizabeth and perhaps still had a grudging respect for the tall, slim, auburn-haired girl of his memory who had somehow survived and, ever protesting friendship, had defied him so long.

There had in fact already been landings on the Irish coast. In 1579 Papal volunteers under Dr Nicholas Sanders had arrived there, together with Spanish and Italian volunteers. A serious insurrection had developed, but it had been put down by the English in the following year.

In the meantime in the Low Countries, the Duke of Alva, whose savage tyranny had provoked the civil war it was designed to prevent, had been supplanted, after an intermediate period under Requesens and Don John, by Alexander Farnese, the greatest soldier of his day.

Farnese, who became Duke of Parma on his father's death in 1586, was the son of Ottavio Farnese and Margaret of Austria, the illegitimate daughter of the Emperor Charles. Philip II's father was therefore Parma's grandfather; and Farnese was eighteen years younger than Philip. Parma, a strategist and a tactician of the first order, was a man of great personal bravery, ruthless towards his enemies but tolerant and humane as an act of policy to those he conquered; and he very quickly perceived and took advantage of religious and political differences within the revolutionary states of the Netherlands and was able to split them. Where a swift and decisive use of his troops in battle was likely to achieve his end, no one was his equal in deploying and leading them. Where his charm or the offer of money or a title or an appeal to an old religious prejudice would do the work better, he used them.

For a time it seemed that this adroit combination of conquest, moderation and pacification would win the day, and that all, or nearly all, the revolting States would again come under the authority of Spain. Only the iron will and dedication and equally gifted diplomacy of one man appeared to prevent it. William Prince of Orange had begun life as a Lutheran and the son of Lutherans, but on the order of the Emperor Charles had been brought up a Catholic and had played his full part in the brilliant court life of Brussels. Until his mid-twenties he lived the easy-going extravagant life of a prince of the blood, and his splendid Nassau palace was the meeting place for gay and dissipated young noblemen like himself. In his youth William was a personal favourite of the Emperor, and at first was on terms of friendship with Philip too. But gradually as he perceived the tightness of the Spanish grip upon all aspects of life and administration and he witnessed the terrible persecution of the Protestants, his attitude changed and he found himself becoming an antagonist of Philip and of all Philip's policies in the Netherlands. After the judicial murder of Egmont and Hoorn, he became the principal antagonist and indeed the one figure around whom the forces of revolt and independence could centre. So his life changed, he left his palaces and his lands and his rich living and became the head of a forlorn but dedicated group of men and states determined to throw off the Spanish tyranny. He lived in the harsh world of soldiering, with the simplicity of a peasant, sometimes in want, always in danger. In 1582 he narrowly survived a first attempt at assassination when a pistol was fired into his head so close that the powder set fire to his hair and beard. In the following year four more attempts were made, and in 1584 a sixth was successful when he was shot dead in a disused convent known as the Prinsenhof which he was then using as his home. The assassin, a young clerk called Gérard, was tortured to death, and therefore could not receive the twenty-five thousand crowns Philip had offered as a reward for this 'laudable and generous deed'; so instead Gérard's parents were granted three seigniories in the Franche Comté and at once elevated to the landed aristocracy.

Well before William of Orange's death, Parma's brilliant combination of warfare and diplomacy had been regaining lost ground for Philip. One fortress after another had fallen and one town after another had been captured or gave way. Nowhere now was there sign of the 'Spanish fury'. Troops entering a town behaved with discipline and restraint; fair terms were offered everywhere. Protestant worship was suppressed but Protestants were allowed to leave and given time to leave, and could take their goods with them. In many towns Catholics were in a large majority and had been themselves oppressed by fanatical Calvinists who had desecrated their churches and murdered their priests. So it was half a conquest, half a liberation.

Soon after William's death Ghent fell, and then Brussels. Bruges had already gone, and one could see that Antwerp was doomed. The Protestant secessionists were falling back everywhere leaderless and in disarray. It looked like the end of the war. Philip thought so. The States General in despair approached Henry III of France, offering him the crown in return for his aid. But Henry, who not infrequently dressed as a woman, loved to play with little dogs, and wore his hair in ruffles, was embroiled in the first stages of a civil war in which two other and altogether more formidable Henrys fought across his kingdom: Guise to try to drive the last Protestants from France, Navarre to try to prevent him and to survive as the heir to the throne. So Henry of Valois refused the honour. The States General thereupon offered it to Elizabeth.

She too refused. But now she offered more aid than she had ever done before, and of a different kind. Hitherto it had been money, reluctantly squeezed out, volunteer regiments led by gentlemen adventurers and soldiers of fortune, a trickle of supplies and some naval help. Now, after long negotiation, she signed a treaty in September 1585, by which she undertook to send an army of six thousand men, a thousand of them mounted; and their commander was to be her first and oldest favourite and close adviser, Robert, Earl of Leicester. At the same time she published and had distributed an apologia, a justification, an announcement of her reasons for this action, which, in its statement of ideals and the ideals worth striving for, has been likened to the American Declaration of Independence. It was printed in English, French, Italian and Dutch, and she saw that Parma received a copy.

It was not a declaration of war but it was as near as Elizabeth was ever prepared to get. It was a declaration of intent; and it must have helped Philip to concentrate his mind wonderfully on the final issues which separated him and his sister-in-law.

The ultimate issue was whether she could be allowed to continue to attack and damage the priceless convoys bringing their treasure from the New World, and at the same time to prop up with her own army the rebels in the Low Countries. One of these activities could have been tolerated. Not both.

47

So Philip no longer continued to toy with the idea of invasion, to listen to other people's suggestions. He began to make his own plans.

The early historians of the Great Armada, because most of them were Protestant, depicted a tiny England, with its simple godly seamen fighting David-like against the great Goliath that Spain launched upon her. Only God, one felt, and the rightness of the Cause, and the splendid bravery and skill of the sailors enabled a few brilliantly handled but undersized warships to take on this great fleet and defeat it. The running battle up Channel, the fireships of Calais, the destructive infighting of Gravelines, and the great gales which followed, were all part of a divine pattern. Patriotism and religion triumphed together; great courage and simple faith walked hand in hand and the colossus was shattered.

Most later historians, suffering no doubt from the reaction from this medieval legend, have learned in greater or less degree the other way, estimating that the fleets were roughly equal in size, with a great mobility and fire-power advantage to the English, depicting the Armada as a clumsy almost useless assembly of unseaworthy galleons, over-manned and undergunned, herded together into a great unmanageable fleet and sent to keep an impossible rendezvous on the directions of an absolute monarch writing out his impractical orders from a cell in the Escorial.

Was it really like that at the time? Which is nearer the truth?

One tries to push the mists back another half millennium and wonder what would have happened if King Harold had not had to fight Hardrada at Stamford Bridge and had come fresh to meet William – later known as the Conqueror – at Hastings. If William had been defeated, as he probably would have been, there is no doubt that the Anglo-Saxon chronicles would have hailed this as a victory for faith and English bravery and God. But it is not impossible to imagine later historians pointing out that from the beginning William's invasion plans were ill-organized and hopelessly optimistic and that from the beginning he hadn't stood a dog's chance.

A bastard Duke of Normandy with a tenuous claim to the English throne tries to enlist the help of his barons in making a piratical landing on the Sussex coast. At the great council of

Lillebonne they turn his proposition down flat and he has to persuade them individually with bribes and threats. After his mass of tiny ships, laboriously built through the summer, have been held back for more than a month by contrary winds and storms and many of them wrecked, there is sickness in his camp and many desertions among those of his troops who see that the hand of God is against them. Eventually he sails with his heterogeneous collection of fellow Normans, together with drop-outs and adventurers from Maine and Brittany, from Flanders, from Burgundy, from Aquitaine, from Piedmont, and from the Rhine : the idle, the unsuccessful, the unscrupulous, the dissipated, all looking for land and loot and easy plunder.

He sails thus, knowing that a large and active English fleet has been patrolling the Channel all through the summer waiting for just such an opportunity to attack him, and that all through the summer Harold has maintained a standing army in Sussex and Kent under his personal leadership, ready to do him battle. When he lands, if he lands, he is faced by a population comprehensively hostile, and united under a popular king.

No wonder he came to grief, the historians would say. For the enterprise was the dream of a desperate gambler, unaware of the strength of the forces that he challenged, an adventure badly thought out and clumsily executed. Even the blessing of the Pope could not help him . . .

There were not people lacking, with access to Philip, who could urge him that *his* enterprise would be much more surely organized, with a far greater certainty of success than any of his predecessors had had. Among them the English Jesuit, Father Parsons, listed the times England had been invaded in the history of the island. The number was sixteen, of which all but two had been successful. It was a country with many good landfalls, with bays and harbours, and rivers easy of access, capable of taking large ships into the heart of the land. Most of Philip's advisers believed also that two-thirds of the English were still Catholic at heart (and perhaps they were not far wrong : you do not change a whole nation's religious beliefs in a few generations). The English had long had peace in their land, the castles were in decay, their swords and pikes rusty, their indiscipline a by-word.

No doubt someone also drew his attention to the fact that almost exactly one hundred years earlier the founder of the new Tudor dynasty, an exile and a fugitive for most of his life, a man described by Commines as 'without money, without power, without reputation and without right', had landed with a few supporters at Milford Haven, together with a band of three thousand Normans lent him by the King of France, and had marched to Bosworth and gained a crown. No seer was able to foretell to Philip that exactly one hundred years after the Armada another man, a Dutchman, was to land at Torbay and proceed without battle to London to turn the last of the Stuarts off the throne. But there were enough precedents without this.

For some time the Marquis of Santa Cruz, Spain's great veteran admiral, had been pressing his King to allow him to sail with his navy to invade England. Philip asked Santa Cruz for an estimate of what he would need.

When the estimate came it was a monumental one. The admiral said he would want five hundred and fifty-six ships of which one hundred and eighty were to be front-line galleons, with a total naval personnel of thirty thousand, and an army of sixty-five thousand men. There was also to be included two hundred flat-bottomed boats, to be carried in the larger ships, and a wealth of other provisions calculated to last eight months, which would cost in all nearly four million ducats. This equalled all the income Philip could expect to receive from his treasure house of the New World for about three and a half years. The King read it carefully and made his precise notations in the margins. It was an impossible demand. He filed the estimates away alongside Don John's plan to invade England across the Channel from the Low Countries, and various other ideas which had been put to him from time to time. Then early in 1586 a detailed scheme was submitted to him by the Duke of Parma, elaborating and yet simplifying Don John's plan. Parma's proposal was that he should launch his veteran army swiftly across the Channel in flat-bottomed boats in a single night. With the element of surprise and a screen of twenty-five warships, an army of thirty thousand men with five hundred cavalry could be thrown ashore in Kent or Essex, and the first crossings could be effected in eight or ten hours.

It was an exciting proposal, coming as it did from Europe's greatest soldier, and it would not be ruinously expensive, since the army was already in being. Philip reasoned, however, and noted so in the margin, that an element of surprise was not possible where the mustering of thirty thousand men was concerned, and only surprise could see them across without inviting weighty counter-attack at sea. Santa Cruz's plan, on the other hand, was entirely feasible, but there was not, and there never would be, the material or the financial resources to launch it.

Could not the two be combined? A naval force from Spain large enough to drive off or defeat the English warships. A military force under Parma ferried across the narrow waters and covered by the Spanish fleet. It was an idea with a good deal to commend it, since it integrated the suggestion of his two most brilliant captains. As the crisis deepened and the need for some military action became more imperative, Philip can hardly be blamed for seeing this combined offensive as a likely solution. It was to be an Enterprise, an *Empresa*. The Enterprise England, it would be called.

He directed Santa Cruz accordingly. And he directed Parma accordingly.

Whatever naval force Santa Cruz would be able eventually to assemble, Parma's army was already the most formidable in Europe. Indeed nothing like it had tramped across Europe since the Roman legions of the time of Christ.

It was a purely professional army, comprising men who had taken up soldiering as their career and expected to live as soldiers and die as veterans. They garrisoned frontier towns or fought where they were told to fight, seeing their enemy where they were instructed to see him. Their discipline in defence was only equalled by their *élan* in attack. The infantry regiments, which comprised a thousand to fifteen hundred men, were known as *tercios* from their custom of forming up into three ranks to do battle. In Spain, to become a military man was considered a thoroughly honourable vocation. Even the hidalgos and lesser nobility were proud to serve in the infantry – a very different matter from any form of manual labour or despicable trading. It matched their sense of heroism and their sense of dignity. The fields and vineyards of Spain went untended while the men who owned them fought in Brabant or in Brittany, in Lombardy or Peru.

But of course the Spanish army was a polyglot one, as befitted the army of a widespread empire. In April 1588 Parma's army of sixty thousand men was roughly divided in the proportion of 34 per cent German, 31 per cent Walloon, 18 per cent Spanish, 12 per cent Italian and 5 per cent of other nationalities. It also enjoyed a local autonomy, and at times its very discipline, as when turning to thoughts of mutiny for lack of pay, made it the harder to control. The 'Spanish Fury' of 1576, in which eight thousand men, women and children were savagely slaughtered in Antwerp and a thousand buildings burned – a blow from which the city never recovered – was not an act of policy like other, and lesser, massacres, it was an uncontrollable revolt, a mutinous outburst by an army shut up too long in its fortresses, unpaid and neglected. There had been other mutinies before and since, and at the taking of any city at any time the soldiers usually got out of hand; but under Parma the authority of the commanding officers had been restored, malcontents weeded out, and some of the back pay made up. Troops, particularly professional troops, will always give of their best for a brilliant and personally fearless general; they are quick to recognize the master touch.

If a force of thirty thousand such infantry could be landed in England, there was virtually nothing to stop them. A few miscellaneous, hastily gathered forces of militiamen, town trained bands and farmers who had been drilling once a week on coastal defence; these were the best that could be thrown up behind the dyke of forty miles of sea. The towns were undefended and ripe for the sacking. How many more Spanish Furies might there be?

Even the new English army now operating in the Netherlands had met with indifferent success. Although when they fought they did so with their customary obstinacy and refusal to retreat – a characteristic which resulted in Parma always ascertaining from his spies the proportion of English among the troops in any fort or strong point before he attacked it – Leicester himself had quarrelled with everyone, even with 'Black' Norris, England's ablest soldier, who had been in the Netherlands on and off for ten years and had forgotten far more than Leicester would ever know of war. The States General, from first greeting him as a saviour and a future sovereign, now saw him as a meddler, an incompetent and even, eventually, as a betrayer of their cause.

This last with some reason, for when returning to England in November, he left, in spite of the protests of his allies, two of the most important outposts in the hands of Catholic-English commanders. These were Sir William Stanley, in charge of the city of Deventer, which had recently been captured from Spain; and Rowland York, commanding the fort of Zutphen, overlooking the town of that name. Hardly was his back turned than both went over to the Spanish, Stanley taking twelve hundred Irish troops with him. Later the Scotsman, Pallot, did the same in Gelderland. The French historian Mariéjol says that Stanley was a former soldier of the Duke of Alva, and that, although he had three times sworn fidelity to Elizabeth, he was secretly under engagement to the King of Spain in the Low Countries. Whatever the truth of this, he was far too sincere a man to turn his coat for gain. He did so to serve God, as he understood it.

This, in January 1587, must have been a great encouragement to Philip to believe that there were many others of like mind and heart in England who were only waiting the opportunity to declare themselves. Let the Catholic standard once be raised . . .

And now the English Lutherans shocked the civilized world by bringing Catholic Mary of Scotland at last to the block. The plot which finally resulted in her execution was led, if not engineered, by a wealthy young Derbyshire nobleman called Sir Anthony Babington, who had known and served Mary when he was a page to Lord Shrewsbury in the 1570s. It was coldly designed to accomplish the assassination of Elizabeth by six young Catholic friends of Babington, while Babington himself and a hundred others freed Mary and raised the standard of the new queen at Chartley.

In two decades of imprisonment Mary had outlived the obloquy of Darnley's murder and the Bothwell marriage and had become a heroine to many English and foreign Catholics, a romantic princess locked away in a tower. Certainly she was still this to Babington and his friends, though in fact she was now forty-five and her notable good looks had faded. An eye-witness at the time of her trial – probably an unfriendly one – writes: 'She is of stature tall, of body corpulent, round shouldered, her face fat and broad, double chinned, with hazel eyes and borrowed hair.' When the Babington plot was uncovered she was so obviously incriminated that there was little chance for her this time. Indeed Burghley and Walsingham and others of the Council for their own sakes simply had to see Mary go to the block, for if Elizabeth died and Mary succeeded, their own heads would be the first to fall.

Mary was moved to Fotheringhay Castle in September 1586, and in October was brought to trial before thirty-six noblemen, privy councillors and judges of both religions. At first she refused to recognize the validity of the court, but later, encouraged by a curt note from Elizabeth holding out a bare hint of clemency, she appeared before her judges and defended herself ably for two days, until the trial was adjourned. When it was resumed at the Star Chamber, Westminster, two weeks later, Mary was not present, and the verdict was a foregone conclusion. Yet the signature of Elizabeth to the death warrant had still to be obtained. While she struggled with her agony of indecision Mary wrote – and was allowed to send – letters appealing for help to Pope Sixtus V, to the Duc de Guise, to Mendoza in Paris, to the Archbishop of Glasgow and others. She also wrote a dignified and touching letter to Elizabeth which made Elizabeth cry and no doubt added to her hesitations. The French and the Scots sent emissaries to the English court to appeal for clemency. Yet behind Elizabeth all the time was her formidable Council presenting to her the inescapable truth – which she herself fully recognized – that only Mary's death would now suffice.

There is no question that at this juncture Elizabeth would have been glad of four knights such as Henry II had had at court waiting to misunderstand his words and ride off to murder Thomas à Becket. Indeed, she more than hinted as much to Mary's jailers; but they were upright men as well as Protestants and gave her no help. So at last, four months after the trial and two after the verdict, she signed the warrant and later, in a tormented struggle to placate her own conscience and to evade responsibility in the eyes of the world, she tried to throw the final blame on one of her secretaries for having borne the document away without her permission.

When it was known that Mary's head had at last fallen, there was rejoicing in the streets of London and in many other parts of the country. To all English Protestants she had been the ever-present danger to their new and prosperous existence, a menace to their Queen's life, a possible successor of Mary Tudor's calibre and a threat to the whole future of the Reformed Church. Elizabeth had hesitated so long over the drastic decision that, now it had finally been taken, there was an overwhelming sense of relief in the country. The die was cast, the knot was cut, there was no going back even if the way forward might lead to outright war with Spain. It was what the country wanted and was psychologically prepared for. To her own great surprise, Elizabeth found her personal popularity increased.

In Scotland there was a brief national outcry in which James as briefly joined. But he had long since let it be secretly known that the execution of his mother would not be allowed to injure his own alliance with England, made in the hope of succeeding to the English throne. The news took several weeks to reach Paris. There the court went into deep mourning and a·requiem Mass was held at Notre Dame attended by all the royal family. Henry III had lost a sister-in-law, the aged Catherine a daughter-in-law, the Guises a cousin. It was a dastardly act, but France, as ever in those days, was in too great a disarray to do more than protest.

In Rome the shrewd, vigorous, tactless, uneducated Sixtus had just succeeded his old enemy Gregory as Pope. He greeted the news of Mary's death with lamentation, but added in an aside about Elizabeth: 'What a valiant woman – she braves the two greatest kings by land and sea. A pity we cannot marry, she and I, for our children would have ruled the world!' To the Spanish Ambassador he repeated his promise to give Philip one million ducats as soon as Spanish soldiers landed on English soil, but would not advance a single one by way of a forward loan.

From Brussels Parma wrote to his King advising him not to break off peace negotiations with Elizabeth out of anger or shock but to continue them as a cloak for the preparations being made. 'One cannot help feeling,' he went on, 'and I for my part firmly believe, that this cruel act must be the last of many which She of England has performed, and that Our Lord will be served if She receives the punishment which She has deserved for so many years . . . For the reasons I have so often put before your Majesty we must be able to achieve our aims if we are called on to undertake any of the many parts which fall to us. Moreover, the aims of your Majesty as a most powerful and Christian king oblige you to try to end this affair as the service of God requires . . . Above all, I beg your Majesty that neither on this nor on other occasions will you relax in any way in regard to your preparations for the prosecution of this war and the *Empresa* which was conceived in Your Majesty's heart.'

5
Drake at Cadiz

Many reports had reached England during the last year or so
of the preparations going ahead in the Spanish and Portuguese
sea towns, and in Naples and Genoa too. Old galleons were
being repaired, new ones laid down. Foreign ships were being
commandeered, ships belonging to Danes and Germans, Nea-
politans and Ragusans, some impounded, some chartered. The
King's agents were out and about fixing up new contracts for
cordage and sail, for biscuit and dried fish, for barrels and
timber and tar. Galleys were being refurbished. New ships
called galleasses, which attempted to make the best of both
worlds by using wind and oar together, were being built in
Naples. All Europe was being scoured for cannon and ball and
shot. For first-quality Dutch guns the Spanish were paying as
much as £22 a ton. A substantial quantity of arms was also
bought in England, and Ralegh complained bitterly of this
traffic. The Privy Council did its best, but the prohibitions
were constantly evaded. Ralph Hogge, of Buxted in Sussex,
who was the first man in England to cast iron and became
the Queen's 'gonstone maker and gonfounder of yron', wrote
to Walsingham in 1574: 'There is often complaints coming
before your honours about the shipping and selling of ordnance
and cast iron to strangers to carry over the seas, they say in
such numbers that your enemy is better furnished with them
than the ships of our own country are.' He then explained
that no licence was needed for shipping guns from port to
port along the English coast, and therefore it was perfectly
easy for ships to load supposedly for another English port and
then slip over to a foreign one.

As the demand increased, so did the price, and so did the
flow of contraband. One Sussex ironmaster sold a hundred
pieces of cannon to the Spaniards, and Bristol merchants sold
them nine shiploads of culverins cast in the forest of Dean,

together with powder, muskets and shot – all this during 1586 and 1587, and mainly routed through Naples.

With a military commitment in the Netherlands, however reluctantly maintained, and Mary executed, the forward party in the Council was in the ascendant. Drake had just returned from his great West Indies raid, during which he had first impudently called in and watered at Vigo, challenging the King of Spain to come and fight on his own doorstep, then had sailed to the Cape Verde Islands where he captured and burned Santiago and Porto Praya. Then he had crossed the Atlantic, and, although beset by sickness in his ships, had attacked and captured the supposedly impregnable city of San Domingo and lived there in luxury for a month with his crews before revictualling with Spanish stores and departing with additions to his fleet, two hundred and forty extra guns and a large number of freed galley-slaves, Turkish as well as Christian. From there he had sailed to Cartagena, the capital of the Spanish Main, which, being warned of his coming, had been heavily reinforced. But by a manœuvre of sheer genius he had captured the place, had stayed there six weeks unmolested and had finally returned to England, after many other adventures, laden with spoil.

This voyage was in a real sense the one great setback to the Counter-Reformation in the years following the death of William of Orange, when all over Europe Spain and Rome seemed triumphant. It confirmed Drake as the foremost and only successful champion of the Protestant cause which everywhere else was in retreat. 'El Draque' was famous throughout Spain, being at once dreaded and respected; and 'many princes of Italy, Germany and elsewhere, enemies as well as friends, desired his picture.' The moral effect of this great adventure was much greater than the immediate physical damage done. It struck at the empire from which Philip drew so much of his wealth and authority, it damaged Spanish credit by preventing the treasure ships from sailing and thus starved Parma of the money to pay his army; it was rumoured that the Bank of Seville would be broken and that Philip would become bankrupt.

But Philip survived and quietly went ahead with his preparations while Parma continued to negotiate with Elizabeth. Drake, in spite of the various dramatic proposals he put forward for his own employment, was kept on a leash after his return; and it was nearly a year before the forward party at court succeeded in persuading Elizabeth to let her lion free again.

On the 2nd April 1587 Drake sailed with a mixed fleet of sixteen ships and seven pinnaces to do mischief upon the Spanish ports. His instructions were 'to prevent or withstand such enterprises as might be attempted against her Highness's realm or dominion', and these instructions he proceeded joyfully to carry out. After reaching Lisbon on the 16th, he learned that there was a great concourse of shipping in Cadiz just getting ready to sail, so he fled south under all canvas, instructing his fleet to follow to the best of their sailing abilities. Arriving off Cadiz in the afternoon of the 19th, accompanied only by those few who were as fast as he, he called a council aboard his flagship, the *Elizabeth Bonaventure*, and announced his intention of sailing in and attacking the harbour at once – this in spite of the strong opposition of his vice-admiral, William Borough, who considered the defences of Cadiz too strong, with batteries commanding the narrow entrance to the harbour, and at least a dozen powerful galleys in harbour, and one or more galleons much larger than the English ships.

According to the orders laid down by Henry VIII, it was obligatory that an admiral in charge of a fleet should call a council-of-war and fully discuss policy and strategy with his captains before taking any such grave step as landing on enemy territory or forcing the entrance of an enemy harbour. But Drake's councils were always perfunctory. It was said of him by a friend that though he was a willing hearer of other men's opinions he was mainly a follower of his own. This time he barely listened. He gave his captains his instructions, and even Borough's urgent request that they should wait until nightfall – not an unreasonable one – was unregarded.

Even while the 'council' was in progress, the ships were nearing Cadiz, and, barely giving his captains time to leave, Drake stood in. The wind was favourable, the sky clear, the time four o'clock. The ancient town drowsed like a white cat in the afternoon sun. In the harbour was a scene of peaceful industry appropriate to a warm spring day. Something like a hundred ships, from small barques to armed merchantmen, were in port, of every type and nationality, loading up stores, being repaired, or ready and waiting orders to sail. Foreign ships which had been commandeered had no sails, for this was a useful way of ensuring that they should not slip away in the night. Others were without guns and some were without crews.

As soon as Drake's ships were sighted two galleys put out to challenge them, but these in the open spaces of the bay were driven off. Once in the harbour it might be different – this sort of combat in an enclosed space had never taken place before. Galleys, though lightly built and lightly armed, were swift and dangerous and could out-manœuvre any sailing ship – they could turn on their axis in their own length – and they had been the traditional ships of war for three thousand years.

Elizabeth Bonaventure sailed in under the barking cannons of the Matagorda fort, followed by *Golden Lion*, *Rainbow* and *Dreadnought* – the four Queen's ships – and a group of armed merchantmen led by Captain Flick in *Merchant Royal*. In the port all now was sudden panic and chaos, as every ship that could move at all cut its cables and tried to find some sort of escape from the attack. Many collided, some went aground, a few smaller ones were able to retreat into water too shallow for the English ships to follow.

From opposite the town ten galleys appeared to attack the intruders. Drake ordered his armed merchantmen to deal with the panic-stricken ships in the harbour and turned the attention of the four Queen's ships to combat with the galleys. The galleys opened fire as they approached from the single gun platforms mounted forward. Drake, handling his five-hundred-ton warship like a skiff in the fresh breeze, came about and discharged broadsides of demi-cannon and culverin, the guns firing eight at a time, into the packed benches of oarsmen. As one galley fell away the others pressed in to the attack, and were met with the same devastating fire from the English warships. In fifteen minutes it was all over, and history had been made. The long pre-eminence of the galley as a ship of war was ended. (Or at least the results of the very rare clashes between galleys and sailing ships during the last few years had been heavily and dramatically underscored.) One galley was sinking; the other nine retired under the shelter of the shore guns.

Of the many ships captured in the harbour, those with full equipment were taken as prizes, those without sail or otherwise thought unsuitable were set afire. As night fell Drake ordered his ships to anchor out of range of the town guns, which had been firing on him for three hours, and told his captains, who had come to consult him, that they must stay where they were until the morning. Vice-Admiral Borough, who was anxious to finish the work and move away from this land-trap while they were still free to do so, was not heeded.

At dawn, instead of making off with his prizes, Drake organized and personally led a flotilla of pinnaces into the inner harbour where he took and destroyed one of the largest Spanish galleons of the day, belonging to the Admiral, Santa Cruz, himself. In the meantime Borough, finding himself under fire from a shore gun, had edged farther and farther out of the harbour, until six galleys, seeing him separate from the rest, attacked him, and Drake had to send eight of his ships to the rescue. The galleys were beaten off, but Borough continued his slow retreat, taking with him the ships which had been sent to his aid, and finally anchored at the mouth of the harbour, where he could catch the fitful wind, and waited petulantly for Drake.

Drake was nearly ready. The galleon was burned down to the water line; thirty other ships had been destroyed and six captured; his own ships were laden with whatever could be seized from deck or quayside, and food and wine to last his fleet three months. His loss in ships was nil and in personnel quite small. By now more and more Spanish troops were arriving from the mainland and marching across the narrow isthmus into Cadiz: it was time to go. And at that moment the wind dropped.

It was an awkward situation. A sailing ship without wind is an unwieldy hulk which can only be moved laboriously by oarsmen in ship's boats straining to keep way on her. Or in shallow water anchors may be dropped and she can be warped forward or aft a few yards at a time. But her wings are suddenly clipped, and it is not comfortable at such a time to find oneself in an enemy harbour, almost surrounded by land which is rapidly being occupied by hostile troops. This was the time, too, for galleys to come into their own. Also it was known that somewhere not far away Juan Martinez de Recalde, after Santa Cruz the most experienced and notable Spanish admiral of his day, was abroad with a squadron of Biscayan galleons and might be nearing Cadiz. A calm, of course, is a calm; but there is more chance of light airs out at sea. There were also other squadrons about the coast, the main concentration being at Lisbon, where Santa Cruz, superintending the Armada preparations, now knew of Drake's presence on the coast and might be coming to seek him. Ill fortune could bring a sufficiency of ships to Cadiz to imprison

Drake's fleet in the harbour and sink them.

It is not to be wondered if some of the English captains, and perhaps even Drake himself, watched the declining sun with an anxious eye. Borough was certainly in no doubts as to their danger, although his partial retreat had put him less at risk.

In the afternoon the Duke of Medina Sidonia reached Cadiz with another three thousand infantry and three hundred cavalry. The people of Cadiz, some of whom had trampled others to death in the panic of yesterday, breathed again, and began to help to manhandle new guns into position where their shot could reach the English ships. The galleys made another concerted onslaught on their now unwieldy adversaries. It was like dogs attacking a circle of bears. But by warping and paying out skilfully the English ships presented their broadsides constantly to the enemy, and the galleys after some hot exchanges again retired.

Then just before dark fire-ships were tried. These could have been disastrous, but they suffered from the prevailing lack of wind. They had to be towed in the direction of the English ships, and once they got within range they were necessarily abandoned, so the English small boats could take them in tow and beach them out of danger. About nine the galleys tried again, but again without success. Meanwhile the guns barked regularly, but only a few shots hit the English ships.

At midnight, just twelve hours after the wind dropped, a light breeze began to blow off shore, and Drake and his ships with flags flying, kettledrums beating and trumpets strident, slipped out to sea.

The adventure was not over yet; for, after further brushes with the opposing galleys, Drake sailed back to Cape St Vincent, landed a force of a thousand men on a sandy beach nearby and at the second attempt captured the impregnable Sagres Castle, the fortified monastery of St Vincent, and Valliera Castle, together with all supplies and guns. These the English carried away after burning the forts. They also captured and destroyed over a hundred fishing boats and coastal barques, thereby ruining the Algarve tunny fishing industry, on which any Spanish armada had to rely for its salt fish, and at the same time destroying the seasoned barrel staves being carried by many of the coastal vessels. The navies of the world relied on such casks for storing water and wine and salt meat and biscuits, and the lack of good barrels to keep provisions sweet was one of the notable deficiencies in the Armada when it sailed in the following year.

Nor was this all. Having appeared next off Lisbon and vainly challenged Santa Cruz to come out to fight him, Drake then with a part of his fleet – Borough in the meantime having mutinously sailed for home – succeeded in capturing the *San Felipe*, a huge Portuguese carrack homeward bound from Goa, laden with spices, ivories, silk and gold to a value of £114,000.

The voyage was an astonishing achievement, a success in everything it was sent out to do – in which it was so different from most enterprises of those years. It disrupted Spanish plans and communications – no one knew where Drake was going to turn up next – and no one dared to take a chance, so no one moved. It hit precisely at the weakest links in the Spanish preparations for the invasion of England – indeed it delayed the sailing of the First Armada for a year – it shook Spanish confidence and added to the legend of *El Draque*; and finally it made a thundering profit for the Queen. As a model of its kind, as an example of how much a small fleet may achieve, if brilliantly handled, in breaking up the preparations and organization for war of a powerful nation, it has probably not been equalled in history.

The adventure has come to be known as 'Singeing the King of Spain's beard', from Drake's famous comment. Drake had all the arrogance of genius, but, as Mattingly has pointed out, this was not intended as a boastful remark. After the Spaniards with their allies defeated the Turks in the great battle of Lepanto in October 1571 the Sultan said: 'When the Venetians sank my fleet they only singed my beard. It will grow again. But when I captured Cyprus I cut off one of their arms.' Drake was claiming a small victory, not a large. He knew the danger and he had seen the preparations afoot. He was under no illusions about the danger to England. And his great concern over the next twelve months was to dispel the illusions that still lingered in England, especially at court.

He had returned reluctantly from patrolling off the coast of Spain; weather, lack of reinforcements, sickness in his crews, the desertion of Borough, and lastly the capture of the great treasure ship, had brought him home. He expected to be allowed to resume his commission as soon as he had refitted and refurbished his fleet. The overwhelming success spoke for

itself; this was the one sure – and wonderfully economical –
way of continuing to disrupt Spain's preparations. Indeed,
with such tactics it seemed likely that an armada never *would*
be got ready to sail against England. Although virtually an act
of war, it made outright war less likely by preventing a confrontation. The Queen, of all people, must appreciate the
brilliant logic of this.

But the Queen, influenced by Burghley, who had a temperamental antipathy to Drake and his bravado, was still intent on
appeasing Philip rather than on fighting him. Whatever she
may have felt privately, she hypocritically expressed strong
displeasure to the Spanish at Drake's violation of their coast,
and Drake found himself a national and international hero in
temporary eclipse.

Then by October the pendulum swung again and the English
fleet mobilized, expecting the Armada that autumn. In the
week before Christmas Lord Howard of Effingham as Lord
Admiral took command of the English Fleet, and two days
later Drake became his vice-admiral and was given command
of an independent fleet to be based on Plymouth. (In January
the English again partly disbanded: mainly in the interests of
economy, but with some regard too to the impracticability of
keeping large groups of men cooped up for months without
epidemics; and Drake's fleet did not materialize as promised
but became a makeshift group that he assembled as and where
he best could.)

Then on the 9th February 1588 the Marquis of Santa Cruz,
Spain's great admiral, died, followed a few days later by his
vice-admiral, the Duke of Paliano, and it seemed for a time
that the whole armada project would be abandoned. At least
Elizabeth, on false intelligence from Spain and from France,
allowed herself to be persuaded so, and peace commissioners
were sent to Flanders to discuss terms with Parma. At the
same time Drake was forbidden to leave the English coast.
Philip, however, never had the least intention of abandoning
his Armada, now it was so far forward. Nor was he to be
deterred then or later by complaints from his commanders
that all was not at a peak of readiness for the great adventure.
Precisely similar complaints had reached him before Lepanto,
that other great and victorious crusade. Slow to make up his
mind, he was not a man to change it because of a few setbacks. The young prince of Elizabeth's memory, cautious but
statesmanlike, wise, and essentially a lover of peace, had long

since been submerged by the years; and it was a cardinal error on her part – one of the few she had made – to think of him as unchanged. To Philip the sailing of the Armada had become as holy an enterprise as any crusade of the middle ages. Indeed at one time he had intended to sail in it himself, so that he could be on the spot to dictate terms when the English collapsed.

To many Spaniards, high born and low, it was the same. To join the Armada was to join the popular cause, to embark on a Crusade. To proceed against the Infidel and try to recapture Jerusalem was an undertaking no more blessed of God than one to reunite Christendom and bring all Europe back into the bosom of the Church of Christ. Indeed, the people they were to fight were more ignoble than infidels, for they were 'fallen angels'. Lutherans condemned the belief that one could pray to the Virgin and the saints to intercede for them with God. They condemned the worship of images and holy relics, and wherever they conquered they ruthlessly destroyed them. They condemned the confessional. They condemned almost everything that was fundamental to the Catholic religion. They were people who sinned not out of ignorance but who, having known the light, had set their face against it.

There were also of course the practical considerations mentioned already – and these were becoming more urgent with every year that passed. The Iberian mercantile economy would founder if a stop were not put to the depredations of the English pirates. The economy of Spain itself might collapse unless the Netherlands were regained. So Philip cast around among his distinguished admirals and his generals and his noblemen for the most suitable man to take the place of Santa Cruz.

Like Elizabeth – only even more so than Elizabeth – Philip was compelled to place an aristocrat of great distinction at the head of his fleet. Elizabeth was lucky in Howard, who had served at sea when his father was Lord High Admiral, whose family in the past had given four admirals to England in Tudor times alone, and who had had separate command of a squadron of ships as early as 1570. (As further recommendation, he was first cousin to Anne Boleyn.) The death of Santa Cruz deprived Philip of just such a man; one of unimpeachable nobility and of high enough birth to take precedence over all others, but born to the sea. After consideration Philip chose to succeed him Don Alonso Perez de Guzman, Seventh Duke of Medina Sidonia, Count of Nebla, Marquis of Casheshe in Africa, Lord of the City St Lucar, Captain General of Andalusia and Knight of the Honourable Order of the Golden Fleece.

It was a formidable title for a man of formidable means and position. But the Duke of Medina Sidonia – then aged thirty-seven – suffered all his life from one of the gravest and rarest afflictions known to man : he had a poor opinion of his own abilities. He was also more than a trifle melancholic. He underestimated himself; and his contemporaries and most of his successors have taken their cue from him – they always do. But lately some historians, notably Mattingly, have done something to rehabilitate his reputation.

He was a sturdily built, rather short man of fresh complexion, with brown hair and beard, and dark intent eyes which certainly did not lack determination, though they may have lacked the self-certainty of a leader. At the time of the Armada his reputation stood high. Not only was he the largest and richest feudal landowner in Spain, but his career up to this time showed him to be a man of ability and distinction. He had served in several military capacities, and had led troops into battle on two occasions – though the occasions as it happened had not resulted in much fighting. He had been responsible for fitting out the Spanish fleets which sailed to the Indies and the Magellan Straits; and for two years he had been active behind the scenes helping with preparations for the Armada. On many of the most vital questions of recruitment, provisioning and finance his advice had been constantly sought by the King and followed. He was probably the best administrator in the kingdom.

We know that other names were considered along with his, among them the Duke of Savoy and the Grand Duke of Tuscany. Juan Martinez de Recalde suggested his own appointment. In his well-known letter to Philip asking to be relieved of the honour of leading the Armada, Medina Sidonia, after listing the reasons for his own unworthiness, suggested as a substitute Don Martin de Padilla, Adelantado of Castile.

Padilla, who had been a group commander at Lepanto and had had a distinguished fighting career, was later chosen by Philip to lead the Second and the Third Armadas of 1596 and 1597. It is stated by Duro that he offered the King a thousand men for the First Armada, with wages paid for six months.

But it is possible that in 1588 Padilla was under something of a cloud, for, although the actual commander of the galleys that fought Drake was Don Pedro de Acuña, Padilla was Captain-General of the galleys of Spain, and so bore over-all responsibility. It is usually the case, if some part of a nation's services fails, that the man in charge bears some of the odium, however little it may be deserved. So Padilla was left in the Mediterranean to keep an eye on the Turks.

I. A. I. Thompson has recently put forward some additional reasons for Philip's choice of Medina Sidonia in 1588. Portugal, only recently conquered, was growing very restive under the burden of the Armada preparations with its ruinous demands on their shipyards and their grain supplies. Whereas Santa Cruz was hated, Medina Sidonia was popular in Portugal, his wife being half Portuguese and his grandfather having been on terms of close friendship with the Portuguese royal family. The Duke was also known in England and had friends among the Catholics there, and if England should collapse it was essential to have someone apart from Parma to represent the King on the spot. The Duke was also a man of the highest reputation and honour, and with him as leader many would flock to follow him, not merely his vassals and dependants but adherents and friends, and even strangers, knowing of his financial repute.

And of course there was the money. If one takes the value of the maravedi at this time as being roughly five hundred to the pound sterling, and multiplies by forty to bring nearer present-day standards, one can estimate that the Duke of Medina Sidonia contributed about £650,000 – or about $1,600,000 – to the cost of the Armada out of his own pocket. No other could have done so much.

Indeed, whatever he thought later, Philip may not have been too upset at the time in having to make this vital change in the leadership of the *Empresa*. Philip's dry comment when he heard that the Marquis of Santa Cruz had died was, 'God has shown me a favour by removing the Marquis now rather than when the Armada has put to sea.' He does not sound heart-broken or appalled. In fact from the inception of the Enterprise Philip had worked with two difficult yokefellows. His intention was, and he had made it plain all along, that the Armada's role should be mainly defensive and should be there only to defeat the English fleet if it attacked. Mainly its purpose was to serve as a massive covering force for the passage of his veteran soldiers under Parma into England. Parma was to take command. At the juncture of the two forces he was to become the supreme general.

But Parma of late had been dragging his feet. Enthusiasm had given way to caution. Philip had certain suspicions of Parma. Also Santa Cruz with his sea prestige and knowledge of war might react in some unpredictable way to a crisis which arose far out of reach of the Escorial. They might indeed quarrel, Parma and Santa Cruz, and endanger the success of the Enterprise.

Medina Sidonia was more to be trusted than either. He would obey Philip's orders; he would do exactly as he was told; at the juncture of the fleet and the army he would gladly and modestly surrender the supreme command to Parma. But if he carried secret instructions from Philip – as Philip determined that he should – then these too would be faithfully carried out if the need arose. It looked like a guarantee against failure. At least it was a guarantee against failure to obey instructions.

Perhaps Philip was looking for someone like Eisenhower in the Second World War – not the best general but the best generalissimo.

So the Duke – a home-loving man and a pessimist – protesting that he was unequal to the task, went down to Lisbon, where he found chaos. It was no wonder that the Armada had not sailed under Santa Cruz. It looked as if it never would have done under him. In four short months of toil Medina Sidonia composed jealousies, abolished the worst abuses, increased recruitment, stockpiled food and ammunition, and created a central administration and something like a fleet ready to sail against England.

So as the spring of 1588 drew on, and the windy unseasonable summer broke, the portents of conflict threw deepening shadows across Europe. It was the year of ill-omen, predicted more than a century before by Regiomontanus, the great German astronomer and astrologer, who said that in 1588, if total catastrophe did not befall 'yet will the whole world suffer upheavals, empires will dwindle and from everywhere will be great lamentations'. These predictions had been confirmed by other learned philosophers since that time.

A Latin verse of the time, freely translated into English, runs:

When after Christ's birth there be expired
Of hundreds, fifteen year, eighty and eight,
There comes the time of dangers to be feared
And all mankind with dolors it shall fright.
For if the world in that year do not fall,
If sea and land then perish nor decay,
Yet Empires all, and Kingdoms alter shall,
And man to ease himself shall have no way.

If not the end of the world, was it to be the end of England?
In the Low Countries Parma after a long and bitter siege had
taken Sluys and had dug fifteen miles of new canals, making
it possible to haul barges to the invasion coast at Nieuport.
From there one could reach Dunkirk without exposing the
barges to attack from the sea. Dunkirk to Deal is about forty
miles – in good weather an easy night crossing. Parma's troops
were slowly massing in that direction, and he was assembling
and having built hundreds of flat-bottomed canal barges.

France, still ravaged by civil war, was for the time being
too weak to take sides at all. Her Catholic nobles, financed by
Spain, were now in control of Paris, and King Henry had fled
to Blois. It meant that for the duration of the coming summer
France would be completely neutralized. She could not menace
Parma's flank if he crossed the Channel and left the Netherlands weakly guarded. Nor could she aid England, even if she
wished, by sea.

As for Scotland, Parma had for two years been toying with
the idea of a Catholic insurrection, led by the Earl of Morton
and Colonel Semple, but this idea had been allowed to lapse.
Nevertheless King James and his puritan ministers were in no
position to help 'the Englishwoman'. Scotland, whatever her
true feelings, would militarily be neutral. Denmark, the then
naval power of the north, was highly apprehensive of a possible Spanish conquest of England; but her King had just died,
the new King was ten years old; and her offer of help, if any,
was likely to be too little and too late to sway the issue.

So it augured well for the crusade. In Lisbon the vast array
of ships was weekly growing. All Europe was waiting for the
coming trial of strength, and not many gave a great deal for
England's chances. Pope Sixtus, chattering away in the Vatican,
remarked that it was strange that a man who was emperor of
half the world should be defied by a woman who was queen
of half an island.

In that half island musters were being called and trained in villages and towns throughout the land. They were a motley lot, some armed with pikes and pitchforks, others with ancient swords or bows and arrows, all making do with what weapons they could find, like the Home Guard of 1940. Stow, in his *Chronicles of England*, speaks of 'certain gallant, active and forward citizens of London, merchants and others of like quality, to the number of three hundred, who voluntarily exercised themselves and trained others in the ready use of war'. They met every Tuesday.

From Gravesend to Tilbury Fort a chain and a bridge of boats was to be thrown to bar the enemy's passage up the river and to provide a ready communication from one bank to the other so that troops could move quickly to meet a threat to the north or south. Peter Pett, the engineer in charge of this operation, was still consulting with Leicester about completing the bridge when the Armada was off Torbay.

In the west country, where the main blow might come, five deputy lieutenants were appointed for Devon, two for Cornwall. Ralegh, as Lord Lieutenant of Cornwall, was much assisted by his cousin, Richard Grenville. Throughout England old forts were repaired as best they could be in a short time and field trenches were dug. Beacons were built all along the coast and far inland. A map of the beacons erected in Kent and Sussex shows that almost every high point was utilized, so that once the alarm was given the whole countryside would be alive with tiny fires spreading the alarm. A great wave of patriotism ran through England. High and low rushed to offer their arms to the Queen. Aged noblemen got out of their beds, put on armour and led their retainers to join the army camps. It was a bad time for aliens – of whom there were many in the City of London. Ubaldino says that it was 'easier to find flocks of white crows than one Englishman who loved a foreigner'.

An anonymous author lists the men available in each county in 1588, the numbers trained, the numbers untrained, the weapons available, the leaders of each regiment. In sum it looks a formidable total, but spread throughout the land it is wafer-thin, a paper-bag defence capable of being punctured at any point by a strong and resolute blow. Of course, once the Spanish landed, the country would have resisted to the last breath, but it is impossible to believe that the musters, however obstinate and bravely led, could have held out at a local level against disciplined and well-armed soldiers. So long as Spain retained the vital initiative she could strike anywhere along hundreds of miles of coastline.

The Queen was left in no doubt about the feelings of Drake. He besought her and her council in a stream of letters to allow him to descend again on the Spanish coast before it was too late. 'If there may be such a stay or stop made by any means of this fleet in Spain,' he wrote, 'so that they may not come through the seas as conquerors – which I assure myself they think to do – then shall the Prince of Parma have such a check thereby as were meet . . . My very good lords, next under God's mighty protection, the advantage again of time and place will be the only and chief means for our good; wherein I most humbly beseech your good Lordships to persevere as you have begun; for that with fifty sail of shipping we shall do more good upon their own coast than a great deal more will do here at home.'

This was in March. On the 13th April he wrote personally to the Queen : 'The advantage of time and place in all martial actions is half the victory, which being lost is irrecoverable. Wherefore, if your Majesty will command me away . . .' On the 28th April, again : 'Most renowned Prince, I beseech you to pardon my boldness in the discharge of my conscience, being burdened to signify unto your Highness the imminent dangers that in my simple opinion do hang over us . . . The promise of peace from the Prince of Parma and these mighty preparations in Spain agree not well together . . . these preparations may be speedily prevented by sending your forces to encounter them somewhat far off and more near to their own coasts, which will be cheaper for your Majesty and her people and much dearer for the enemy.'

Still Elizabeth hesitated. She was a woman born to hesitate and prevaricate, and thirty years on the throne had proved to her how often prevarication and delay had been her friend. There was another reason : the Queen was trying to buy Parma off by offering him the independent sovereignty of the Netherlands. It would have been a betrayal of her Dutch allies, and her Dutch allies suspected this; but it would have prevented an Anglo-Spanish conflict and would probably have terminated the war in the Netherlands, which, as it was, still had many bloody generations to run. But even if this offer failed – and she must have known that even with Parma's emotional commitment to the Netherlands it was likely to fail – she was not altogether won over by Drake's aggressive views. If the Armada did eventually sail, the seas were wide; might not Howard and Drake if cruising off the Spanish coast miss the Spanish fleet and allow it to reach an undefended England? (That this was not an academic objection was proved by the events of 1597, when this was precisely what happened.)

In May, however, Drake was able to leave Plymouth and visit the Queen at court. There, with all the ebullience and confidence of his genius, he was able to bring Elizabeth to his way of thinking, and Lord Admiral Howard, though unconvinced at first, also came to accept the aggressive ideas of his lieutenant. Howard was dispatched to Plymouth to take command of the much augmented fleet there, and he arrived on the 23rd May, Drake now becoming his second-in-command in fact, as he had been since December in name. It was a situation that seemed bound to lead to disharmony; but from the first they worked together without jealousy or ill-will.

Drake, throughout all the adventures which had made him the most famous commoner in the world, had *always* been his own supreme commander, yielding to no one, arrogant in his rightness because he had so often proved to be right. Strict, religious, jolly, dynamic, beloved, he must have faced one of the sternest tasks of self-discipline to have accepted graciously the arrival of a supreme commander to take charge of his fleet at this time of all times. Howard, born to the sea but knowing himself to be looked on by the fleet as something of a figurehead, knowing that throughout the world his name and his very real naval talents meant little enough; that the Spanish if they came would come to fight Drake and that if the English lost he would get the blame, while if they won Drake would get the credit. Howard, knowing this and knowing the explosive, prideful genius of his second-in-command, must equally have shown admirable tact and self-discipline in the weeks of inactivity that lay ahead.

For inactivity there still was, occasioned by a pitiful lack of all supplies, despite Howard's six-months-long campaign to get them; by atrocious weather that kept his ships stormbound; by reports – true enough – that part of an Armada had been sighted off the Scillies and had been driven back by the great gales; by further impossible instructions from Elizabeth to beat up and down and try to protect the whole of the English coastline from invasion; by genuine uncertainty now as to the target the Spanish might aim at if they were already so near; and by further storms. The initiative, it seemed, was lost. Drake's offensive plans had been agreed to too late.

Then at last reliable information reached England that in fact the Armada had sailed, that parts of it had reached the Lizard and Mounts Bay and then all had been battered by the storm, and the great fleet was back in Coruña licking its wounds and replenishing its supplies. With the news came – wonder of wonders – permission from the Queen to move, so move they did, nearly a hundred ships, scantily provisioned, the men already having been on half rations for some time, but all so eager to be off before another countermanding order should reach them. They fled with a favourable wind, and in two days were within a hundred miles of the Spanish coast. Had the wind stayed fair there can be no doubt that there would have been a battle in or around the approaches to Coruña, for by now, after a period of depression and discouragement, the Armada and its captains had regained their resolution and were awaiting a favourable wind to sail.

But at this point the wind backed right round to the south, and Howard and Drake, having gambled on picking up extra provisions from their raids in Spain, found themselves beating into the wind, making small progress, dangerously short of supplies, and all too aware that what was an adverse wind for them was ideal for the Spanish. They could do only one thing, and this they did, which was to turn about and return to Plymouth. As they reached Plymouth the Armada began to leave Coruña.

Froude writes of that departure: 'It was a treacherous interval of real summer. The early sun was lighting the long chain of the Galician mountains, marking with shadows the cleft defiles and shining softly on the white walls and vineyards of Coruña. The wind was light and falling towards a calm. The great galleons drifted slowly with the tide on the purple water, the long streamers trailing from the trucks, the red crosses, the emblem of the crusade, showing bright upon the hanging sails. The fruit boats were bringing off the last fresh supplies and the pinnaces were hastening to the ships with the last loiterers on shore.'

That was on the 12th July. By the afternoon of Friday the 19th they were off the Lizard. At sight of land the Duke of Medina Sidonia ordered his great flag to be hoisted, showing the crucifixion, with the Virgin Mary and Mary Magdalene kneeling beside the cross. It was the banner which had been blessed by the Pope. On that same afternoon Captain Thomas Fleming in the *Golden Hind* (fifty tons, with a crew of thirty), one of the screen of barques keeping watch in the Channel, returned in haste to Plymouth with news that the Armada, which was still thought to be in Coruña, was in fact in the Sleeve and advancing towards Plymouth.

Its arrival was a complete surprise – of the sort that Drake was fond of springing on his enemies – and it found the English fleet in the worst possible position: desperately low in all essential supplies, with the enemy to windward of them, themselves trapped in a harbour with an impossible south-west breeze blowing full into the port, and a neap tide flowing against them.

The story that Fleming found Howard and Drake playing bowls is substantiated by people who wrote within living memory of the occasion, and by the Spaniards themselves in 1624. Drake's comment, made before his superior officer could speak, that there was time to finish the game and beat the Spaniards after, accords with the nature of the man. A quick tongue is almost as much an essential of leadership as a cool head. It was precisely the right thing to say to avoid the risk of panic. And, as so often with Drake when he said things which did not conform to the normal run of probabilities, he was absolutely right.

6

The First Armada

The Christian Catholic crusading Armada was at last upon the English shores. All flags flying, bands playing, unscathed from its days at sea except for the four galleys, which had turned back, and one other ship, the *Santa Ana*, which had been unable to weather the storms of Wednesday. But otherwise intact, in good spirits and ready for battle. The *Empresa*, as Philip first called it. Then the *Felicisima Armada*. Then the *Armada Invencible* – a name later picked on by its foes and immortalized in much the way that one speaks of the Old Contemptibles.

What did this fleet, after all the early losses through storm and last minute additions, actually consist of? And who were the men, apart from the Duke, who commanded it?

The total of the fleet which eventually reached the Channel was about one hundred and thirty-seven, of which one hundred and nine were combat vessels, the others supply ships. The combat vessels varied from full war galleons of upwards of a thousand tons, with fifty guns and five hundred men; through ships of five hundred to eight hundred tons which were virtually converted merchantmen with rebuilt forecastles; to hulks – heavy built, slow-moving auxiliaries – and patches and zabras, which were sloop-rigged, fast, and lightly armed.

This fleet was divided into nine squadrons. The first squadron under the direct command of the Duke of Medina Sidonia consisted of twelve ships: ten of the Royal Galleons of Portugal and two zabras. The Duke himself sailed in the *San Martin*, the fleet flagship, a vessel of one thousand tons with forty-eight guns and a complement of nearly five hundred men. The second was the Biscay Squadron of ten galleons (now reduced to nine) and four patches, under the command of Admiral Juan Martinez de Recalde; the third consisted of the Galleons of Castile: fourteen fine ships, with two patches, under Admiral Diego Flores de Valdes; the fourth was the

Andalusian Squadron: two large ships, three galleons, five hulks and one patache under Admiral Pedro de Valdes; the fifth was the Guipuzcoan Squadron of nine big ships, one hulk and two pataches, under Miguel de Oquendo; the sixth was the Levantine Squadron of ten big ships under Martin de Bertendona; the seventh was the fleet of hulks – twenty-three of them, ranging from two hundred to eight hundred tons under Juan Gomez de Medina; the eighth was a full squadron of zabras and pataches, twenty-two in all, under Don Antonio de Mendoza; and the ninth was the four galleasses under Don Hugo de Moncada – these last each carried a mixed crew of around three hundred and fifty men, with three hundred galley slaves as oarsmen. The total tonnage of the fleet was about fifty-eight thousand – immeasurably the largest fleet that had ever sailed the seas – and it was manned by eight thousand sailors and nearly nineteen thousand soldiers. There were also some four thousand others aboard, of whom twelve hundred were the galley slaves in the galleasses, and the rest non-combatants of one sort or another: a hospital staff of sixty-two, one hundred and eighty monks, four hundred and fifty-six servants of the gentlemen adventurers – these adventurers including four English, one Irish and one German. (There were also among the salaried officers eighteen English or Irish and an Irish priest.) Many of the noblemen had long retinues of servants; the Duke of Medina Sidonia had fifty, the Prince of Ascoli – a natural son of Philip II – had thirty-nine, Don Alonso de Leyva had thirty-six, and so on down the list of diminishing nobility and importance.

And the men in command? For all Medina Sidonia's administrative ability, even Philip's commission could not make a seaman of him, so someone must stand at his side, someone who could support and guide him in the day to day conduct of the fleet at sea. For this post Philip had chosen Don Diego Flores de Valdes, the commander of the Galleons of Castile. Diego Flores was a very experienced officer (much older than the Duke) who had been responsible for the design of some of the latest galleons and who for more than twenty years had commanded the fleet known as the Indian Guard – that is the warships detailed to protect the treasure ships. He was also an expert on tides, seas and currents, and the choice so far seemed a good one. Yet his record was marred by a succession of quarrels with his brother officers, not least that one which had led to the failure of the expedition to the

75

Straits of Magellan in 1581; and it is surprising that Philip did not know he was one of the most unpopular men in the fleet. He had a permanent feud with his cousin Pedro de Valdes, an equally distinguished officer, who commanded the Andalusian Squadron; and the King's choice meant that, standing next to the skilled administrator, the noble figure-head of Medina Sidonia, was this narrow-minded, acrimonious man who by his mere presence would automatically undo much of the conciliatory work of his chief. Most of the time Flores de Valdes sailed aboard the *San Martin* beside the Duke.

By the wording of this appointment Philip also took something from the authority of Medina Sidonia's second-in-command, who naturally was Recalde, Spain's greatest living sailor. Born in Bilbao in 1526, Recalde had been Superintendent of the Royal Dockyards, had been second-in-command to Santa Cruz and had also commanded the Indian Guard. In 1579 he had been the admiral in charge of landing a thousand Spaniards in Ireland, and after doing this he had reconnoitred the English coast before returning to Spain. He had had considerable other experience of the northern seas and the Channel. It was he whom Drake had missed near Cadiz. If one thinks of a better alternative to the chief commander one looks no further than Don Juan Martinez de Recalde, Knight of Santiago. It is a view with which Recalde himself would have agreed.

Recalde did not sail in a ship of his own squadron either, but in the vice-flagship of the Duke's squadron, the *San Juan de Portugal*, a galleon of one thousand and fifty tons, with fifty guns and a crew of five hundred.

Pedro de Valdes, commanding the Andalusian Squadron, was also a seaman of long experience, having been in numerous fights against the French and the Portuguese, and having been seriously wounded in a grim little battle with two English ships which in 1580 took refuge in the estuary of Ferrol, near Coruña. He had had, however, one or two vicissitudes in his career, being imprisoned in 1582 on the King's orders, on the failure of his attempt to land in the Azores and his loss of a large part of the soldiers he landed there. He sailed now in the *Nuestra Señora del Rosario*, one of the largest and newest of the galleons of the fleet.

It would be incorrect to assume that Spain derived no benefit from Drake's raid on Cadiz. The fighting there finally demolished the belief that galleys could hold their own against sailing ships. Without that demonstration a considerable number of galleys would have certainly accompanied the Armada. (Santa Cruz had asked for forty.) With it, even the most conservative of naval men were constrained to see the light, and even the four that eventually were sent were turned back by Wednesday's storm. But a small squadron of four powerful galleasses accompanied the fleet, those oar and sail vessels which it was hoped would combine the best of both worlds, being heavily armed – as galleys could not be – and as manœuvrable as galleys and independent of wind. This squadron was under Don Hugo de Moncada, a high-born veteran of the Netherlands campaign, with a long experience of galley warfare, sailing in his flagship, the *San Lorenzo*. But it was the *Gerona*, the third of these great ships, which was to make the saddest history for Spain.

Two other men had inevitably been appointed to high command. One, Don Miguel Oquendo, commanded the Guipuzcoan Squadron, sailing himself in his flagship, the *Santa Ana* (not the one that turned back). He was a sailor of great skill and dash, handling his ship, it is said, as if she were a light horse. In the battle of Terceira in 1582 he had fought beside Santa Cruz and had saved the Admiral from destruction by running his own ship under full sail between two of the enemy ships and boarding and capturing the French flagship, hoisting his own flag on her masthead above the smoke of the battle.

The other was Don Martin de Bertendona, commanding the Levantine Squadron, and sailing in his flagship *La Regazona*. The most gifted of the younger captains, his was a name which was to occur a number of times in English history. His father, an earlier Don Martin, had been in command of the Biscayan great ship which had brought Philip to England to marry Mary thirty-four years before. Three years hence, the younger de Bertendona was to take the leading part in the great fight off the Azores when Sir Richard Grenville in the *Revenge* took on the Spanish fleet single-handed and was at last overwhelmed. Between the first Armada of 1588 and the second and third of 1596 and 1597 a new generation of Spanish seamen grew up. De Bertendona is the only officer who commanded a squadron in all three armadas.

The last officer needing mention did not command a squadron but was in fact designated by Philip to take charge of the Armada if Medina Sidonia should die or be killed. This was the Lieutenant-General of the Fleet, a brilliant young soldier called Alonso de Leyva. A tall, slender, handsome man with a blond beard and smooth flaxen hair, he was a favourite at court, a hot-head, a dashing soldier; one thinks of him as the Spanish parallel to the Earl of Essex. De Leyva had already commanded the Sicilian Galleys, had been Captain-General of the Milanese Cavalry, and had resigned his high position in order to lead the army which was to sail in the Armada against England. His ship, the *Rata Encoronada* of eight hundred and twenty tons, complement four hundred and nineteen, was part of de Bertendona's squadron. In her sailed the flower of Spain's young noblemen.

Let us make no mistake: these men and the captains who sailed under them were not indolent gallants, not inefficient officers, not fair-weather sailors. It is true that they carried more than their share of 'passengers' – noblemen of high spirit but no knowledge of the sea; the servants of these dons; and a high proportion of trained and well-equipped soldiers who, because of the tactics of the English, were never to be utilized. It is also true that the sailors themselves were more used to the Mediterranean and the long runs with the trade winds to the West Indies and back. But anyone who supposes these waters are always calm can never have sailed on them. Mediterranean storms can be sudden and vicious; the Atlantic is the roughest ocean in the world; and the Bay of Biscay, which was home territory to the Spaniards, is as nasty as the English Channel any day. That a new style of sea warfare was in the process of being evolved and that their ships were ill-designed for this evolution is not a reflection on the people who manned them.

First among the admirals on the English side was the fifty-two-year-old Howard of Effingham, a personal friend as well as a cousin of the Queen's. As soon as Elizabeth came to the throne his good looks and ability, together with his kinship, had brought him advancement and high office. Ambassador to France at the age of twenty-three, General of Horse under the Earl of Warwick in putting down the northern rebellion, Member of Parliament for Surrey from 1563 to 1573, a Knight of the Garter, Lord Chamberlain of the Household, a commissioner at the trial of Mary Queen of Scots and one of the strongest advocates for her execution; a grandson of the second Duke of Norfolk, the victor of Flodden, he was, unlike many of the Howards, a staunch Protestant.

There was no doubt about the family religion of his vice-admiral. Born about 1545 at Crowndale Farm near Tavistock, Francis Drake was the eldest of twelve children whose father, Edmund, having become a passionate Lutheran, was too ardent in his advocacy of the New Religion during the Prayer Book Rebellion of 1548 and had to decamp with his family to the safer areas of eastern Kent. There, during the reign of Mary, he lived with his multiplying family in one of the hulks on the river, in considerable poverty – and no little danger, since he read prayers and preached religious sedition to the seamen in the Queen's ships. Young Francis was brought up in an aura of persecution where the identity of the persecutor was quite clearly the Scarlet Woman of Rome; and all through his life his utterances bore the mark of religious conviction and were adorned with the metaphors of the Reformed Church.

When only twenty-two he had sailed with his cousin John Hawkins on the voyage to the West Indies which ended in the disastrous events of San Juan de Ulua, where warships of Spain, under the direction of Don Martin Enriquez, the new Viceroy of Mexico, having first given the small English fleet a promise of safe conduct, treacherously set upon them; with the result that the English returned home with a hundred and fifty men alive of the six hundred who ventured, and about a quarter of their ships. From this point forward Spain became the practical enemy to Drake, 'the wolf with the privy paw', the embodiment of all that was worst in the Catholic faith. The results had since been plain for all to see. By nature an individualist, by necessity a privateer, Drake had so exercised his naval genius that the Spanish credited him with supernatural powers – powers of darkness of course – and felt they needed God's help when fighting him. It was a considerable moral disadvantage for them.

Of equal importance in the English fleet – some would even say greater – was John Hawkins. A man of fifty-six at the time of the Armada, Hawkins had been born in Plymouth of a prosperous ship-owning family, and, almost more than Drake's, the history of his career traces the burgeoning of English maritime enterprise in the sixteenth century. Always well dressed, unfathomable, courteous and charming, he claimed friendship with King Philip of Spain and argued that he was a loyal subject of Philip's, dating from the time of the King's marriage to Mary. Directly involved in the Ridolfi plot of 1571, which was one to assassinate Elizabeth and put Mary Queen of Scots on the throne, in which he was to provide naval cover for an invasion of Spanish troops under Alva, Hawkins had contrived to keep Elizabeth and Cecil informed of every step and yet was apparently adroit enough to avoid suspicion by the Spanish that he had betrayed them, even when the plot was uncovered and the main conspirators arrested.

Partly as a reward for these services, Elizabeth two years later had appointed him Treasurer of the Navy, and in this position not only was he able to attack the abuses and dishonesty that he found at every level, but he was largely responsible for building the ships which these last tense months had floated in dockyard and harbour, half-crewed and ill-provisioned, awaiting their greatest test. However starved they were of men, rations, gunpowder and shot, these vessels were in design ahead of any others in the world.

Compared to those which preceded them, and to the Spanish ships they opposed, they were longer in relation to their breadth – a proportion of something like three to one – deeper in keel, and lying 'low and snug' in the water, with the forecastle and sterncastle greatly reduced and with the deep waist decked over. The mainmast was stepped further forward, the sails were flatter, and there was a reappearance of top gallants. Such ships could sail nearer the wind and were more manœuvrable than any warships that had been built before. The English had not previously been renowned for original or creative ship design, and the predominant influence of sailors of great experience at the dockyards during this period of building and rebuilding was as vital to the survival of England as the development of the Spitfire three and a half centuries later.

Hawkins was fortunate, since he was able to take a prominent part in the battles in which his ships were put to the test. But perhaps too the spirit of Henry VIII breathed down over the scene. For it was Henry who introduced the broadside which so revolutionized war at sea; Henry who initiated the policy of putting guns of longer range into his ships so that future battles might be won by gunfire; and Henry who had laid down the dockyards without which it would have been impossible to build the ships of 1588.

The last of the great trio of seamen adventurers was also in his middle fifties at this time. Martin Frobisher was a Yorkshireman, though the family was originally Welsh. He had gone to sea as an orphan with Wyndham in 1553, and was one of only forty to survive the voyage. The following year, when sailing under John Lok, he had been captured by Negroes and spent some months in a Portuguese gaol. When Queen Elizabeth came to the throne he was living as a merchant's factor in Morocco. There was a smack of real piracy about his middle years, when he used southern Ireland as a base of operations and combined with like-minded gentlemen of the sea issuing from the Cornish coves and creeks. In the 1570s he had made three voyages to the Arctic, where Frobisher's Bay is named after him, and he had sailed as Vice-Admiral under Drake, commanding the London merchantman *Primrose*, on the great West Indian voyage of 1585-6. A tough, irritable, unruly man, he combined ill with Drake; but when the Armada came he commanded the largest English ship of the time, the *Triumph*, of eleven hundred tons with a crew of five hundred, and was always in the thick of the fight.

In the first stages of the battle the English did not divide into squadrons. Howard was aboard his flagship, the *Ark* – sometimes called the *Ark Ralegh* because she had been designed for Ralegh and sold by him to the Queen – a vessel of eight hundred tons with a crew of four hundred, and Drake sailed in the *Revenge*, of five hundred tons with a crew of two hundred and fifty. As against a Spanish total of one hundred and thirty-seven ships of all sizes, the English had, in the neighbourhood of Plymouth at the beginning of the fight, about sixty-four. (Another fleet of forty-odd vessels under Lord Henry Seymour was guarding the Thames and Dover against a surprise landing there.) But, in order to have such ships as he brought out of Plymouth fully manned, Howard had to strip some of his ships bare and leave them to be provisioned and crewed later, so that only a proportion of the sixty-four was at first in the battle. If, however, the total fleets of England and Spain confronted each other, as they did in the battle of Gravelines, the Spanish still had a big advantage in fire power. The average Spanish ship had a broadside twice as heavy as the English, and while the English had many more smaller long-range pieces, the Spanish carried three times as many heavy cannon as the English and nearly eight times as many perrier types. So that at close quarters they had every chance of crippling the English ships and boarding them. Nor is there much to be said for the theory that the Spanish guns were inferior to the English. The Armada, as has been seen, carried a considerable proportion of English-made guns, and the rest came from the finest foundries in Europe. The Spanish personnel outnumbered the English by two to one, though the superiority lay in soldiers, who in the event were never used.

These comparisons are of the two fleets when both fully engaged. So it is clear that the Spanish superiority at the outset, when engaged by about half the English fleet, was overwhelming.

Not only were they superior but they had the English at the worst possible disadvantage, catching them in harbour while still re-provisioning after their own voyage, and embayed by wind and tide. It will be remembered what Drake did in a not altogether dissimilar situation outside Cadiz. Vice-Admiral Borough's concern as to the hazards of going straight in, and a plea that they should at least wait until dark, were blown away by the wind as *Elizabeth Bonaventure* cast off her captains one by one to return to their own ships and follow as best they could.

Medina Sidonia, when only ten miles off Plymouth, hove-to to allow his straggling fleet to close up. It was thirty-four years to the day since Philip had landed at Southampton to marry Mary. After prayers 'when all our people kneeled down, beseeching Our Lord to give us victory against the enemies of His holy faith', and while they could see the clouds of smoke blowing across the land as the beacons flared to give warning of their coming, the Duke called a council-of-war. It was an act of which Vice-Admiral Borough would have approved.

There are varying reports of what happened at that council, but the best founded is that de Leyva, the handsome young Lieutenant-General of the Fleet, supported by Recalde and Oquendo, the two most aggressive admirals, urged an instant attack on Plymouth. They were not absolutely certain that Drake was there, but their wide sweeping of the seas on their way from Spain had made no contact with English forces, so that it was a reasonable inference that he was in the port. If not he, certainly a substantial part of the English fleet. An attack pressed home now with fire-ships and a favourable wind might very well destroy that fleet and so provide a first resounding victory for Spain. Medina Sidonia – like Borough – saw danger in entering a fortified harbour which would only allow entry of three vessels abreast and an impossibility of retreat – with the present wind – if the attack did not prosper. Other admirals – including Pedro de Valdes – were against the venture; but the debate ended when the Duke told them of his personal instructions from the King. These instructions were to defeat the enemy if or when he attacked or attempted to impede the progress of the fleet, but not to seek him out – the overriding objective of the Armada being to arrive off Margate intact and to make juncture with the Duke of Parma to cover the landing of his troops.

As evening drew on and the Spanish council-of-war broke up, the English fleet, in the eye of the damp wind, began to warp laboriously out of Catwater. By dusk most of the big vessels were out and struggling close-hauled to beat out of and down the Sound towards the comparative safety of Rame Head. The decision not to attack Plymouth having been taken, the Armada proceeded on its way, thus assisting the English in their efforts to claw to windward of them. Dark fell and all the headlands were aflame with their warning bonfires, spreading the alarm throughout England faster than an express train. The Spanish were here at last. About one in the morning a Spanish pinnace returned with captured fishermen who told that Howard and Drake were now at sea, and the Duke decided to come to anchor until morning, in the meantime dispatching orders to his great fleet to close up into battle formation.

By dawn the wind had veered to west-north-west and the two fleets sighted each other for the first time. The English were now to windward, having performed a feat of which the Spanish ships however handled would have been quite incapable. This English fleet was still hastily assembling, being joined from time to time by some of its larger ships which were only now able to get free of the land. It was a straggling formation stretching from north to south in a line of about nine miles, with some of the largest warships nearest the land, a group of vessels of all types in the centre, and a wide screen of smaller ships, armed merchantmen, pinnaces and the like, sweeping south far beyond the enemy.

The Armada had already adopted its famous crescent formation, and, besides being so much more numerous and formidable to look at, was more closely concentrated, the bulge facing away from the English ships, and the tips of the crescent like the pincers of a crab about six miles apart and arching to close. Duro says that all the contemporary writers, especially the foreign ones, agree in describing the consternation of the English when they saw the mass of ships. He then goes on to quote the Italian, Bentivollo: 'You could hardly see the sea. The Spanish fleet was stretched out in the form of a half moon with an immense distance between its extremities. The masts and rigging, the towering sterns and prows which in height and number were so great that they dominated the whole naval concourse caused horror mixed with wonder and gave rise to doubt whether that campaign was at sea or on land and whether one or the other element was the more splendid. It came on with a steady and deliberate movement, yet when it drew near in full sail it seemed almost that the waves groaned under its weight and the winds were made to obey it.'

This was a confrontation such as had never happened before in the history of the world. No such forces had ever faced each other; all the old rules or principles of attack or defence were discarded. Communication between one ship and another was by flag or by hailing trumpet; no opportunity existed for working out new tactics to counter the manœuvres of one's foe or the accidents of war or weather; discipline in ships was good but between ships depended on the personality and impulses of the varying captains. Understanding on this score was better on the English side because it was a homogeneous fleet; the Spanish included various nationalities sailing with varying degrees of communication and conviction.

Yet at this stage the Spanish formation was the stronger and much the better controlled. It was slow moving but tightly knit, like a battle square on land; and equally hard to attack. In the most exposed positions at each end were some of its largest and best-gunned galleons; while no lighter fleet – or part of a fleet – would willingly attack the centre, for it could immediately be surrounded. The left end of the crescent – that is the one nearest the land – was defended by Recalde with his Biscayan squadron, with Pedro de Valdes in support. At the right end was Bertendona, with Oquendo in support, both officially under de Leyva in the *Rata Encoronada*.

The English without hesitation decided to attack both ends of the crescent, since these could be more easily isolated than the rest and because the wind would make them hardest to succour if they became so isolated. While Howard in the *Ark* led his ships into an attack on the right wing, Drake in the *Revenge*, followed by several others including Frobisher in the *Triumph*, attacked Recalde on the left. The two sorties met with very different results. Howard, the first to close, engaged in a furious cannonade with de Leyva's *Rata Encoronada*,

Bertendona's *Regazona*, the *Lavia*, and the other seven ships of the Levantine squadron, which had come about to meet them. The thunder of the guns was carried widespread over the little flecking waves, to fishing smacks far out at sea, and to the land for miles around Plymouth, greeting the new ships as they beat out of the port to join Howard's fleet, telling the anxious watchers on beach and cliff that the battle was at last joined.

Sailing in line ahead, the English ships swept past the Spanish, but they did not attempt to close the distance, and even their own guns, lighter but of longer range, fell short, so that although the exchange was fierce no damage was done on either side. When the attack was made on the other wing, however, Recalde himself in the *San Juan de Portugal* came about to meet the English fire as the first wing had done, but only the *Gran Grin*, his vice-flagship, followed suit; the rest of his squadron sailed on leaving the two big galleons isolated and to be quickly surrounded. Various reasons have been given for this event: (a) that the rest of the captains panicked at the heavy firing of the English fleet, (b) that Recalde in the emergency of the moment failed to make the proper signal to his squadron. The first seems improbable, since the Biscayan squadron was one of the best in the fleet; the second quite impossible for a sailor of Recalde's eminence.

It has also been suggested that Recalde deliberately disobeyed the Duke's orders so as to create a *mêlée*. It is true that Recalde, of all the officers, had the least faith in the idea of joining up with the Duke of Parma; and yesterday he had been cheated of his chance of catching Howard and Drake embayed in Plymouth. With such a massive fleet it was probably intolerable for him to retreat slowly up Channel while the English dogs barked at his heels. And all the captains knew – even Philip II knew and had so written in his orders to Medina Sidonia – that the English would *try* to keep their distance, attacking from long range, refusing the invitation to board the enemy, doing what damage they could without being damaged themselves. Well, here was a chance to break the deadlock before the deadlock had begun to grip.

If this is a fair interpretation of Recalde's actions, it is worse than Nelson's blind eye, for by going contrary to the whole of the Armada strategy Recalde played directly into the hands of the English. But his was a bluff which might have succeeded. Two of the biggest galleons were an enormous prize: the sort of prize that Drake or Frobisher would be unable to resist. Let them but come within range and the fight would be on. Even if the galleons were heavily pounded, the English guns were not likely to be able to finish them off. To capture them they would have to be boarded, and the *San Juan* and the *Gran Grin* carried between them nearly six hundred trained soldiers. In the meantime other units of each fleet would be drawn in, and once locked in combat . . .

Whether this was his reasoning or not, or whether the rest of his captains did panic at a cannonade such as they had never heard at sea before, no doubt the isolation of the two galleons did present a terrible temptation to Drake and Frobisher. But it was a temptation they resisted. They closed only to a range of about four hundred yards, where their fire could be effective and the Spanish fire would fall short. So for nearly two hours the *San Juan* and the *Gran Grin* were bombarded, and both were damaged, though this damage was largely to personnel and superstructure, for the English shot was not heavy enough to hole the enemy between wind and water. As soon as Medina Sidonia saw his rearguard in trouble he came about in his galleon the *San Martin* and, followed by his squadron, sailed to the rescue. But since he was well in the van of the whole Armada, it meant not merely beating back into the wind, a difficult enough operation in itself, but skirting the whole crescent front of the fleet in order to get to the southernmost tip.

When eventually about midday the *San Martin*, the *San Marcos*, the *San Felipe* and the *San Mateo* reached the battle area, the English ships fought them for another two hours, but always giving sea room when they had to, never closing the range, ignoring the Spanish invitations to grapple and board, avoiding the rushes of the Spanish squadrons and snapping at their heels. But as more and more of the galleons arrived on the scene Howard gave orders to break off the engagement and to retire to a safe distance. Still needing reinforcements and still sounding out the strength of his opponent, Howard hesitated to commit himself further, and so the first clash came to an end. Recalde was gathered into the fold of the Armada, and the fleet began slowly to re-form and move up channel again. But while the regrouping took place in a rising wind and sea, Pedro de Valdes in the *Rosario*, the flagship of the Andalusian squadron, making towards Recalde with the intention apparently of helping him, collided with another

Biscayan ship and then, swinging round, fouled a galleon of his own squadron, the *Santa Catalina* of eight hundred and eighty-two tons, and lost his bowsprit and brought down the stay of his foremast.

For a while all was confusion; and almost before it could be sorted out there was a tremendous explosion aboard the *San Salvador*, which tore out her stern castle, splintered her masts and killed two hundred of her crew.

Many romantic stories have been told of the cause of this explosion, the most picturesque being Ubaldino's of a Flemish gunnery officer who took exception to an army captain making free with his wife, 'who was with him, as is the custom of the country'. The army captain ordered the Fleming to be beaten, whereupon, when he was released, the gunner plunged a lighted taper into a barrel of gunpowder and wrecked the ship. However, a more mundane explanation is far more likely, namely that the ship had been in action and a gunner's carelessness resulted in a spark reaching the gunpowder in the rear hold. Whatever the cause, the *San Salvador*, a vessel of nine hundred and fifty-eight tons with a crew of three hundred and ninety-six, belonging to Oquendo's squadron, became almost a total wreck, and in the confusion caused by the explosion and the flames, Howard saw another opportunity to attack, and led a dozen of his best ships back into action.

Once again the Duke and his squadron came to the rescue, driving away the English ships to a respectable distance and with the help of two galleasses, which could make greater headway into the wind, came up with the *San Salvador* and got a line aboard her and was able to salvage the bullion and put out the flames. In the growing sea the *Rosario* was in further trouble, for her foremast gave way at the hatches and fell on the main yard. The *San Martin* herself got a line aboard the *Rosario* and took her in tow. But the line parted; and now Diego Flores, appointed by Philip as Medina Sidonia's chief adviser, was at the Duke's side angrily reminding him that it was his duty to command the fleet, not to succour all its lame dogs, and that anyway the bulk of the Armada was now so far in advance of him that if he did not follow soon the fleet would be split in two, and that with dusk falling any attempt to recall the van of the Armada would fail.

The Duke, who had eaten nothing all day – the first of many such days to come – would not at first accept the advice of his chief of staff; but as the ships pitched ever more dangerously around the damaged *Rosario*, with an increasing risk of further collision, he sent word to Pedro de Valdes asking him to leave his ship and come aboard the *San Martin*. De Valdes vehemently rejected the invitation. At length, having appointed six smaller ships to attend the *Rosario*, the Duke gave the orders to follow the slow progress of the rest of the Armada eastward.

The first day's fighting had brought losses to the Spanish, but not from enemy action. It had brought some depression to the English. They could outsail the Armada but not outgun it, and the discipline of the Spaniards was impressive. Howard wrote to Walsingham: 'We durst not adventure to put in among them, their fleet being so strong. But there shall be nothing neglected or unhazarded that may work their overthrow.' Drake wrote to Admiral Lord Henry Seymour, chafing in the Narrow Seas on watch for Parma: 'The fleet of Spaniards is somewhat above a hundred sails, many great ships . . . as far as we perceive they are determined to sell their lives with blows.'

At least the danger to Plymouth was past, and the present course of the Armada did show that their objective was not to be Ireland or any of the extreme western ports. It might still be Torbay or the Isle of Wight or some other harbour along the south coast. By refusing battle on the advice of his more experienced captains, Howard had delayed the final clash at the expense of leaving the initiative with Spain. The English still retained the 'weather gage' – that is, they remained to windward of the enemy, and were therefore at a great advantage, being able to choose their time and place of attack – but this also meant that they could not prevent the Armada from assailing any English port or harbour it might choose. The question was, would the Spaniards dare to do this with the undefeated English fleet still at their heels? It was a possibility which had to be faced. Therefore above all things contact with the Armada must not be lost. There would be about six hours of darkness. After a council-of-war in the gathering windy dusk, with a short choppy north-westerly sea, and clouds obscuring the stars, each captain returned to his own ship with precise and absolute instructions as to his station and course. Drake had been appointed to lead the way, showing his big poop lantern to the ships astern for their guidance.

Yet by dawn, which was before four a.m. and further lightened by the rising gibbous moon, the English pursuit had completely broken up. Drake had quenched his light and had veered south in quest of some unknown and mysterious sails, had come with his usual astonishing nose for a prize upon the crippled *Rosario* and had taken her and her commander Admiral Pedro de Valdes prisoner, with all crew, forty-six guns and fifty-five thousand gold ducats intact.

Most of the English fleet, missing his lantern, had heaved to or shortened sail, and so were far behind; but Howard in the *Ark*, accompanied by Lord Edmund Sheffield in the *White Bear* and Edmund Fenton in the *Mary Rose*, had closed with the Spanish fleet, in the dark mistaking their lights for the lights which Drake should still have been showing. At dawn they found themselves off Berry Head, near Brixham, and almost within the crescent of the Spanish fleet, certainly more part of that fleet than of the English, which was hull down on the brightening horizon. They had to go about sharply, into the slackening wind of dawn, to avoid being surrounded and attacked. Hugo de Moncada, commanding the galleasses, requested that he might pursue them, for he had a chance of overtaking them and holding them until the rest of the Spanish fleet closed in; but for some reason he was refused, and the three English ships escaped.

Drake's utter disregard of discipline, which would have ensured a court-martial in Nelson's time, was scarcely criticized then, and we have to see it in the context of its age. He was more envied for his uncanny ability to know where a rich prize was to be taken than blamed for breaking formation in the night. After all, Howard himself in the final battle of Gravelines did nearly the same thing, though not with such profitable results.

But one thinks of Philip's written instructions to Medina Sidonia: 'You should see that your squadrons do not break battle formation and that their commanders, moved by greed, do not give pursuit to the enemy and take prizes.'

If Drake has been judged more harshly since by standards which did not altogether then apply, Pedro de Valdes's surrender was treated too kindly at the time and has been ever since. No doubt he was unlucky to lose his bowsprit and later his foremast when attempting to go to the help of another ship. No doubt he felt he had been unjustly deserted and left in the lurch as the rest of the Armada proceeded on its way.

No doubt he was beside himself with anger that his cousin Diego Flores, with whom he had this continuing feud, should have been able to convince Medina Sidonia that his duty was to sail on. But about twelve hours had passed between the loss of his mainmast and Drake's arrival; some sort of repair or jury rig must have been possible in the time. No account speaks of any being attempted. And the *Rosario* was eleven hundred and fifty tons, one of only six ships in the Armada over the thousand tonnage; she carried, as has been said, forty-six guns, many of them the biggest cannon, capable of firing fifty-pound cannon balls and holing an enemy ship or wreaking the greatest damage if she came within range. She had one hundred and eighteen sailors and three hundred and four soldiers aboard; she had so far fired few shots. She would not be easy to handle in a beam wind but she had suffered no other hurt. Her forecastle and poop were much higher out of the water than the English, which would have made boarding a murderous business.

Instead of fighting, Pedro de Valdes, when he found that Drake was his adversary, considered it proper that he might gracefully surrender to a man 'whose valour and felicity was so great that Mars and Neptune seemed to attend him'. It was a knightly act, a chivalrous and courteous yielding to superior forces, and Drake accorded his enemy all the honours of war, entertained him in his cabin to dinner and presently saw him given every comfort before being conveyed to an honourable internment in England.

Drake was always a man who believed in the full etiquette of war. When on his voyage round the globe Thomas Doughty rebelled against him and was condemned to death by Drake for mutiny, Drake took Communion with him and then entertained him to dinner before leading him out to the block to be executed.

More reason here for all possible chivalry. One of the greatest galleons, surrendered without a fight! No doubt they could have pounded her for ever from a distance, but would they have had time, with Howard calling for all aid and the Armada likely to land in Torbay? Could one have imagined Drake meekly surrendering if positions were reversed? Or Recalde? Or Oquendo? Or Medina Sidonia? One thinks of the traditions of the Spanish navy summarized nearly three hundred years later by Admiral Mendez Nunez off Callao: 'My country prefers honour without ships to ships without honour.' De Valdes should have hanged himself.

7

The Battles in the Channel

But the Armada was not going to land in Torbay. All day, the wind gradually dropping, it crawled across the smiling blue water of Lyme Bay towards Portland Bill, and the English fleet reassembled itself after the confusions of the night and followed.

In the afternoon Medina Sidonia called a council and appointed Don Diego Enriquez, son of the Viceroy of Peru, to command the Andalusian Squadron in place of Pedro de Valdes. He also appointed Alonso de Leyva commander of all the rearguard, which was to consist of forty-three of the best ships of war. Recalde, his galleon still being repaired, was to be sheltered until he was fighting fit again. Medina Sidonia, aware of the risk of panic among ships exposed for the first time to the violence and rapidity of the English fire and of the disorders of yesterday which had cost him two capital ships, issued new orders. If henceforward any ship broke formation the captain would be hanged immediately. The provost marshal and the necessary hangmen were appointed and three majors were told off to each squadron to carry out the order without delay. (This order ten days later accounted for the execution of Don Cristobal de Avila, and for the arrest and near execution of Captain de Cuellar of the *San Pedro*.) At this time the Duke was expecting a frontal attack from Lord Henry Seymour – actually far away off Margate – so he put himself and the rest of his best ships in the van. The hulks, the supply ships and the victuallers were thus as usual protected on all sides. By retaining so tight a formation Medina Sidonia made himself most difficult to attack; but he limited his progress to the speed of the slowest. So far, from the time they sighted the Lizard they had progressed at the rate of three knots. But this infinitely slow progress did mean that the galleons with any sort of favourable breeze at all could move backwards and forwards among their flock and go to the help of any in peril.

As Monday afternoon wore on the light airs dropped, the sails of the galleons flapped and hung motionless, flags drooped and the opposing fleets drifted gently with the tide. Only the galleasses had motive power, but Don Hugo de Moncada, smarting under his rebuff of the morning from Medina Sidonia, refused to use them in attack. It had been a brilliant day since noon, but in the long light evening a few clouds assembled to obscure the sunset and to promise a change on the morrow.

All night the dead calm persisted, and well on into dawn. As light grew the look-outs reported that the relative positions of the two fleets were unchanged. The Armada was just east of Portland Bill. But at five a.m. a breeze sprang up; and it blew from the north-east. The change provided the Spaniards with what for two days they had been seeking, the weather gage.

By minutes the English fleet was the first to move, and Howard swung north-west towards the land, hoping to out-flank the Spanish. But this time Medina Sidonia was too quick for him and led his own squadron to intercept. Howard presently was forced to come about on the opposite tack, steering south-east, and tried instead to attack the southern wing of the Armada. Now the powerful Spanish rearguard took a hand. De Leyva in the *Rata Encoronada*, Bertendona in *La Regazona*, followed by their squadrons, with the wind in their favour, cut across the English path and fierce exchanges took place.

In the meantime a small part of Howard's fleet, Frobisher in the *Triumph*, together with five armed merchantmen, had mistaken or disobeyed Howard's orders and had come so close in to Portland Bill that they could not weather it and dropped anchor to avoid going aground; and there they were attacked by Hugo de Moncada and his four galleasses, coming into action at last. These ships in addition to their oar motive power were perhaps the best armed of any of the Spanish fleet, carrying over forty brass guns each, a large part of their armoury being fore and aft, but a considerable number of guns being mounted on the deck above the rowers, and a few even between the rowers.

While this was going on the main battle drifted back slowly westward into Lyme Bay. Here the greatest cannonade in naval history took place, with the more cumbersome and unwieldy Spanish ships straining every nerve and every sail to take advantage of the wind and close with their English opponents. Many times it looked as if individual English ships or groups of ships would be cut off in the *mêlée*, but every time their superior sailing qualities got them out of trouble.

And now the wind was beginning to hesitate and to veer. Drake, who so far had been disengaged, knew the likely properties of an easterly breeze at dawn and the prospect of its veering later, and he had manœuvred his squadron into a position where he could take advantage of the change. When it came he launched a sudden and fierce attack on the Armada's seaward wing. His ships, appearing out of the smoke of battle like a new fleet, broke up the seaward wing and turned the whole battle front.

As the wind picked up from the south-south-west the Armada began to re-form to meet this new attack. It had attempted two things – to isolate Frobisher and to bring Howard to battle. Now a third front had opened, and in the early exchanges many of the Spanish ships suffered. Recalde, who could not be kept out of any fight, again found himself isolated, and was surrounded by English ships which pumped shot into the *San Juan*. Medina Sidonia, who saw that Howard was going to take advantage of the change of wind to rescue Frobisher, now directed his Portuguese galleons and five others, himself in the van, to intercept this move; but, suddenly informed of Recalde's plight, and seeing that all except his own galleons were to leeward of Recalde and therefore unable to lend immediate aid, he instructed the whole of his squadron of fourteen large galleons to go to Recalde's aid, and alone in the *San Martin* continued on his course to intercept Howard. He thus presently found himself isolated from the rest of his fleet and bearing down alone upon the *Ark*, the *Elizabethan Jonas*, the *Leicester*, the *Golden Lion*, the *Victory*, the *Mary Rose*, the *Dreadnought*, and the *Swallow*. Although he saw himself likely to be surrounded, the Duke would not bear away and attempt to escape from a squadron flying the Lord Admiral's flag, so he came up into the wind and backed his foretopsail, inviting the English to grapple and board.

It was the conventional, the knightly thing to do; but the day for such gestures was over. Howard came no nearer than to bring the galleon within the range of his guns, and as he passed he discharged broadsides into the *San Martin*. Again sailing in line – the new order which was to become the classic order for centuries to come – the rest of his squadron did the same. Then they wheeled about and came back. In the meantime, Drake, having withdrawn before the might of the

Portuguese galleons coming to Recalde's aid, had doubled round them and he too came to attack the *San Martin*. The Spanish flagship was blazing away with all her forty-eight guns, but it was nearly an hour before she could be rescued, by which time the holy standard had been ripped in two, her masts were damaged, and torn rigging was hanging among the dead and wounded on her decks.

Long before the *San Martin* was finally extricated, Howard and his squadron had left her to Drake and had gone on to rescue Frobisher. How far Frobisher wanted to be rescued is a debatable point. He and his London merchantmen, after a fight, had finally dealt with the four big galleasses. The English shot was not sufficiently heavy to hole the galleasses, but their aim had been directed at the rowers, who had been cut down in swathes, and the galleasses had broken off the fight before Howard arrived.

If Medina Sidonia instead of attempting two objectives had swung round as soon as he saw Frobisher isolated, and, after leaving a screen to ward off Howard, had set about the destruction of the six embayed ships, there might have been a different story to tell, for Howard could hardly have kept his distance while the six ships were destroyed. But it has been suggested that Frobisher, hard-bitten, sea-wise and as pugnacious as Recalde, may just as deliberately have offered himself as a prize in order to lure the main Spanish fleet into the treacherous waters of the Portland Race and the Shambles. Whatever his secret purposes, if any, in becoming so surrounded, his fight with the galleasses made him the hero of the day.

In the first light airs of Wednesday's dawn a Spanish straggler was discovered, the *Gran Grifon*, the flagship of the urcas, which during the night had drifted out of the protective range of the rest of the fleet. She was a ponderous, moderately powerful but slow-moving vessel; and she was immediately attacked by Drake, who showed his usual ability to be in the right place at the right time. A considerable action blew up, with Recalde again in the fray, and Bertendona and Oquendo. After damage on both sides the *Gran Grifon* was eventually rescued by one of the galleasses which took her in tow, and Drake and Howard then withdrew before the approach of Medina Sidonia and his Portuguese galleons. Although the action lasted for less than two hours, it seems to have been at closer quarters than on Tuesday. The *Gran Grifon* was quite badly damaged, with forty of her crew killed and an unknown number wounded, and Drake lost his mainyard and a number of men.

(Perhaps it should be mentioned here that all through the Armada battles the English understated their losses in personnel, for the simple reason that if a ship reported, say ten men killed, a due proportion of victuals and back pay was automatically deducted from the next meagre allowance.)

But, after that early morning battle, there was little further action on Wednesday. All day in light airs and fitful breezes, the Armada continued its slow, stately progress up channel towards the Isle of Wight. All day the English fleet shadowed it. Howard held a council-of-war in the afternoon, and for the first time divided his fleet properly into squadrons. Howard himself, Drake, Hawkins and Frobisher were the natural choice for command. Until now it had been something of a free-for-all on the English side; ships more or less followed whom they liked; Drake's friends kept close to him, and any others who saw Drake's flag and fancied his leadership did the same. Now the English had learned the value of grouping from the Spaniards, and some order began to appear in the fleet. They were coming bitterly to appreciate the fact that the better discipline of the Spaniards was preventing them from breaking up the Armada or indeed seriously damaging it. So far two vessels only had fallen out after all this fighting; and neither had been from enemy gunfire. The Armada was scarred but intact.

The English were almost out of shot, and still short of men and ordinary victuals. Howard in his *Relation of Proceedings* speaks of the enormous expenditure of great shot on the Tuesday and says that although the musketeers and the harquebusiers (who fired a heavier type of musket) were discharging their weapons as rapidly as they could, the sharper bark of the hand weapons could never be heard because of the rapid firing of the cannons and the culverins. Sir George Carey writing to the Earl of Sussex says: 'The shot continued so thick together that it might rather have been judged a skirmish with small shot on land than a fight with great shot on sea.' Both fleets indeed had blazed away in the heat of the first engagements as if ammunition were unlimited. 'We sent,' writes Howard, 'divers barques and pinnaces on to the shore for a new supply of such provisions.'

But a nation which had been at peace within its own bound-aries for over a hundred years could not produce powder and shot anywhere for the asking. Some ammunition was ferried out from Portsmouth, Weymouth, and the little towns along the coast, but there was never enough, scarcely enough for another major engagement. Indeed without the ammunition salvaged from de Valdes's *Rosario* there might not have been enough to go round at all. Meanwhile Howard's fleet was constantly being reinforced by volunteer vessels which were emerging enthusiastically from all the little harbours. But their presence was an embarrassment rather than a help to the main fleet, which could really make no use of them in a fight against a close-knit and disciplined enemy who proceeded on his way and protected his weaker ships within a hard ring of galleons.

As for the Spaniards, they had been provided by Philip with one hundred and twenty-three thousand round shot of varying sizes and five hundred and seventeen thousand pounds of powder. It should have been enough for all emergencies. And they had ample yet. They were more than half way up the Channel; but these constant running fights were eating into their supply. And unlike the English they were on an unfriendly coast. As they neared the Isle of Wight Medina Sidonia sent off messages to Parma, telling him of his approach and requesting that new supplies of powder and shot should be made available to him when they linked up.

The Spanish even more than the English were guilty of firing too often while out of range. Most of the engagements so far had taken place at a range approximating to an average par-4 hole at golf. At this distance the English ships were just out of effective range of the heaviest fifty-pound balls that the Spanish guns could fire, and it would have been a great tactical stroke for the Spanish to have refrained from firing them, once it was seen that they were not reaching their mark. But it would have required a superhuman restraint which would have been psychologically impossible. To wait until you can see the whites of their eyes is good tactics when the other side is getting ever nearer. The English never got nearer. They continued to turn away and refuse all contest at close quarters.

But this very policy, well though it paid off in the end, meant that even the English gunfire was erratic and had the minimum of serious effect. It brought down a few spars and killed some men but it never completely disabled and it cer-

1. ELIZABETH I AS A GIRL
(Oil painting by an unknown artist, c. 1542–7)

2. PHILIP II OF SPAIN
(Oil painting by Titian, 1551)

3. MARY I
(Oil painting by
Antonio Moro,
1554)

**4. MARY QUEEN
OF SCOTS**
(Drawing by
François Clouet,
c. 1560)

5. DON ALONSO PEREZ DE GUZMAN
Duke of Medina Sidonia
(Oil painting, 16th century)

6. JUAN MARTINEZ DE RECALDE
(Oil painting by Alcalá Galiano)

tainly did not sink. Something more had to be concerted to break up the Spanish discipline, to prevent them reaching their destination.

The gentlest of breezes persisted through Wednesday night, but dawn broke in a complete calm with the two fleets drifting a mile or two apart and about ten miles off the Needles, the westernmost tip of the Isle of Wight. Daylight showed a situation not unlike that of the day before. This time two Spanish ships had lagged behind: a Portuguese galleon, the *San Luis*, eight hundred and thirty tons, thirty-eight guns, and another hulk, the *Duquesa Santa Ana*, nine hundred tons, twenty-three guns. Nearest to them of the English fleet was the dreaded 'Juan Achines', as the Spaniards called him, commanding the *Victory*, of eight hundred tons and sixty-four guns. Thereupon began a battle in dead calm between ships dependent on wind for movement.

As soon as he saw game so near Hawkins put down boats, which began laboriously to tow him into range of the enemy. The rest of his squadron followed suit. Medina Sidonia at once countered by dispatching three of the four galleasses to the rescue, but, having noted how vulnerable the galleass, unsupported, was to saker and culverin fire directed at the banks of rowers, he had them tow along one of the great carracks to add to their firepower. This was de Leyva's *La Rata Encoronada*, in which so many of Spain's young noblemen sailed. It also, according to Artiñano, carried fifty-three guns and was 'the Spanish ship with the most artillery'.

The Duke, watching the considerable conflict which now developed between a few heavy ships of both sides while the rest of the fleets looked helplessly on, had something on his mind greater than the outcome of this immediate action. He had already during the night called and listened to one council-of-war. For this was the day to seize the Isle of Wight if it were to be done at all. In his letter to the King of last Saturday, before any of the fighting began, the Duke had expressed himself quite plainly as having no intention of proceeding farther up the Channel than the Isle of Wight until he had made contact with the Duke of Parma. It made good sense. It was a reasonable precaution to wait here until he received a reply to the messages he had sent on ahead. So far he had preserved his fleet splendidly intact. He should know Parma's precise intentions before venturing into the narrows of the Channel, with no port of shelter or replenishment and the uncertain weather of the North Sea to face. Most of his officers were in favour of this plan.

But the Armada could not very well just anchor for several days in the Solent. The island could be captured, though at considerable cost, at considerable wastage of strength, especially with the English fleet still at large and undamaged. Yet, once the Isle of Wight *was* in his possession, the Armada had a sure base from which to emerge to meet Parma, a base to return to if things went wrong.

But the King's letters were on the table before him. One was headed: 'Secret Instructions for you, the Duke of Medina Sidonia, my cousin, my Captain General of the Ocean' and signed 'I, the King'. It said: 'If God gives the success which is desired, as it is hoped that He will, you are to follow strictly the order of my public instructions to you. If, however, through our sins it should fall out otherwise, and the Duke, my nephew, should not be able to cross to England, nor you for that reason meet him, after communicating with him, you will see whether you are able to capture the Isle of Wight.' Philip then goes on to outline the advantages of having a secure base but concludes by saying emphatically: 'On no account should you try to capture the island on your journey eastwards without first having made a supreme effort to achieve success in the main task.'

So there it was – the precise instructions. So far the Duke had obeyed all his instructions, and had done so with complete success. Was he now to go against these instructions at the very last, and perhaps leave Parma high and dry, for lack of the courage to go on? All the King's advice so far had been good. His knowledge of the English coast had proved correct in every detail, so had his predictions as to the tactics of the English fleet. The sailors and soldiers of the Armada were clearly anxious about their position, but not in poor heart. The swiftness of movement of the English fleet dismayed them, but losses so far had been slight. The weather, after the appalling early summer, was seemingly set fair; so far nothing could have been more favourable for their journey up the Channel. How many great military enterprises had failed for lack of resolution, from over-caution on the part of the commander-in-chief?

It is not clear what the Duke – or his council – would finally have decided, for the events of Thursday, operating on indecision, took the choice gradually out of their hands. The local battle in the calm of dawn gradually developed into a major clash. Hawkins, for a time outgunned by the arrival of *La Rata* and the three galleasses, was eventually supported by both Howard in the *Ark* and his cousin Lord Thomas Howard in the *Golden Lion*, who got themselves hauled by longboats into the battle area. Then the galleasses, in spite of English harassment, were able to get ropes aboard the two stranded ships and tow them away to safety, though not without damage to the galleasses. The *Gerona* was holed in the bows and had her lantern shot away, while the *San Lorenzo*, with Moncada aboard, again suffered heavy casualties.

The English were of course just as concerned as the Spanish about the Isle of Wight, and during the night Frobisher had edged himself so far forward in order to be between the Armada and the land that he found himself once again isolated and inshore, much as he had been off Portland yesterday. With no wind but a strong eastward current, the stronger the nearer it was to the land, he and a few supporting ships were only a mile or two off Ventnor and within range of the Spanish northern wing. He was quickly engaged by them and seemed in danger of being overwhelmed, so he dropped longboats, and others went to his assistance, there being in all eleven to take him in tow and drag him back out of range of the Spanish.

Then at last a light wind began to stir and, as movement in the fleets became possible, a confused battle developed. The breeze favoured the Spanish, and several of their galleons bore down on the *Triumph* again. But Frobisher's ship, though somewhat damaged, immediately shook off her tow and, although pursued by two of the swiftest galleons in the Spanish fleet, drew away so quickly that, in Calderon's words, 'our own ships seemed to be standing still'. Probably in this the *Triumph* was aided by the currents, which Frobisher knew so well how to utilize.

Meanwhile Medina Sidonia brought his main squadrons to bear on the English centre and in an hour's mixed fighting drove them back westward. Howard in the *Ark* got the worst of this, and Fenner in the *Nonpareil* and Fenton in the *Mary Rose* stood between him and Recalde in the *San Juan* and Oquendo in the *Santa Ana*, who were eager to press home their advantage. There was nothing now, if he so chose, to prevent the Duke from swinging northwards and entering the undefended eastern arm of the Solent – that recommended to him by the King – and seizing Spithead. But again following the pattern of the previous day, Drake, little engaged so far, had used the new wind to claw himself out to sea, and from there with his squadron he now launched a fierce attack on the southern wing of the Armada, where first the *San Mateo* and then the *Florencia* bore the brunt. These ships retreated east and north towards the land, causing disarray in that wing of the Armada and bending the crescent so that its tip straightened and was in danger of breaking away.

There was still nothing to prevent Medina Sidonia from leading his biggest galleons straight up the Solent, but he would have done so at the risk of leaving the ships of his southern wing to fend for themselves and to see the defensive formation that he so much prized disintegrate under pressure. With so rigid a strategy there was really only one course open to him at this stage, and that was to re-group his ships back into their tight formation and sail to the rescue of his menaced southern wing. Once he had re-grouped he could then in theory turn if he so desired and sail up to Spithead.

When eventually the main Spanish fleet came up, Drake and Hawkins broke off the engagement. Their primary objective seems to have been to draw the Spanish fleet farther from the mouth of the Solent and into a position where the flow of tide and current would make it difficult for them to turn and enter the estuary. In this they were successful. They may also, as has been suggested by some modern writers, have been trying to edge at least a part of the Spanish fleet on to the Owers Bank off the Bill of Selsey. If so, they failed in this, as they failed to disrupt the essential Armada formation.

There is no record, however, from any Spanish source that the Duke or his advisers had second thoughts about attempting to double back and take the Isle of Wight after all. We shall never know how far the scattered battles of Thursday, and especially Drake's fierce attack which ended them, influenced the Duke in his decision to continue on his way without news from Parma. He may always have intended to do so. At any rate he sailed on with his four pilots, his sailing master, Captain Marolin de Juan, his naval adviser, Diego Flores, and his military adviser, Don Francisco de Bobadilla, at his side, towards his destiny in the narrows of the Channel.

What that destiny was the English did not know any more

100

than the Spanish. Again there had been a day's inconclusive fighting. Again the Armada proceeded on its way with a few ships damaged, a few hundred men dead and perhaps twice as many wounded. But still virtually untouched, considering its total size. Since the second day not a single ship had fallen out, not one prize for the English to claim. It was no story to tell the Queen.

Yet, rightly, the English celebrated Thursday as a great strategic victory, and on Friday Howard held a council-of-war at which he knighted Martin Frobisher, John Hawkins and several others. The Armada against all probabilities had forced its way up the Channel unbroken, but it was now past the last of the most suitable of invasion harbours and, although its attempted junction with Parma still remained a possibility, Howard knew that ahead of them was a new and unused English fleet under Lord Henry Seymour. This would be a re-inforcement not of brave useless little fishing-boats armed with a pop-gun cannon apiece but of a powerful squadron of about twenty-four capital ships and eighteen others. None of these was large by Spanish standards or those of the *Triumph* or the *Bear*, but two at least were brand-new ships embodying the very latest principles of naval design, and all were fresh and fuming for a fight and might even conceivably carry some powder and shot to use in their guns.

Which Howard notably now had not. Friday was a superb day, brilliant and cloudless and hot; and not a shot was fired either then or on Saturday, when the weather clouded and there were a few showers. The only bombardment was Howard's upon the sea-coast towns : of pinnaces with urgent messages demanding from the Earl of Sussex, Sir George Carey and the captains of the forts and castles along the coast that at all costs they should send him food for his guns and victuals for his men. Quite clearly there would be another and perhaps final trial of strength somewhere off Margate or Dunkirk; for this he must have ammunition and men with food in their bellies.

And men who had had some rest. In none of the accounts of the Armada is mention made of the fatigue and strain that the commanders and men of both fleets must by now have been suffering. For the best part of six days the two great fleets had accompanied each other up channel, never out of sight of each other except at nightfall, when the chance of accidental encounter increased, and almost always in the day fighting or manoeuvring to fight. The opportunity for sleep or even rest for any of the commanders was minimal. Medina Sidonia, it has been said, hardly left the taffrail during the whole time, receiving up there such food as he would eat, constantly consulting his advisers, usually in the thick of the battle or directing his own galleon to steer to that part of his fleet most directly menaced, sometimes snatching a few hours' rest at dusk and then up again and leaning over the stern through the night.

If the strain was perhaps greatest of all for him, it can hardly have been much less for Howard, with all England to lose; and so on down the fleets.

Twice a day Medina Sidonia now sent off fast pinnaces to Parma, but so far had received no reply.

Parma, indeed, who had blown hot and cold over the *Empresa* for the last twelve months, was in no position to answer Medina Sidonia as the Admiral wanted and hoped. After the failure of this Armada and its return to Spain much of the blame for the failure was put on Parma's shoulders for letting Medina Sidonia down. Indeed, from that time on Philip never trusted him again. Later historians, studying the warnings that Parma had sent to Philip and the almost insuperable difficulties involved in ferrying the Spanish troops across the narrow seas with the obstacles that existed, have tended to absolve Parma of blame.

Yet he must bear his full share of responsibility for what happened. Although others – like Alva and Don John of Austria – had thought of invading England from the Netherlands long before Parma suggested it, it was he who in the spring of 1586 first submitted his detailed scheme to Philip, outlining the possibility of a landing in Kent or Essex with thirty thousand infantrymen and five hundred cavalry, in flat-bottomed boats, screened by an escort of twenty-five warships. When later Philip decided to amalgamate this scheme with an Armada under Santa Cruz, Parma at first was in full agreement; and after the death of Mary Queen of Scots he wrote to Philip, as we have seen, assuming that the great *Empresa* would now go forward. Until March 1587 his own drive in the Netherlands had been northward; but from that time on he turned his eyes west, and the maps hanging in his headquarters in Brussels, instead of being of Leiden and Utrecht and Amsterdam, were of Flanders and the ports along its North Sea coast. After weeks of bloody and bitter fighting among the mud and tidal channels of Sluys he had at last forced the town into surrender – one of his dearest-bought victories. What could that victory be intended to further more certainly than the enterprise against England? After the capture of the town his troops began to dig the canals necessary to get the barges to Nieuport, so that from there they could be moved to Dunkirk while still under protection from the shore.

In November 1587 he wrote to Philip telling him that the barges – with fly-boats to escort them – were ready at Antwerp and Dunkirk, and that in two weeks he could launch the invasion – a palpable piece of wishful thinking if one does not use a harsher word. Then he moved his headquarters from Brussels to Bruges and discovered that his exits along the coast were all blockaded by Justin of Nassau, Admiral of Zeeland. He at once wrote to Philip, warning him of this and pointing out that Santa Cruz and the Armada would now necessarily have to clear a way for him before he could stir. He also later emphasized the extreme difficulty of the link-up, because galleons could not approach Dunkirk for lack of sea depth and Justin of Nassau could attack the troop-filled barges in the shallow water before they could gain the protection of the galleons.

Through the spring and summer many barges and fly-boats were certainly laid down at Dunkirk and Nieuport, but work on them proceeded with excruciating slowness. It is difficult to believe that Parma, who could achieve miracles of organization when he chose to, could not have hastened on this building programme. Yet he never appears to have let either Santa Cruz or Medina Sidonia know the true extent of his naval weakness. Certainly no general of Parma's experience would have considered launching his troops in defenceless flat-bottomed barges into a sea patrolled by enemy fly-boats – though he made a token effort to do this when it was too late. But no general of Parma's brilliance could not have advanced his preparations further than he did in the time at his disposal.

Perhaps he half thought the Armada would never come. (He did not know it had left Spain until it was off the Isle of Wight.) But in war you cannot afford to be caught in two minds. And it was Medina Sidonia who paid the price.

8

Gravelines

At its majestic crawl – about the speed of a rowing-boat – the Armada proceeded unharassed all through Friday and Saturday, and in the evening of the latter day it came to anchor off Calais, still unbroken, still in its strong defensive formation. The English fleet dropped anchor half a mile away. The fine week of summer seemed to be over, and a fresh westerly breeze was bringing lowering clouds and a threat of rain.

Before darkness fell the English fleet was reinforced by the arrival of the new squadron of Lord Henry Seymour who, disobeying the Queen's express instructions to continue his patrol duties off Dunkirk, gladly accepted Howard's summons to join him. This meant that the English fleet was now increased by about a third, and that its numbers were for the first time something like equal to the Spanish. At the same time Justin of Nassau took over the guard duties of Seymour; but with his fleet of small tough shallow-draught warships of fifty to one hundred and fifty tons each he was able to keep a closer watch on Nieuport and Dunkirk than Seymour had done.

The night passed quietly, and on Sunday morning both admirals held councils-of-war. They both had cause for anxiety, for Howard, though stronger than he had ever been before, was well aware that the two Dukes were now only twenty-five miles apart by sea and little more by land. He had no certain knowledge of what Parma had been able to build during the last months or how many fly-boats he might have accumulated. A juncture between the two forces was at hand and this must be challenged at all costs. The Spanish had anchored rather dangerously inshore; but they, the English, were only half a mile farther out and might also be in difficulties if the weather broke. Monsieur Gourdan, the Governor of Calais, was a known Catholic and an adherent of the pro-Spanish Guises, and would no doubt give the Spaniards 'all help short of war'.

But Medina Sidonia's anxieties were far greater. At last he had heard from Parma – a message expressing his 'great joy' that the Armada had forced the Channel passage and promising that his forces would be ready to take part in the invasion of England in about six days. But Don Rodrigo Tello de Guzman, Medina Sidonia's relative and envoy, had found Parma in Bruges, not in Dunkirk, and he had a most depressing story to tell of the extent of the unpreparedness he had seen in Nieuport and Dunkirk. His own view was that nothing would be likely to be ready for at least fourteen days.

A fourteen-day stay off Calais Roads – or even six – was an impossibility for the Armada. Indeed Gourdan, who yesterday had driven cheerfully down to the shore with his wife in his coach hoping to be able to watch an immediate battle, sent a message of friendly greeting to Medina Sidonia on Sunday morning, pointing out that his present anchorage just east of Calais cliffs was an extremely dangerous one, because of the strong cross currents at the mouth of the English Channel.

Medina Sidonia dispatched a further urgent message to Parma: 'I am anchored here two leagues from Calais with the enemy's fleet on my flank. They can cannonade me whenever they like, and I shall be unable to do them much harm in return. If you can send me forty or fifty fly-boats of your fleet I can, with their help, defend myself here until you are ready to come out.' Parma had in all fewer than twenty fly-boats, and some of those were not ready for sea.

Medina Sidonia also replied to the Governor of Calais, thanking him for his warning and for the present of fruit and fresh vegetables he had sent, and he requested that Monsieur Gourdan should sell them whatever powder and shot he could spare. Gourdan, sitting on the fence, refused this, but offered to sell them food or any other 'non-combatant' provisions they were short of. Stow in his *Chronicles of England* writes of that Sunday afternoon: 'The Flemings, Walloons and the French came thick and three-fold to behold the Spanish fleet, admiring the exceeding greatness of their ships, and warlike order: the greatest kept the outside next the enemy, like strong Castles fearing no assault, the lesser placed in the middle-ward. Fresh victuals straight were brought aboard; Captains and Cavaliers for their money might have what they would, and gave the French so liberally, as within twelve hours an egg was worth fivepence, besides thanks.'

The figure of five pence was about twenty-five times what an egg was fetching in London at that date, so one perceives that the French, as usual, were not averse from making a profit out of casual callers.

One can visualize the scene, people flocking on foot or by horse or cart or donkey from the town and the neighbouring villages; a fine Sunday afternoon with something to gaze at, as they would have come to stare at a wreck – only this was more dramatic, a real treat, tension growing – sitting on the edge of the cliffs, hurrying down to the beaches with their produce or standing in clumps gossiping and speculating on a possible battle while the little boats went speedily back and forth plying their profitable trade.

Stow goes on : 'Whilst this lusty Navie like a demi-Conqueror, rid thus at anchor, the Spanish faction in sundry nations had divulged that England was subdued, the Queen taken and sent prisoner over the Alps to Rome, where barefoot she should make her humble reconciliation.' The first of many such rumours that spread through Europe during the next few weeks.

Another rumour had spread around the Armada – or had been deliberately started – that Parma was coming out to join them tomorrow. It was perhaps a necessary lie to try to relieve long pent-up tensions and fears and to revive flagging spirits. For now the strain was making itself apparent in the whole Spanish fleet. Throughout the long week up the Channel most of the hulks, the supply ships and the smaller armed merchantmen – that centre core to the Armada – had not been in action at all. Like sheep they had continued on their slow and ponderous way while the ring of galleons, like guard-dogs, had protected them against the wolves. But they had witnessed the battles, they had seen – and reluctantly admired – the speed and mobility of the English fleet, and their nerves were wearing thin. A considerable proportion of the masters and crews of these ships was not Spanish; they had no particular relish for a fight and, being good seamen themselves, they were not comfortable anchored so close to a lee shore. Already there had been one desertion to the English, of the hulk *San Pedro el Menor*, of five hundred tons, and that under Portuguese command. There might soon be others.

Nor was the depression and the tension confined to the weaker members of the fleet. The obvious sailing superiority of the English at all times, the complete failure of the galleons even to close and board one English ship, the English reinforcements, their menacing position now off the weather flank of the Armada, all added to the nervousness and the depression. The greatest single calamity, of course, after the failure of Parma to come out, was the shortage of shot. There was powder in plenty yet, but some of the ships had only shot enough left for one short action, particularly for the heavier cannon which had so far kept the English at a distance. Medina Sidonia had obeyed his instructions and achieved his objective with the maximum fidelity and the minimum loss. But what now? Parma was *not ready*, and Sidonia's pilots warned that to venture farther out into the North Sea would be to add to the hazards of navigation.

It probably never entered Medina Sidonia's head to take Calais. It needed a later century for man to discover the advantage of attacking neutrals. But if one deducts two thousand for sickness and casualties, the Duke still had some eighteen thousand trained soldiers in his fleet. It would not have been difficult to pick a quarrel with Monsieur Gourdan and force the town : the fighting might have been fierce but it would have been brief. Then he could have sailed into a safe harbour, linked with Parma on land, and restored and refurbished his fleet and picked his time for an invasion.

By Monday anyway it was too late for such perfidy, for on Sunday night the English launched the fire-ships.

There was nothing new or original about fire-ships, no stroke of inventive genius bearing the stamp of Drake or some other master mind. They were a common arm of naval warfare, far more lethal to stout wooden ships than the inaccurate cannon of the day. Fire-ships had been attempted against Drake in Cadiz; the Spaniards had contemplated using them a week ago when considering an attack on the English fleet in Plymouth; Philip in one of his letters had expressly warned Medina Sidonia against the risks of such an attack. (He really did try to think of everything.)

The present situation was ideal for their use. A fresh breeze blowing steadily from the English fleet towards the Spanish, the Spaniards still in close defensive formation, a lee shore, the onset of night, and the turn of the tide at eleven p.m.

The decision to use the fire-ships had been taken at the council-of-war on board the *Ark* that morning. As soon as it was known that the Armada was succeeding in its attempt to force the Channel, Walsingham had given orders for a number of fishing-vessels to be relinquished at Dover and laden with pitch and faggots, and immediately the decision was taken to use them Sir Henry Palmer was sent in a pinnace to bring them over. But the day wore on and evening came and there was no sign of Palmer, so it was decided to act without him while the best tidal conditions prevailed and to sacrifice some of the smaller ships of the fleet. Drake gave a two-hundred-ton vessel, the *Thomas*. Hawkins gave the *Bark Bond* of one hundred and fifty tons, and six others were contributed. These were all bigger than anything that had ever been used before; and as soon as darkness fell they were made ready for their work. An old Devonshire captain called John Young, one of Drake's men, was put in charge of the fire-ships, and his second-in-command was a Cornishman called Captain Prouse. All the masts and rigging were tarred, all the guns were left on board double-shotted to go off of their own accord when the fire reached them.

Medina Sidonia and his advisers were alert for some such attempt. With the tide and the wind as it was, a special risk must exist, and they made all the preparations they could to meet it. A screen of patrol-boats equipped with grapnels was thrown out to cover the Spanish fleet from the seaward side, and one of the Duke's most trusted officers, Captain Serrano, was put in charge. At the same time the Duke sent a message to every ship in the fleet that an attack by fire-ships might well occur that night. If such an attack came the fleet was not to panic, for the screen of patrol-boats would protect them; and if by chance a fire-ship should get through they must have their own boats ready lowered to fend it off. Supposing even this failed they were to slip their cables, marking the position with buoys, and stand out to sea, then return to station and to pick up their cables once the fire-ships were past. The Duke could have done no more.

Unfortunately something worse than fire-ships was feared by the anxious captains receiving this message. Three years before at the siege of Antwerp an Italian engineer called Giambelli had devised ships called hell-burners which, when the fire reached the powder within them, had exploded and killed a thousand men, flinging the blazing wreckage of boats and bridges over a square mile of the city. It was the most destructive weapon that had ever been seen by man. And

Giambelli, it was known, was in England and working for the Queen. (In fact he was in London and working innocently on its defences, but no one was to know that.)

Soon after midnight, with the tide racing, the eight ships were lit up and sent away. Almost immediately they were seen by the Armada and the alarm given. The eight ships were sailing in line abreast, and they bore down on the Spanish fleet with the flames already leaping and crackling all over them. Their very size was more than the Spaniards had ever reckoned with. A two-hundred-ton barque, with the wind and the current behind her, and manned by determined men until the last moment, is a very hard obstacle to stop. The Spanish patrol-boats had no motors to aid them, only sail and oar against the wind and the tide, and eight ships to deal with at once, all much larger than they were themselves. They got hawsers aboard one at either end of the line and pulled them off course. An attempt was made in the middle, but the fire on the blazing ships had now reached the guns which began exploding in every direction. This convinced the Spanish that they had not to deal with ordinary fire-ships but with the dreaded hell-burners all over again.

As the six ships came on, Medina Sidonia fired a warning gun and slipped his cables and luffed up close-hauled against the wind. A few others of his squadron did the same. But for the rest the long-imposed discipline at last broke. They did not wait to slip anchors; they cut them and shook out their sails and went with wind and tide, drifting past Calais out towards the North Sea and the low coastline of Dunkirk. In the confusion ship collided with ship and it was every man for himself. The fire-ships in fact did no material damage of themselves at all; they drifted harmlessly on to the beach to burn down to the water-line; but they had achieved what the English fleet in six days of fighting had failed to do, they had broken the disciplined defensive formation of the Armada, and it was never to be recovered.

As soon as he saw the fire-ships safely past, Medina Sidonia in the *San Martin* brought his ship back again to near his original anchorage, put out a sheet anchor and fired a gun to direct the rest of his fleet to follow suit. But very few did. The *San Marcos*, with the Marquis de Penafiel on board. The *San Juan* with Recalde. The *Santa Ana* with Oquendo. Two or three others. The rest had scattered over several square miles of water and most could not anchor if they would; they had

had two anchors out against the swift-running tide and had cut both away in the panic. If they possessed a spare anchor it was stowed away and could not immediately be brought into use.

A gusty dawn showed a half dozen of the great galleons riding at anchor where dusk had left them and the other one-hundred-and-thirty-odd ships strung out eastwards towards the Dunkirk sandbanks. The big galleass *San Lorenzo*, with Hugo de Moncada on board, had fouled her rudder in a collision with the *San Juan de Sicilia* and had then run into another ship, with the result that she was now crawling in a crippled fashion just off the French coast and dangerously far in. The English fleet, of course, had not shifted.

With the first light there was instant activity. The Duke, knowing that the tight defensive grouping had so far been his salvation and that if his fleet were to survive it must at all costs reassemble before the English attacked, had sent off fast pinnaces during the night to make contact with the scattered ships and to order them to reassemble around him. But the dawn showed them still far scattered and a south-westerly wind blowing, which would make their return a difficult and lengthy matter. So the Duke, with the wind in his favour, weighed anchor to catch them up and try to regain formation somewhere off Dunkirk. And with the light the English, seeing for the first time the success that their fire-ships had achieved, at once attacked.

Thereupon began what has been described as one of the great decisive battles of the world. The English order of battle was never put to paper but was agreed orally among the commanders. However, it seems that they attacked by squadrons more or less abreast – with Drake, who had as usual contrived his anchorage nearest to the enemy, slightly in the van. The Duke's small squadron of galleons, seeing themselves being overhauled by the English and perceiving that if they could hold the enemy here it would give time for the scattered Armada to reassemble, came about and formed line abreast also to meet the attack. In the meantime Howard, the commander of the whole English fleet, seeing the great galleass *San Lorenzo* in trouble near the Calais beach, allowed himself to be diverted from his main task of destroying the Armada by the lure of a rich prize and sailed with his entire squadron to attack the *San Lorenzo*. Both he and Drake – on different days – thus conducted themselves in a way which would have led to an instant court-martial in later times.

The injured galleass, crowded with three hundred and twelve oarsmen, one hundred and thirty-four sailors and two hundred and thirty-five soldiers, strained like an injured beetle to gain Calais harbour but ran aground on the bar and heeled over in the surf, pointing a host of slender oars to the sky. The water was too shoal for the *Ark* or any of her companions to reach her, so Howard launched his longboat with sixty men, many of these gentlemen adventurers hot for spoil and to prove their courage. Soon a dozen other small ships were following, including the two-hundred-ton London ship the *Margaret and John* (Captain, John Fisher) which had been in the thick of the fighting throughout the week. This time, however, Fisher overplayed his luck and his ship went aground too, not far from the stranded galleass. Since the tide was still falling they could do nothing yet to refloat her, so half of her ninety crew piled into the boats to make a boarding-party.

In the galleass pandemonium reigned, with the galley-slaves fighting to get free, some of the soldiers and sailors leaping overboard and struggling through the surf to the safety of the beach, while Hugo de Moncada and his officers rallied the rest to resist attack. The English boats in the last fifty yards were fine targets in the bright morning light, and dozens of men were killed and wounded by small-arms fire. Richard Tomson, Lieutenant of the *Margaret and John*, says: 'We continued a pretty skirmish with our small shot against theirs, they being ensconced within their ship and very high over us, we in our open pinnaces and far under them having nothing to shroud and cover us.' After a bitter fight Moncada himself was killed outright by a musket-shot between the eyes, 'and after that resistance collapsed.

Moncada was the first of the high-born Spanish admirals to lose his life.

The English, about two hundred in number, having accepted the surrender of the remaining officers, proceeded to loot the ship and would have taken the ship as well had not the French, who had been watching the whole bloody battle with detached interest from the shore, now put in a claim that the ship was in French territorial waters and ship and guns at least belonged to them. The English, whose temper was up, were prepared to dispute this with their arms, but Monsieur Gourdan reinforced his rights with such accurate gunfire from Calais Castle and the ramparts above the beach that the raiders had to withdraw in haste. Howard now at last directed his squadron towards the main battle. In capturing this one ship he had kept a dozen of the best English ships out of the decisive struggle for more than three hours.

The shape of the great battle of Gravelines is hard to determine from contemporary accounts. Indeed the one fact that emerges is that, after the first hour, it had no shape at all. This was the battle in which the English were determined at all costs to destroy the Spanish fleet. For a week they had been frustrated, knowing themselves more seaworthy but able to turn this to no advantage. Frustrated, aware that they had done nothing that had been so confidently expected of them at home, for ever up against the defensive wall and the Spanish challenge to 'come and board us', they now saw for the first time the Armada scattered and in disarray. Now in these next hours, before it could reassemble, they must tear it to pieces. And this is what they proceeded to do.

Drake in the *Revenge* was the first to close Medina Sidonia in the *San Martin*. It was a meeting of admirals, but this time there was no long-range firing. Drake had to get in to kill and Medina Sidonia was on his last supply of heavy shot. So when they did fire it was at close range, and in the thunderous cannonade which followed heavy damage was done to both ships. Drake's ship was 'pierced through by heavy cannon-balls of all sizes which were flying everywhere between the two fleets, and was riddled with every kind of shot'. Twice Drake's cabin was pierced by cannon-balls, and rigging was brought down on the heads of the sailors. No sooner was the *Revenge* past than Thomas Fenner in the *Nonpareil* took his place. And then Lord Edmund Sheffield in the *White Bear*, and so on down the line while the *San Martin* fought each one in turn. Soon her decks were a shambles and she was holed both above and below the water-line. The *San Juan* and the *San Marcos* also became closely involved.

But this time Drake was not to be caught by the lure of a prize, even the prize of the ship bearing the Armada's supreme commander. Already in answer to Medina Sidonia's commands the Spanish ships were regrouping, forming that hard outer shell of the old crescent behind which the weaker ships could shelter. It was a notable feat in the conditions of the morning and, although never completed, was partially carried out in spite of the English challenge. Drake remained no longer fighting the first line of galleons but by-passed them and drove in to cut up the assembling groups behind. Frobisher, fuming with annoyance at this, took up the battle with the front-line ships, and behind him came Hawkins in the *Victory*, Edward Fenton, his brother-in-law, in the *Mary Rose*, Sir George Beeston in the *Dreadnought*, Hawkins's son in the *Swallow* and a host of others, out-numbering the effective Spanish ships now by four to one.

The bitter confusion of the fight is perhaps best described by an eye-witness, Calderon, who was on board the *San Salvador*, a ship of seven hundred and fifty tons attached to Oquendo's squadron.

The enemy opened a heavy artillery fire on our flagship at seven o'clock in the morning, which was continued for nine hours. So tremendous was the fire that over 200 balls struck the sails and hull of the flagship on the starboard side, killing and wounding many men, disabling and dismounting guns and destroying much rigging. The holes made in the hull between wind and water caused so great a leakage that two divers had as much as they could do to stop them with tow and lead plates working all day.

The galleon *San Felipe* of Portugal was surrounded by 17 of the enemy's ships, which directed against her heavy fire on both sides and on her stern. The enemy approached so close that the muskets and the harquebusses of the galleon were brought into service, killing a large number of men on the enemy ships. They did not dare, however, to come to close quarters [i.e. to board], but kept up a hot artillery fire from a distance, disabling the rudder, breaking the foremast and killing over 200 men in the galleon. This being noticed by the captain of the *San Mateo*, he brought his galleon to the wind and bravely went to the rescue. Then some of the enemy's ships attacked him and inflicted much damage upon him. One of the enemy's ships came alongside the galleon and an Englishman jumped on board, but our men cut him to bits instantly.

In the interim the Duke's flagship, the *San Martin*, and the *San Salvador* luffed up as close as possible and went to the aid of the galleon. The *San Salvador* engaged an admiral's and a commodore's flagships, her bows, side, and half her poop being exposed for four hours to the enemy's fire, during which she had a larger number of men killed and wounded, and her hull, her sails and rigging were much damaged. She leaked greatly through shot holes, and finally the *Rata Encoronada*, under Don Alonso de Leyva, came to her assistance, distinguishing herself greatly. On board the *Rata* there fell Don Pedro de Mendoza and other persons. They had to defend themselves against three flagships, a vice-flagship and ten or twelve other war vessels. This engagement lasted until four o'clock in the afternoon, the *San Juan* and the *San Marcos* suffering very severely. Don Felipe de Cordoba, son of Diego, his Majesty's Master of the Horse, had his head shot off.

The 'Duke's flagship lost 40 soldiers, and Sergeant Juan Carrasco, Alonso de Orozco and others. Diego Enriquez, who succeeded to the command of Pedro de Valdes's squadron, also fought bravely in this engagement, and his ship suffered to such an extent that every one of his sails were destroyed. Don Pedro Enriquez had a hand shot away in this fight, and the ship's company generally behaved with great gallantry.

We sailed between Dover and Calais in the direction of Norway with a W.N.W. wind. The enemy inflicted great damage on the galleons *San Mateo* and *San Felipe*, the latter having five of her starboard guns dismounted. In view of this, and that his upper deck was destroyed, both his pumps broken, his rigging in shreds and his ship almost a wreck, Don Francisco de Toledo ordered the grappling hooks to be brought out and shouted to the enemy to come to close quarters. They replied, summoning him to surrender in fair fight; and one Englishman, standing in the maintop with his sword and buckler, called out: 'Good soldiers that ye are, surrender to the fair terms we offer ye.' But the only answer he got was a gunshot, which brought him down in the sight of everyone, and the Maestro de Campo then ordered the muskets and harquebusses to be brought into action. The enemy thereupon retired, whilst our men shouted out to them that they were cowards, and with opprobrious words reproached them for their want of spirit, calling them Lutheran hens and daring them to return to the fight.

At seven o'clock in the evening, having lost 60 soldiers killed and 200 wounded, the *San Felipe* fired shots for aid to be sent her, and the hulk *Doncella* went to her. She found the galleon sinking and took on board 300 of her men. Captain Juan Poza, who was with them, said he believed that the hulk too was going down. The Maestro de Campo then replied that if that were the case they had better be drowned in the galleon than in the hulk, and they both went back to her. *San Mateo* had her hull so riddled that she was also in a sinking condition, the pumps being powerless to diminish the water. She came alongside the flagship and asked for help. The Duke sent a diver who stopped some of the leaks, but in the end the galleon was obliged to drop astern with the *San Felipe* and their subsequent fate is unknown; but it is said that they ran aground on the banks.

(In fact both ships did drift helplessly into the shore between Nieuport and Dunkirk where they were attacked by three Dutch fly-boats and after a three-hour battle were totally destroyed.)

This is a corner of the battle, the corner of a page turned up and illumined by a narrator who survived. All over the area of sea between Gravelines and Dunkirk equally bitter fights were taking place, in a free-for-all in which the Spaniards were gradually shot to pieces, fighting almost everywhere with great courage but now without formation, in many cases after the first hours their big guns falling silent for lack of shot.

All the time too the English were edging the Spanish fleet nearer to the sandbanks of Dunkirk, the Spanish, under the leadership of Medina Sidonia and Diego Flores, luffing up into the wind and trying to edge farther north.

When Howard himself came on the scene with his dozen fresh ships he charged at once into the *mêlée*. Seymour in the *Rainbow* with Wynter beside him in the *Vanguard* had attacked the enemy's starboard, or inshore, wing – in so far as it remained a wing; and there had done battle with Oquendo in the *Santa Ana* and de Leyva in the *Rata*. The *San Juan de Sicilia*, one of the Levantine squadron, was so badly mauled that half her crew were dead, and eye-witnesses say that 'her port holes were all full of blood'; yet she would not give ground and remained fighting on for three more hours. Martin de Bertendona in his flagship *La Regazona* was engaged alongside, but eventually her battery guns fell silent too as she ran out of shot. With blood spilling from her scuppers she refused to fall out of line but continued to fight with musketeers in her tops and crouching among the dead and the dying on her decks.

As the long day wore on, so the superiority of the English became more manifest. With rare self-control, after the mistake of boarding the galleass in the morning, they made no attempt to capture, or indeed to sink, individual ships; but once they had pounded them into semi-wrecks they moved on to the next target.

By four in the afternoon the battle had almost worn itself out. The English now as well as the Spanish were out of shot. The great Armada galleons were scattered, sometimes in groups of two or three, sometimes alone. For a time the *San Martin* herself was behind the English fleet, and it is said that Medina Sidonia, although wounded in the leg, climbed to the trees to discern for himself what was happening through the clouds of drifting smoke.

It still seemed likely that a total destruction of the Spanish fleet might be achieved, but a heavy squall about six accompanied by blinding rain forced both fleets to look to their sea safety; and when it was past the Armada by running before the wind had got itself temporarily out of range, and a little freer of the menace of the sandbanks. They had also miraculously contrived to re-form, so that once again they were steering in a fairly compact mass, and indeed Sidonia had the courage to shorten sail and wait for another English attack. Howard, however, did not attempt to close again but ordered his ships to shadow the Spanish fleet, of which one after another appeared to be in sinking condition.

Just before sunset the *Maria Juan*, six hundred and sixty-five tons, of Recalde's squadron, which had had a long encounter with Captain Crosse in the *Hope*, signalled for help – she was going down. Somehow the Duke with his battered *San Martin* was still able to put on sail and go to her assistance. But it was too late. He was able to take off one boatload of her men and then she heeled over and sank, carrying with her two hundred and fifty-five men and her captain, Pedro de Ugarte.

So night fell, and the sea rose and the damaged, leaking, defeated fleet drifted parallel with the coast, putting its dead overboard, trying to minister to its many wounded, mopping the blood from its decks, replacing or patching its tattered sails, repairing rudders, stopping and caulking leaks, its unwounded sailors and soldiers in utter exhaustion, trying between tasks to eat such food as there was – much of it rotten biscuit – and drink the sour water.

No sleep for any, least of all for its commanders, with the

English fleet close behind them (and preparing, for all they knew, a new attack at dawn) and the dreaded Dutch-occupied beaches on their starboard wing. It was a prospect which would have daunted any man.

As for the English, they were conscious of winning but not yet that they had won. They knew they had done great damage but only a half dozen of the enemy had gone down. Sir William Wynter, Seymour's second-in-command, wrote to Walsingham: 'Great was the spoil and harm that was done unto them . . . Out of my ship there was shot 500 shot . . . [my ship] was never out of harquebus shot of theirs and most often within speech of one another . . . no doubt the slaughter and hurt was great, as time will discover it; and every man was weary with labour and our cartridges spent and our munitions expended.'

Howard wrote cautiously to Walsingham: 'I will not write unto her Majesty until more be done. Their force is wonderful great and strong; and yet we pluck their feathers by little and little.'

Drake wrote: 'God hath given us so good a day in forcing the enemy so far to leeward, as I hope in God the Duke of Parma and the Duke of Sidonia shall not shake hands this few days; and whensoever they shall meet, I believe neither of them will greatly rejoice of this day's service . . . There must be great care taken to send us munitions and victuals whithersoever the enemy goeth.'

Hawkins wrote: 'All that day Monday we followed the Spaniards with a long and great fight, wherein there was great valour showed generally by our company . . . In this fight there was some hurt done among the Spaniards . . . Our ships, God be thanked, have received little hurt . . . Now their fleet is here, and very forcible, it must be waited upon with all our force, which is little enough. There should be an infinite quantity of powder and shot provided . . . The men have long been unpaid and need relief.'

Richard Tomson wrote: 'At this instant we are so far to the eastward as the Isle of Walcheren, wherein Flushing doth stand, and the wind hanging westerly, we drive our enemies apace to the eastward, much marvelling if the wind continue in what port they direct themselves. Some imagine the river of Hamburg . . . There is want of powder and shot and victual among us which causeth that we cannot so daily assault them as we would.'

When dawn broke on a blustery and showery Tuesday morning, total destruction did indeed face the Spanish fleet. Overnight the wind had come north-west, and with the daylight it was seen that the shore of Zeeland was very close. And not only the shore; for everyone knew that, lurking among the banks and shoals, negotiating them with the familiarity of long experience, was a fleet of fly-boats under Justin of Nassau, whose policy towards the Spaniards – as theirs to him – was one not of ordinary war but of complete extermination. (It must be said, however, in effect that the Dutch were not as merciless as they perhaps had reason to be; from the two big galleons which drifted ashore on the Monday some four hundred prisoners were taken. These of course included the high-born officers, who could be ransomed, but also many ordinary sailors and soldiers as well.)

Behind them, scarcely two miles to windward, were the white sails and bobbing masts of the English fleet.

At the rearguard of the Armada, in the place of greatest danger, ready to meet the first shock of the expected new English attack, were as usual the relatively few fighting ships which had borne the brunt of the battle ever since the first clash at Plymouth: Medina Sidonia and Diego Flores in the *San Martin*, Recalde in the *San Juan*, de Leyva in the *Rata Encoronada*, Oquendo in the *Santa Ana*, de Bertendona in *La Regazano* and about two dozen others. With them were the three surviving galleasses, *Napolitana*, *Gerona* and *Zuniga*. The rest of the fleet struggled ahead under light sail, falling off to leeward ever nearer the shore.

Howard did not attack for the simple reason that he was saving what little shot he had scraped together for the final catastrophe when the Armada took the ground.

The *San Martin* was 'sailing abaft of the rearguard, in consequence of having one of her anchors down, her lead having only reached seven fathoms and she being near the banks'. Various officers now came to Medina Sidonia and besought him to take one of the pinnaces and the much-torn Holy Banner and make for the safety of Spanish-held Dunkirk, but he refused. 'Having confessed himself with his officers he prepared to die like a Christian soldier.' Presently Oquendo in the *Santa Ana* came up and the Duke shouted to him: 'We are lost. What shall we do?' Oquendo said: 'Ask Diego Flores.

As for me I am going to fight and die like a man. Send me a supply of shot.'

The lead said six fathoms and then five. The pilots insisted they were helpless; with the wind as it was, shipwreck was a matter of minutes. It was just a question of which ships would strike first.

Then occurred what appeared as a miracle to the Spaniards: the wind hesitated, gusted for a few moments, and began to back. From north-west it became south-west, and within what must have been only yards from shipwreck the Armada shook out its tattered sails and began to move out of danger towards the safer beaches of the North Sea. 'God succoured us in our distress, as He always does,' wrote Calderon. 'We were saved by God's mercy,' said the Duke. What the English thought has never been recorded. A simple change of wind deprived them by a matter of half an hour of that complete victory which the day before they had gone so far to earn. They were powerless to attack again, they could only fall in and shadow. Even the harassing tactics of the Channel were not possible.

As a result of this, no one knew for many weeks whether the threat to England was really over. And for the Spaniards that God-given change of wind meant the difference between annihilation on the Flanders sandbanks and the long-drawn-out agony of a return round the British Isles to Spain.

9

Irish Ordeal

For long the myth was fostered that the Armada was destroyed not by the English but by the storms of August and September. On the Spanish side it was a better excuse than to admit they had been defeated in battle. On the English side it was preferable to believe that winds provided by God in a righteous cause were more potent than the guns and ships provided by man. Yet the myth really did no honour to either side; neither to the seamanship of the Spaniards nor the gunnery and tactics of the English—nor to the bravery of both. In fact the Spanish were comprehensively defeated in the Battle of Gravelines, shot through, decimated, all but completely destroyed. It was this more than any storms which sank them on the way home.

Another myth is that the Armada was blown relentlessly north by an unceasing south-west wind and could not have returned to the Channel if it would. The wind remained roughly south-south-west from the Tuesday afternoon until Friday. Late on Friday it veered round to the north-west again and presented the Spanish with a favourable opportunity of retracing their course, indeed making it difficult for them not to do so. They did not do so.

On the Tuesday evening before sunset the Duke had summoned his generals and advisers for a council-of-war, and they had discussed the future. It cannot have been a cheerful gathering, and harsh words flew. Diego Flores was for returning as soon as the wind changed and making one more attempt to link up with Parma; but the majority was against him—as indeed was common sense. Without ammunition, and with no friendly port in which to rest and re-arm and re-equip, the move would have been suicidal. But perhaps, like Oquendo earlier in the day, the mood of some of the captains *was* suicidal. Better death in the jaws of the enemy than a long and dishonourable retreat.

But saner councils prevailed, and the pilots were called in.

Theirs was not a hopeful outlook. It would be a long and laborious trek home, fifteen hundred to eighteen hundred miles, days and weeks sailing in possibly stormy seas in that treacherous summer, in waters known only to a few of them, almost every ship damaged, every ship full of wounded men, the whole fleet desperately short of food and water and medical supplies : this prospect was almost as daunting as the first. But it was chosen; there was no other alternative but to surrender, and that course, in spite of the early example of Pedro de Valdes, was not even discussed. So they sailed on ever north and ever shadowed by ninety ships of the English fleet. When the wind changed on the Friday the English took advantage of it and, out of food and water themselves, ran for home, leaving only two pinnaces, one belonging to Drake, to continue to follow the enemy as far as the Northern Islands.

The Spanish made no such change of course. Sharing supplies among themselves, for some ships were better off than others, limiting the thousands of men, wounded and fit alike, to eight ounces of bread, half a pint of wine and a pint of water daily, they beat on slowly – at the speed of the slowest – up into the north.

There was no conviction in England that the danger was past. The very caution and modesty of the dispatches sent by the English captains told against them. The Armada was still in being, and few realized how mortally it had been wounded. The English fleet had parted with the enemy off Newcastle, and there were three dangers still very much in English minds : (1) a return of the Spanish fleet to try again to link up with Parma, (2) a landing in the Firth of Forth, with Protestant James not so sure of the loyalty of his Catholics as Elizabeth had been of hers, or (3) a landing in Ireland, where a Catholic and rebellious population would be waiting to welcome them as friends and liberators.

It took the English fleet several days to reach home, for they ran into a westerly gale, which scattered them along the coast from Harwich and Margate to the Downs. Although casualties had been light – though not so light as was claimed – sickness had spread through the ships, and they arrived in their various ports exhausted and undermanned. Drake thought that possibly a fourth choice existed and that the Spaniards on the wings of the westerly gale might have made for Denmark. 'If they should go to the King of Denmark and there have his friendship and help for all their reliefs, none can better help their wants in all these parts than he; for that he is a prince of great shipping.' Drake perhaps more than anyone had seen at close quarters the devastation wrought in the Spanish ships, and he thought it unlikely that Medina Sidonia would dare to attempt the long northern route home without first trying to recover and refit.

Elizabeth's first letter to Howard, sent to greet him as soon as he reached port, asked as many detailed questions as any modern civil service could devise – most of them unanswerable – about the condition and numbers of her fleet, the amount of powder and shot used and the casualties suffered. It also enquired pointedly what Spanish ships and prisoners had been taken, also what treasure, and why the Spanish ships had not been boarded by the English – at least if the largest galleons were too big, why not some of the smaller ones?

It is plain from the wording of this letter that neither the Queen nor any of her ministers had even begun to understand the strategy adopted by her fleet in this running battle. The last two great naval battles before 1588, those at Lepanto and Terceira, had both seen a grappling of ship with ship and a fight to the finish between boarding parties; and the Queen and her council had clearly expected the same now. (Oddly, Philip had appreciated the probable English tactics better, although he had assumed they could be overcome.)

Ralegh in his *History of the World*, written twenty years later, does not mince his words on this point:

> He that will happily perform a fight at sea must believe that there is more belonging to a good man of war upon the waters than great daring, and must know there is a great deal of difference between fighting loose and grappling. To clap ships together without consideration belongs rather to a madman than to a ship of war; for by such an ignorant bravery was Peter Strozzi lost at the Azores when he fought against the Marquis of Santa Cruz. In like sort had the Lord Charles Howard, Admiral of England, been lost in the year 1588 if he had not been better advised than a great many malignant fools were who found fault with his behaviour.

If one were seeking an example to illustrate 'Gloriana's' meanness, one would look no further than this letter to the battle-worn yet victorious Howard. But in her defence it could be argued that throughout nearly two decades she had grown accustomed to her captains returning with prizes from their private wars with Spain and she had shared in the spoils. It is not perhaps to be wondered at that, not understanding the strategy of the battle, she should expect greater prizes from a national war in which she had sunk so much of her scanty revenues, and one in which clearly there were enormous pickings to be had both in bullion and in ransomable grandees.

For Elizabeth the safety of her realm was paramount; but she did not see at first why her commanders had only been able to ensure this by adopting a policy without profit to her.

In the meantime, though Elizabeth was anxious to take the risk of disbanding her fleet in order to save the expense of keeping it together, her council and her admirals argued hotly against it. While the Armada was in being they could not relax. So the battle-worn ships lay in the little ports, and men died on them from typhus at the rate of a hundred a day. 'They sicken one day and die the next,' Howard told the Queen.

The hideous conditions in which men lived aboard made the spread of disease inevitable if the voyage or the time were long. Because of the complete lack of sanitary arrangements it was practically impossible to keep food and cooking uncontaminated; and when in port this was made worse because so-called fresh water, often itself bad in cask, was kept solely for drinking, and all other water used was drawn up from the harbour, which was filthy with excrement and even corpses.

Disease now spread so sharply that it converted the admirals half way to Elizabeth's line of thought, and it was decided to disband the auxiliaries and split the main fleet into two divisions, one in the Downs (that roadstead off Deal and between the North and South Foreland which is protected from bad weather on two sides by the curve of the coast and from the east by the Goodwin Sands) and the other at Margate. Rumour flew throughout the Continent that Drake was captured, that Medina Sidonia was in London, that the Queen had been dethroned. Rumour in England told that the Armada had landed in Ireland, in Scotland, or was returning, miraculously refreshed, down the English coast to challenge Howard again.

Then towards the end of August definite news filtered through that Parma at least had accepted defeat. He had ordered his men to return to Bruges, the victuals on board his fleet of barges and fly-boats to be unshipped, and the sails to be taken from the yards. Shortly following this, an English pinnace commanded by a man called Anthony Potts reported having sighted the great Armada sailing westward of the Orkney Islands. All immediate danger did at last seem to be truly over.

So the Queen had her way, and most of the fleet was disbanded, with the result that the seaport towns of the southeast were swamped with sick and disabled and starving men begging for food and shelter. West Country ships were packed off home, unpaid and half manned, with sick and dying crews and one day's supply of victuals aboard.

Howard was absolutely furious. 'It is a most pitiful sight to see, here at Margate, how the men, having no place to receive them into here, die in the streets. I am driven myself, of force, to come a-land, to see them bestowed in some lodging; and the best I can get is barns and outhouses. It would grieve any man's heart to see them that have served so valiantly to die so miserably.' He paid some of the seamen out of his own pocket. Greatly daring, he paid more of them out of the treasure found aboard de Valdes's *Rosario*. He pawned his own plate and spent his last guinea to keep the dying sailors alive, while now, all over the land, the victory, seen at last as a victory, was being celebrated with bonfires and processions and the ring of bells.

Elizabeth has been much criticized for this disgraceful neglect of the men who had saved England; and, although in actual fact it was nothing directly to do with her, the payment being sanctioned by the Council and issued at the order of the Lord Treasurer, one cannot but be aware that a sharp intervention by her would have made all the difference. Her care for her homecoming sailors was so much less generous than Philip's.

Yet such was the scarcity of money at this time that she, like Howard, might have had to pawn her plate to pay them. Philip had nearly bankrupted himself to launch the Armada; Elizabeth with all her cheeseparing had come near to bankrupting England to defeat it. Philip had a wide empire to draw on for his revenue; Elizabeth had much smaller resources and she had no private fortune. She could not compel her people to pay their taxes – at least, not the rich ones – it was done on a semi-voluntary basis. A few years later Francis Bacon was to write: 'He that shall look into other countries and consider the taxes and tallages and impositions and assizes and the like that are everywhere in use, will find that the Englishman is most master of his own valuation and the least bitten in purse of any nation in Europe.' In fact in 1588 by exceptional methods which could hardly be repeated Elizabeth had been able to raise her revenue for the year to £392,000. Her expenses in the Netherlands alone that year amounted to £120,000 and the cost of the Navy was £153,000. This left her about £120,000 for all other calls on her purse: the court, the army, the Yeomen of the Guard, the royal residences, the mews with its three hundred horses and one hundred and thirty grooms, the ambassadors, Walsingham's spies, subsidies, rewards for faithful service, the hundreds of incidental expenses falling upon even the most frugal monarch.

It was of course not nearly enough. But during the pre-war years when the risk of war was monthly growing, the Queen and Burghley had adopted a policy of retrenchment; the repair of the royal palaces was postponed, players and musicians at the court were disposed with, the royal progresses through the land abandoned or curtailed, every detail of expenditure watched, so that by 1588 Elizabeth had built up a reserve fortune of about £300,000. This too went, and by the end of her forty-five years on the throne she had been compelled to sell nearly £900,000 worth of Crown lands to pay her way. Over all, her reign does not look like the reign of a mean woman but of a wise one who knew how to husband her resources and not oppress her subjects.

So while responsibility lies on her for the unnecessary suffering of so many good men – immensely more died than were killed by the Spanish – it is a responsibility which everyone in the Council must share.

In August there had been the great procession of the Queen to Tilbury with her review of the troops and her marvellous speech to them. There has probably never been another monarch with such a command of words, and few commoners: one thinks of Ralegh and Lincoln and Churchill. In November came the service at St Paul's. It was another magnificent occasion; but whereas Tilbury had been a promenade of defiance, a splendid appearance before her people in their hour of greatest peril, this procession was before a victorious people who were joining with her in thanksgiving.

She drove from Somerset House to the City in a chariot drawn by two white horses. Above the chariot was a canopy topped by an imperial crown, and a gold lion and dragon flanked the coach. With her were the Privy Council, most of her notable lords and the judges of the realm, the admirals who had won the victory, and heralds and trumpeters, all on horseback. The Earl of Essex, Master of the Horse, rode directly behind her, and he was followed by all the Queen's ladies of honour. The streets were gay with blue streamers, and at the gate of the Temple the Lord Mayor and aldermen in scarlet robes were waiting to greet her and hand her the sceptre. Then with the City Livery Companies added to the procession she was drawn to St Paul's, where at the great west door she knelt a time in prayer on the steps. Dr Pierce, Bishop of Salisbury, preached the sermon, and afterwards she dined in the bishop's palace, and then returned in the falling November dusk in a torchlight procession to Somerset House. She was in truth Gloriana to everyone who saw her at that time. It was thirty years since her accession, and this might have been her jubilee.

Earlier in the month she had with her usual aplomb and versatility composed a poem for the occasion, and this was sung at St Paul's during the service of thanksgiving.

Look and bow down thine ear, oh Lord,
From thy bright sphere behold and see
Thy handmaid and thy handiwork;
Amongst thy priests offering to thee
Zeal for incense reaching the skies
My self and sceptre sacrifice.

My soul ascend to holy place,
Ascribe Him strength and sing Him praise
For he refraineth Prince's spirits,
And hath done wonders in my days.
He made the winds and waters rise
To scatter all mine enemies.

This Joseph's lord and Israel's god,
The fiery pillar and day's cloud,
That saved his saints from wicked men
And drenched the honour of the proud,
And hath preserved in tender love
The spirit of his Turtle dove.

Before His Turtle Dove could quite relax there was one more alarm for the English. The Armada had disappeared into the northern seas, no one knew whither. No one at that time could safely calculate that it would return home with a further attempt to justify its coming out. After it had been sighted off the Orkney Islands there was clearly little risk to the Channel ports. But England has a long and vulnerable sea-board. And there was still Scotland with its dissident Catholics. And there was still Ireland, passionately Catholic and already in semi-revolt.

When therefore the news first reached England that great numbers of the enemy fleet were off Ireland, it was thought that the Spanish were about to land their troops there and begin a large-scale invasion. Twenty, forty, sixty ships, many of them still crammed with trained soldiers: it was a likely enough event. Only after a few days, as more messages came through, did it become clear that these were ships in distress seeking only succour. Some of the ships were already wrecked among the treacherous rocks off the Dingle and Donegal coasts. Some came in seeking food and water. Some were in a sinking condition and were just making landfall in time.

Many of these ships had suffered from the rough weather, but it is not clear how rough the weather really was. What is evident is that crews and ships together had been so mal-treated at Gravelines that they were in a condition to succumb to the first gale. Medina Sidonia's orders, given to the fleet when north-east of Scotland and later taken from one of the wrecked vessels, ran:

The course that is first to be held is to the north-north-east, until you be found under 61 degrees-and-a-half; and then to take heed lest you fall upon the Island of Ireland, for fear of the harm that may happen unto you upon that coast.

Then parting from those Islands, and doubling the Cape in 61 degrees-and-a-half, you shall run west-south-west until you be found under 58 degrees; and from thence to the south-west to the height of 53 degrees; and then to the south-south-west, making to the Cape Finisterre, and so to procure your entrance into the Groyne or to Ferol, or to any other port of the coast of Galicia.

The last direction is a mistake: south-south-west should have been south-east; but any ships which followed the instructions that far were not likely to fall into error.

In the cold northern waters between the Faroes and Ireland, some two hundred and fifty miles north of the northernmost tip of Scotland, the limping damaged fleet was finally split by storm and it never came together again. Medina Sidonia's *San Martin*, which, whatever the Duke's detractors may say, had been in the thick of every fight since the beginning and the special target of the English whenever they could attack her, kept to the prescribed course, and those who stayed with her and followed her reached Spain safely again, albeit in however terrible a condition. Perhaps she was the strongest-built ship in the whole Armada; we do not know. (In fact, about the 4th September, Diego Flores transferred from the *San Martin* to another galleon, the *San Juan de Avendano*, and took Medina Sidonia with him: this because of the typhus and dysentery raging aboard the *San Martin*.) But at least they all arrived home together and apparently only had two days of storm, although the weather was constantly rough and blustery, with south-west winds prevailing.

Whatever the cause, it is hardly Spanish seamanship that was at fault, though often their charts were inaccurate, and of course nine out of ten were sailing in waters they had never been in before. Some sixty-odd ships splintered from the main body of the fleet and drifted or were blown towards that island against which the Duke had expressly warned them. They came in 'like flocks of starlings', were wrecked or fought for their lives or were slaughtered as they struggled ashore. Most of them were killed by – or on the orders of – the English.

The arrival of floods of Spanish soldiers – in whatever straits – upon the shores of this conquered but rebellious island threw the English on the spot into an understandable panic. They had fewer than two thousand troops in the whole of Ireland at the time, many of them half-trained, and with ancient muskets and rusty cannon, and gun carriages 'rotting for want of men to maintain them' and the universal and inevitable shortage of powder and shot. This force had to keep the peace in a country thirty-two thousand square miles in area, a country full of mountains, wild moors, lakes and treacherous bogs, and populated by about a million temperamental and quarrelsome Gaels who hated the Anglo-Saxons and all they stood for.

The Lord Deputy Fitz William, writing on the 22nd September, paints an even gloomier picture: 'There are not 750 foot in bands in the whole realm. We cannot impress the few soldiers for the shoeing of their horses. We feel rather to be overrun by the Spaniards than otherwise.'

England was at war with Spain. These were invaders, in whatever guise they came. If the position had been reversed English survivors would certainly have fared no better at the hands of the Spanish. What does stain the record is that the English on several occasions accepted the surrender of the Spanish survivors on fair terms, and then proceeded to hang them just the same. Of course the Spanish so far outnumbered their captors and there were so few stockades or keeps in which they could be safely imprisoned that their being merely alive was a menace to the security of the country. So at least argued – however inexcusably – Fitz William, Bingham and the rest; though Christopher Calleil was a noted and humane exception.

It was fashionable for many years to put all the blame for the slaughter on the wild Irish who were said to have killed and robbed the Spanish as they came ashore. Now it is as fashionable to put all the blame on the English, where in truth most of it rests. But the accounts of the few Spanish survivors who have left their stories do not leave the Irish blameless – though essentially the natives mostly wanted Spanish clothes and gold and ornaments more than they wanted Spanish blood. All through these accounts the Spaniards refer to the native Irish not as potential allies but as 'the savages', much as a shipwrecked sailor would write of being cast away on the coast of Borneo. The Calendar of State Papers (Ireland) records the claim of one Melaghlin M'Cabb who stated that he killed eighty Spaniards with his galloglass axe.

Among the commanders of the Armada, Bertendona followed the Duke, as did Oquendo, though Oquendo died of typhus soon after he reached Spain. Diego Flores was of course with the Duke and was tried and imprisoned in Spain for the 'bad advice' he had given Medina Sidonia.

The veteran Recalde was one of those who lost touch with the Duke and, in company with two other ships, found himself off the dreaded Blasket Islands at the jagged tip of Dingle Peninsula, the westernmost point in Europe. His ship, the San Juan de Portugal, like the San Martin, had been in the thick of the fighting all through and appears to have suffered more. Calderon says: 'He was dreadfully in need of everything and his ship was in a very injured state.' It is at least fairly to be assumed that Recalde would not have put in to the Irish coast willingly or unless driven by sickness or shortage of supplies.

Of the two ships with him, one was a Castilian galleon, the *San Juan Bautista*, of seven hundred and fifty tons, with a complement of two hundred and forty-three men. On board her was the Paymaster and Controller of the galleons of Castile, Marcos de Arumburu, who survived to give an account of his adventures and also ultimately to command a Spanish squadron in the Armadas of 1596 and 1597. The second ship was the *San Pedro el Mayor*, a vessel of five hundred and forty-one tons and a complement of two hundred and forty men : one of the only two hospital ships in the Armada. No doubt at this date she was crowded to the ports with sick and wounded men. The two ships had sighted the *San Juan de Portugal* through the driving mists of a windy September morning and had attached themselves to her, recognizing Recalde's ship and knowing his seamanship.

At first Recalde anchored between the Great Blasket and the shore, but this was no place to stop. In Irish waters the long Atlantic swells often run counter to the winds ruffling the surface, and this made navigation for sixteenth-century sailing-ships a matter of peculiar peril, even when in the peak of condition. Now Recalde, after edging his galleon closer to the inhospitable cliffs, veered away and approached the island of Inishvickillane, which is a smaller island than the Great Blasket about three miles to the south-west. This has a tiny rock-bound harbour big enough to take fishing-boats. In Arumburu's words, Recalde ran into the port of Inishvickillane 'through an entrance between low rocks, about as wide as the length of a ship, and so anchored. We came in behind her, and after us the tender . . .'

It was a superb piece of seamanship performed with a badly damaged vessel and a half dying crew. How far an anonymous Scottish pilot was responsible, how far Recalde himself – who knew the coast – we can never be sure. Recalde at once sent a longboat to the mainland several miles distant with eight men under a Biscayan officer called Licornio to reconnoitre the situation. They were captured and after being questioned were executed by the small band of English soldiers guarding the coast. After waiting vainly for their return Recalde sent a bigger boat containing fifty arquebusiers, and these men, out-numbering the English, proceeded to spend three days ashore, obtaining fresh water and what little else might be gleaned of the bleak countryside. The English and the Irish watched them in enmity but did not attack.

There then blew up one of the worst winds of that windy month, and the two *San Juans* dragged their anchors in the tiny harbour and collided, doing each other further damage. On the wings of this storm the galleon *Santa Maria de la Rosa*, vice-flagship of Oquendo's squadron, drifted in, her sails in ribbons, and sank before their eyes with the loss of the entire crew except for one man. Following her came yet another *San Juan*, which tried to anchor in the shelter of the island while the last of her tattered rigging blew to shreds. Presently, in spite of Recalde's efforts to save her, she too went down with most of her crew.

As soon as the wind blew itself out Recalde, who was now almost too ill to rise from his bed, gave orders to set sail, and the three remaining vessels, still in bad condition but at least re-watered and their crews rested, crept out of the narrow harbour in the dark and began the next leg of their long journey home.

It was each one for himself. The *San Juan Bautista* after a hazardous and sickly voyage was the first to make port. Recalde and his *San Juan de Portugal* reached Coruña on the 7th October, one of the very last to come home; but Recalde was so far spent that he died four days after his return. So disgusted and humiliated was he at the fate of the great Armada that he did not wish to see even his family and friends before he died. The *San Pedro el Mayor* was even less fortunate. She was blown by contrary winds back into the English Channel and wrecked in Hope Cove, off Salcombe. Some of her crew and patients were drowned but the majority got ashore. Although not important enough to be ransomable, none was slain : they were hauled out of the water by the sturdy Devonshire villagers and were fed, albeit scantily, by the local magistrate, George Cary, at his own expense until the country took them over.

Higher up the Irish coast, in Clare, in Galway, in Sligo and in Donegal, the other Spanish ships had drifted in in their dozens, a few to shelter and to water and to be off again, but the vast majority to founder, with the whole of their crews either drowned or killed as they came ashore or hanged after capture. Among these ships was the *Rata Encoronada*, with de Leyva aboard and his cargo of dashing young men. De

Leyva, like Recalde, and Medina Sidonia, had all the time been in the thick of the battle, and his great carrack, less stoutly built than the Portuguese galleons, had suffered the more. Separated from the main body of the fleet, he led three other ships to an anchorage in Blacksod Bay in Galway, far to the north of Recalde. It is a wild coast, smiling and green in fair weather, grim and deadly in bad, and for some reason he chose an exposed anchorage off Ballycroy.

De Leyva, like Recalde, sent a boat ashore to reconnoitre, and these men were set upon by one of the petty chiefs, Richard Burke, who robbed and maltreated them. A gusty wind and a heavy tide meanwhile snapped the hempen rope of the one serviceable anchor and the *Rata* drifted on to the beach. Almost all her crew landed safely, and with them brought such possessions as they could carry: plate, money, clothing, some armour, but precious little food. They camped one night on the beach and then took possession of a ruined hill-fort, called Doona, from which they began to scour the countryside for food and water. Presently scouts brought news of another Spanish ship, that hulk of Andalusia, the *Duquesa Santa Ana* of nine hundred tons, anchored beyond the next headland. This was the ship which on the Thursday morning of the Channel fight, together with the *San Luis*, had drifted out of the protective range of the rest of the fleet and had had to be rescued from the clutches of John Hawkins by three of the galleasses and the *Rata Encoronada*. Perhaps it was fitting that she should now offer hope of escape to the *Rata*'s distinguished company. De Leyva marched his men across and found the *Santa Ana* in fair condition but with already more than her full complement of men, for she had saved some from another sinking ship.

A council-of-war was held, at which the captains of both ships and the pilots were of the opinion that to attempt to sail to Spain with eight hundred men aboard and scanty provisions, and with the prevailing headwinds, would mean certain disaster. De Leyva therefore decided to sail *north* again, to skirt the savage Irish headlands and try to land on the west coast of Scotland. This being a neutral country, if not actually a friendly one, there was a good chance of making one's way in due course to Flanders and thence back to Spain.

So at the first favourable wind the hulk weighed anchor and began to creep up the coast. Past Annagh Head and Erris Head and Benwee Head, each one as dangerous as the last, and then across the fifty-mile gaping mouth of Donegal Bay to Rossan Point, about a hundred miles in all, before another strong wind coming up out of the north-west drove the ailing *Santa Ana* on the rocks of Loughros More Bay.

This was a nastier shipwreck than the last: rocks, not a sandy beach; some were drowned and de Leyva himself 'was hurt in the leg by the capstan of the ship in such sort as he was able neither to go nor ride'. But some of their arms were ferried ashore, and most of the men survived and once again made some sort of camp in the rainy September twilight and committed their souls to God.

The next morning the usual scouts were sent out. This force under de Leyva was the most dangerous to England of any that landed or attempted to land. Not only did it still contain all the vigorous and enterprising young noblemen but, in spite of its sore straits, it was the only one, because of de Leyva's guidance, that kept a degree of cohesion and discipline; and if it were allowed to consolidate itself it could well become the nucleus of a major revolt. But the English, although aware of its existence, had not yet located it, and de Leyva was able to send his scouts out without hindrance. Once again there was a convenient ruin near, and the great mass of men set about converting it into a defensive position, de Leyva being carried about in a chair and directing operations. The neighbouring Irish, those who were friendly, gave what help they dared.

So they stayed for eight days until an Irishman brought information that just south of them across the mountains of the Malin Mor peninsula in Donegal Bay was the *Gerona*, one of the galleasses, not too badly damaged and with a complement of crew and galley-slaves. The following day de Leyva struck camp and made a forced march in rain over the steep pass of Ardara to Killibegs with his seven-hundred-odd men, he being carried in a chair by relays of four soldiers at a time.

When they arrived they found the *Gerona* in a poor condition and most of her crew camping on the beach beside her. Near them were the remains of yet another Spanish ship, and de Leyva at once ordered his men to strip her of everything useful to their purpose and with the timbers and ironwork and ropes to set about repairing the *Gerona* and making her ready for sea. His position here was eased by his making contact with the local chieftain, one of the O'Neils, who offered de Leyva the hospitality of his home. This de Leyva refused, on the grounds that when he was gone his host would suffer at the hands of the English; but he gladly accepted supplies and after fourteen days of hard work the galleass was repaired and declared fit for sea.

By now the English were in full alarm, and the Lord Deputy Fitz William was directing as large a force as he could muster to attack them. So on the 14th October de Leyva put to sea again, this time in an even more overcrowded ship, there being eleven or twelve hundred men in all. This time in addition to his patched-up sails he had the oars to propel him and not more than three hundred miles to go.

But the galleass, heavy with fore and aft superstructure and weak in fundamental design, particularly of the rudder, was the prey to every wind, and they made but slow progress, inching north and east day by day. Then in the dark of the night, when they were past almost all the worst hazards and only about forty miles from Scotland, the rudder broke in a sudden squall and the great ship drifted on the rocks near the Giant's Causeway. In the shadow of Dunluce Castle the ship broke to pieces and all but nine common soldiers of her enormous crew were drowned. Hardly a noble house in Spain did not lose a son or a nephew or a cousin in this great disaster. Philip, brooding over his defeat in the Escorial, said when the news was brought to him that the loss of Alonso de Leyva meant more to him than the loss of all the Armada.

One other story of the shipwrecks – a remarkable example of human endurance – concerns Captain Francisco de Cuellar, captain of the galleon *San Pedro*. During the retreat from the English fleet in the North Sea, his and another ship disobeyed the explicit instructions of Medina Sidonia and broke line by sailing ahead of the others. He was brought before that harsh and hated disciplinarian General Bobadilla, who sentenced him to be hanged. This was repealed by Medina Sidonia, but de Cuellar was relieved of his command and transferred under open arrest to the Levantine vice-flagship *La Lavia*.

Nearly a month later, in company with two other ships, *La Lavia* found herself unable to make headway against the southerly winds, so put into the Irish coast near Sligo Bay and dropped anchor off Streedagh Strand, a five-mile stretch of pale sand flanked by cliffs. There she stayed about a mile offshore for four days, hoping for better weather but with the surf too heavy for anyone to land. On the fifth day, instead of the wind abating, it grew worse and broke the frail cables which held the ships. With the sea 'as high as heaven' all three ships were driven ashore, and in an hour were broken up by the thunderous surf. Of the more than fourteen hundred men on board fewer than three hundred reached the shore alive.

Diego Enriquez, the Camp Master aboard La Lavia, and a half dozen aristocrats carrying sixteen thousand ducats' worth of jewels and coin, took to the ship's tender, which had a covered deck, and ordered the hatch to be battened down and caulked behind them. This was done, but as usual in the panic more than seventy men clambered aboard hoping to reach the shore, with the result that the tender capsized and all were drowned. Later when she drifted ashore the Irish seized her and began to break her up for the sake of the nails and the ironwork, when they discovered not only the drowned men inside but the treasure. Joyfully they stripped everything and left the corpses unburied on the sand, anxious to get away before someone surprised them in their rich find.

As for Cuellar himself, he could not swim, but clung to the poop watching others drown around him, saw them clinging to rafts, hatches, spars, barrels, anything that would float, and saw the few who were lucky enough to reach the shore being set on by a horde of two hundred hungry Irish, dancing and leaping with delight, who knocked them down as soon as they reached shallow water and stripped them naked. Presently with the Judge Advocate beside him – that Judge whose prisoner he still officially was – he found a hatchway as big as a table, and between them they contrived to float themselves away on it. On the way ashore the Judge was washed off and, weighted down as he was with crown pieces sewn into his doublet and hose, was instantly drowned. But somehow Cuellar kept afloat, though by now his legs were crushed and bleeding from collison with a piece of wreckage.

When he landed on the beach, gasping and half drowned, there were so many others coming in around him that he was ignored by the 'savages' for more promising prey, and he was able to crawl away through his naked and groaning countrymen and find shelter among some rushes growing in the sandhills near a stream. He stayed there until dark, when he was joined by another Spaniard, naked and shivering with the cold. Together the two crouched there, half dead with pain and hunger, while they heard a search in progress. A small English garrison at nearby Grange had now taken charge and was rounding up such of the enemy as were left alive.

After about half an hour the two Spaniards were discovered by a couple of villainous-looking Irishmen, one with a captured sword, the other with a great iron axe. They stared at each other in the light of a lantern for a few seconds, and then the savage with the sword swung it to cut down the rushes. These, with grass and reeds from near by, they piled on top of the two fugitives until they were hidden from sight; then they passed on.

All night lights flickered and horses neighed and there were the shouts of men and the crash of axes as the great crowd on the beach broke up and dragged away whatever was left of value on the wrecks. Cuellar at last fell asleep, and when he woke at dawn he saw that the young man beside him had died in the night. The beach was still occupied with a few scavengers picking among the remnants, but the great crowd had gone. The only other population was the hundreds of dead and naked bodies piled in heaps waiting for the ravens and the wolves.

He crawled away and began to limp inland, searching for some monastery or Catholic retreat where he might hope for succour. Two miles inland was Staad Abbey, a small monastic church, and Cuellar saw its grey stone walls through the misty sunlight and hastened towards it, hoping to find at least one kind monk to help him. When he pushed open the door he saw the inside of the church had been wrecked, images destroyed and crosses broken, and hanging from the iron grilles of the church were the bodies of twelve Spaniards.

In sick despair he fled from the place and began to make his way back to the beach in the hope that now it would be quite empty and there might be biscuits or bread being washed up by the tide. As he neared the shipwrecks he met two more Spaniards and together they returned to the beach. Here Cuellar came upon and recognized the body of Diego Enriquez, and he and his new companions made an attempt to bury their noble commander. While doing this they were surrounded by Irishmen who did not molest them, being chiefly interested in their occupation; but later in the day Cuellar was robbed of his clothes and the money that he had carefully secreted about himself: forty-five crown pieces and a gold chain worth a thousand reals. Then, through the intervention of a 'beautiful girl of about twenty', some of his clothes were restored to him, and he was at last given a piece of oaten bread to eat with butter and milk, and his wounds were dressed.

I set about putting on my doublet and coat again, but they had taken away my shirt and also some precious relics that I was carrying in a little vestment of the order of the Holy Trinity. The young savage woman had taken these and hung them round her neck, making signs to me that she wished to keep them, and telling me that she was a Catholic, though she was no more a Christian than Mahomet was.

The following night he was given shelter in a hut by some men, one of whom was able to talk to him in Latin, and in the morning he was lent a horse and boy to guide him on his way. The road was so bad that there was 'mud up to the girths'. But they had gone no distance before they had first to hide from a troop of English searchers, and then were discovered and surrounded by 'forty savages on foot' who wanted to hack him to pieces. The boy's intervention saved his life but did not prevent him from being beaten with sticks and robbed of every stitch of clothing. After they had gone he found a piece of old matting and some bracken to try to protect himself from the cold, and went on alone.

All day he made north-east for the Darty Mountains and finally came on a lake, Lough Glenade, where he found thirty huts, all of which were empty except for three naked men who, after the initial alarm, embraced him as another ship-wrecked Spaniard. For supper they ate blackberries and water-cress and then bedded down together in the straw, burying themselves in it to keep out the cold.

In the dawn, however, the 'heretic savages' returned to work in the fields about the huts, and the four Spaniards lay hidden in the straw all day, unable to stir, while men came in and out of the hut. At nightfall, as the moon rose, they wrapped themselves in the straw and slipped away, and after another long trek during which they were at their 'last gasp for thirst and hunger and pain', they found a village belonging to Señor de Ruerque (Sir Brian O'Rourke) where they were given shelter at last. O'Rourke was away fighting the English, but Cuellar was given 'a rotten old blanket swarming with lice, and I covered myself with it and somewhat relieved my plight'. There were in fact already seventy Spaniards in the village, many wounded and all semi-naked, so it is not to be wondered at that supplies of clothing ran short.

News reached the village next day that a Spanish ship lay offshore and she was waiting to pick up fugitives; so Cuellar and twenty others set off to join her. But Cuellar's leg, once injured and once wounded, let him down and he lagged behind, and when he got to the shore the other nineteen men had embarked and the ship, fearful of attack from the land, had sailed. Cuellar's utter despair was later mitigated when he learned that the ship had been wrecked farther along the coast and those not drowned in her had been slaughtered by the English.

A chance meeting with a monk directed him to a village and castle belonging to a native chieftain, one M'Glannagh, eighteen miles distant. There at last he was well treated – 'the womenfolk wept to see me so ill used' – and there he stayed three months, living as one of them.

It is the custom of these savages to live like wild beasts in the mountains. They live in huts made of straw; they . . . eat only once a day and that at nightfall, their usual food being oaten bread and butter. They drink sour milk for lack of anything else; water they do not drink, though theirs is the best in the world. On feast days it is their custom to eat some half-cooked meat without bread or salt. The men dress in tight hose and short coats of coarse goat's hair; over this they wear a blanket, and their hair falls low over their eyes . . . Their great desire is to be thieves and plunder one another, so that hardly a day passes without a call to arms among them, for as soon as the men of one village discover that there are cattle or anything else in another village they come armed by night and attack and kill each other. The English garrisons get to know who has rounded up and stolen most cattle and at once fall upon them and take away their spoils . . .

They sleep on the ground on freshly cut rushes, full of water and ice. Most of the women are very beautiful but poorly dressed; they wear nothing but a smock covered with a blanket, and a linen kerchief folded tightly round their heads and fastened in front . . . These savages liked us Spaniards well . . . indeed if they had not taken as much care of us as they did of themselves not one of us would still be alive. We were grateful to them for this, although

138

they had been the first to rob and strip naked any man cast alive upon their shores, from whom these savages gained great wealth in jewels and money.

After Cuellar had been living in the village for three months, news reached M'Glannagh that a force of English infantry was advancing on them, and the Irish chief decided to evacuate the castle and take to the mountains where he and his family and his people and their cattle could hide until the English had retired again; but Captain Cuellar and eight other Spaniards refused to leave and said they were prepared to defend the place with their lives. The keep was in fact in an extremely defensible position, being on an island in the middle of a deep lake about two miles across and ten long, with an outlet to the sea. The Irish chief agreed to their remaining, and they were left with six muskets, six arquebuses and enough food to last them for a prolonged siege.

When the English arrived they sacked the village and encamped before the castle for seventeen days but could not take it; then December storms and a heavy fall of snow decided them to return to winter quarters. The Irish reappeared and M'Glannagh in his gratitude offered Cuellar one of his sisters in marriage. Cuellar tactfully refused, but asked instead for a guide to take him and his compatriots across the mountains to some port where he could take sail for Scotland. M'Glannagh returned an evasive answer, having by now decided that his Spanish allies were too valuable to release.

So once again it meant a secret departure, stealing away at dead of night in company with the only four of his compatriots who would accompany him, and putting as big a distance as they could behind them before their escape was discovered. They left shortly after Christmas Day 1588 and for twenty days fought their way across the savage mountains of Tyrone and Londonderry to reach one of the tiny villages at the extreme north-east of Ireland, from which it is only a matter of twenty-five miles to the Mull of Kintyre in Scotland.

Missing one boat by a day, and losing his companions, who could walk faster, Cuellar was befriended first by some 'exceedingly beautiful girls', who hid him in the huts of their families for a month and a half, and then by a bishop, who, living in disguise, was sheltering twelve other Spaniards. Through him at last a boat was found, probably something like a ship's longboat, and eighteen people embarked in it.

First they were blown to Shetland, their boat waterlogged and their sail torn, and then venturing again they reached Scotland after three more days. 'Blessed be God who delivered us from so many and such sore trials.'

Captain Cuellar was disappointed in the reception he received in the 'neutral' country. He lived in Scotland for six months, destitute and begging for food and shelter. 'The King of Scotland is of no account, nor has he the authority or dignity of a king, and he takes no step nor eats a single mouthful except by order of the Queen of England.' However, eventually contact was made with the Duke of Parma, who had offered to pay a Scottish merchant five ducats per head to ship Spanish refugees to Flanders. A large party of Spaniards sailed in four separate ships, which had apparently received a safe conduct from the English, for the ships called at English ports and left unmolested.

But whether by a deliberate act of perfidy on the part of the English, as Cuellar thought, or whether Parma could make no such bargain with his more hated enemies, the Dutch fly-boats were patrolling off Dunkirk and instantly attacked the four Scottish ships. Two ran aground, and Cuellar again found himself clinging to a spar in the pounding surf and being washed up on a beach while the Dutch guns cannonaded the fugitives and all who tried to rescue them.

Almost in front of our eyes the Dutch were cutting to pieces two hundred and seventy Spaniards arriving in the boat which had brought us to Dunkirk, and leaving no more than three alive. This deed they were now paying for, as more than four hundred Dutchmen taken prisoner since then have been beheaded. I desire to write to you concerning these things.

From the city of Antwerp, 4th October, 1589

10

Attack on Portugal

An English spy called Anthony Copley wrote an account of what happened when Philip was told of his total defeat.

> When news of the disgrace of the King's late Armada was brought unto him, being at Mass at that very time in his Chapel, he sware (after Mass was done) a great Oath, that he would waste and consume his Crown, even to the value of a [last] Candlestick (which he pointed to standing upon the Altar) but either he would utterly ruin her Majesty and England, or else himself and all Spain become Tributary to her. Whereby it was most evident that his Desire for Revenge was extreme and implacable towards England.

This account is at variance with other reports which describe Philip as accepting the disaster calmly and sadly and ascribing it all to the will of God. Yet Copley's version does seem to accord better with later events.

It must have been an excessive humiliation for Philip, more especially because for a month and more after the sailing of the Armada all Europe echoed with reports of its victories. The Queen was deposed. Drake was captured while trying to board Medina Sidonia's flagship. Mendoza, the Spanish Ambassador in Paris, had publicly announced this and lit bonfires to celebrate the victory. The Ambassador in Prague ordered a Te Deum Mass to be held at the cathedral in celebration. The Ambassador in Rome went to see the Pope and requested a similar Mass in St Peter's, together with the first part of the million gold ducats Sixtus had promised to pay Spain as soon as Spanish troops landed in England. The Pope, according to the Ambassador, 'heard me out without interruption, although he writhed about a good deal with inward impatience; but when I finished his anger leapt out, and he replied that he told me now, as he had told me before, that he would more than fulfil all he had promised, but I was not to worry him any more about the matter until positive news of the Armada was received.' But all the sad English exiles in Rome, led by Cardinal Allen and Father Parsons, accepted the tidings as true and prepared joyfully to return.

By now, however, the English had already held their own first thanksgiving service in St Paul's – this was in September, not the big November one – and twelve captured flags and banners had been paraded through the streets. There were circumstantial reports from Holland and from England about the prisoners held. And Medina Sidonia's emissary had reached the King. Then came the battered fleet, drifting in all along the west Spanish coast like ghost ships, full of sick and dying men.

For weeks the people of Spain could hardly accept the reality and the extent of the defeat. They had been accustomed for so long to war in the form of religious crusades which they had almost invariably won. It was a blow to national pride, to religious belief, to historical precedent and to reason.

The actual losses sustained by Spain in the first Armada are difficult to estimate. Something like fifty-five ships never returned, but of the eighty which did come home many were in such a condition that they were past repair. Of the thirty thousand men who sailed about ten thousand survived. Of the twenty thousand lost, possibly half were killed in battle or were drowned, the other half died from typhus, dysentery, scurvy or sheer privation.

It was a stunning loss, but Philip refused to be stunned. When the starving, dying men drifted in at every port, where there were no medical supplies to deal with them, the King assumed full responsibility for all relief work. He had no word of rebuke for Medina Sidonia, or for anyone except Diego Flores. When the Duke came to see him to explain the disaster, the King said: 'I sent you to fight against men, not against God.' He issued orders that there was to be no mourning 'for heroes who had died gloriously in the defence of religion'. Quietly he docketed the fact that the Duke of Parma had let him down, and resolved only to make use of him so long as he could find no substitute in the Netherlands. Quietly he absorbed the lessons of the defeat. Because of his sins and the sins of the nation, God had not been on their side. But Philip, as well as being deeply religious, was also essentially practical. God might have been more favourably disposed had there been a Spanish-controlled deep-sea port – such as Calais – available for his fleet. God would certainly have been better pleased with him if his ships had been built on the lines of the English.

There was only one way to remedy these defects – not by acquiescing in a position where the heretics ruled the seas, but by striving more vigorously than ever to redeem the situation and by coming to a bitter, dedicated resolve that next time would be different. By the end of the year timber as far afield as the Adriatic was being felled for the construction of new galleons in the shipyards of Lisbon, Cadiz, Santander and San Sebastian.

In this, as in many other matters, he expressed the sentiments of the Spanish nation. The cities voted immediate extra money for his military and naval use: Castile eight million ducats, Toledo one hundred thousand; even Milan a quarter of a million. Too often it is implied that Philip, the absolute monarch, made his own decisions as it were in a vacuum and the Spanish people suffered for them. His popularity in Spain – which survived even this defeat – shows that he acted more often than not as his people wanted. In this case they united behind him in a determination not to accept defeat.

The Spanish downfall was greeted with an enormous wave of relief in the Protestant countries of Europe. The collapse of the Huguenots in France, and Parma's victories in the Netherlands, followed by and following the assassination of William of Orange, had dismayed dissenters everywhere; Drake's West Indian and Spanish victories had been a single sharp flame of defiance in a dark world. But the defeat of the whole might of the Spanish fleet was an achievement which altered men's thinking overnight. Men saw that God was not necessarily on the side of the powerful and the mighty; indeed in a religious age it proved to many that God was a Protestant too. The victory put new heart into the hard-tried defenders of the Netherlands, into the war-torn French Protestants, into the Danes and the Germans and the Swiss; and it raised Elizabeth's prestige to dizzy heights. It was the apogee of her reign – a triumph blighted for her only by the sudden death of Leicester, the one man in her life who was quite irreplaceable. Bereaved and sad at heart, she gathered the plaudits of the world and of her people; but at their best they were comforting embers at which to warm her hands and keep away the sudden chill of age. Essex was young and dashing and handsome and temporarily made one forget the passing of the years; but he was headstrong, conceited and frequently — almost invariably — took too much on himself. Ralegh was by turns brilliant and sombre; but as Aubrey says, 'he had that awfulness and ascendancy in his Aspect over other mortals', which perhaps was what prevented the growth of true warmth between himself and the Queen. Others about her grew old and grey in her service; trusted men, dedicated men; but she had loved none of them.

Even some of the Catholic countries took Spain's defeat philosophically. Elizabeth's religion was deeply offensive to Pope Sixtus, but he admired her courage and intellect. Philip II was his brother in religion, but a personal antipathy existed between the two men that a common cause could not bridge. The failure saved the Papacy a million ducats, shook Spanish hegemony in Europe and a general wish on Spain's part to dictate Catholic thought and policy from Madrid.

In Italy generally, and especially in the Venetian republic, which had always been too civilized to become deeply involved in religious wars, it looked like a welcome shift in the balance of power; and possibly, it was reasoned, this in the end would lead to a return to the older and more subtle political power diplomacy which all Italians understood.

In France a profound change took place. Henry III had recently made Henry of Guise his Lieutenant-General and had been forced to declare all Protestants incapable of trust, office or employment; but as news of the defeat of the Spanish fleet came in he began to reassert himself. This was of course a struggle between two Catholics, but Guise was subsidized by Spain, while Henry III, though a weakling, strove for national independence and a united France. In October he dismissed all his ministers and threw off finally the influence of his too oppressive mother, who had come to favour Henry of Guise more than she did her own son. In December, still struggling to free himself from the dominance of a man so much stronger than himself, the King arranged for and superintended the assassination in his own bed-chamber of his great rival. Then in January 1589 Catherine de' Medici died, leaving the King apparent master of France. But the murder of Guise, who was widely popular throughout France, left Henry III even less master of the realm than he had been before. As James Stephen has said: 'Heaven and earth rose against the murder of Blois.' Just as sixteen years before the massacre of the Huguenots virtually left his brother a prisoner of the Spanish-dominated

Catholic League, so Henry found himself now forced into the hands of the Huguenots, who alone could help him to preserve a part of his violently erupting kingdom. It paved the way for friendship with Elizabeth and for the succession of the Protestant Henry of Navarre.

There are various reports about Philip's health at this time. Some say that the last blond streaks disappeared from his beard and hair, that this beard grew untidy, that he was ill from the shock of all the bad news. Yet he does not seem to have suffered from anything worse than a return attack of gout in his right hand. His fourth wife had been dead eight years, and all the children of their marriage had died except young Philip, the heir to the throne. Catherine, the younger of Philip's two daughters of whom he was so fond, was married and gone, so he was much alone except for his confessor and his secretaries. When he went to Aranjuez early in 1589 one of his doctors asked him why he insisted on going there. 'For companionship,' was the reply. It was the companionship of memories. He drove around the ponds in a small carriage, did a little shooting, sniffed the orange blossom and the spring flowers. Back in Madrid he spent a while adding to his vast collection of paintings, visited the Academy of Architecture which he had founded six years earlier, attended a concert given by the choir of picked singers he had recruited from the Netherlands, inspected the illuminated manuscripts created for him by the monks for the new church of San Felipe el Real in the Puerta del Sol. At the Escorial for Easter, he washed and kissed the feet of twelve beggars on Maundy Thursday, and afterwards waited on them at table.

After Easter he returned more fully to considering preparations necessary to meet the expected English invasion of Portugal that summer. Mendoza in Paris had written as early as the previous November to warn him that it was coming.

Don Antonio of Crato, the claimant to the Portuguese throne, now a man of fifty-seven, had been in England for some time, having been compelled to leave France because of Philip II's attempts to have him assassinated. He had become friendly with Drake and had stayed at Drake's home in Devon. For years Don Antonio had been urging that the English should land him in Portugal with a supporting army, and claiming that the Portuguese were only waiting for his arrival to rise and overthrow their Spanish conquerors. As long ago as 1581 he and Drake had made plans to seize the Azores; later he had attempted it with the assistance of a French fleet under Admiral Strozzi and had been comprehensively defeated; but all through the years he had kept his claim alive.

Now with the Spanish fleet out of action the time seemed ripe for a really serious attempt to install him. With the jewellery and gold he had brought with him when he left Portugal he had been able to maintain spies working for him in the Iberian Peninsula and elsewhere for nearly a decade, and they reported now on the great discontent in Lisbon and Oporto. (Two of these spies incidentally, de Escobar and de Endrada, worked both for him and for Philip II, but were so skilled that though they often met they never suspected each other, nor did either employer suspect that their men were receiving money from the other side. Contrary to what is generally believed, the age of the double-spy did not begin in the present century.)

Don Antonio's offer to Elizabeth was that two months after his attaining the throne he would defray the full cost of the expedition and would pay England a further three hundred thousand ducats annually, and that he would give England full trade privileges in Portugal and her possessions. It was enough to tempt anyone as near bankruptcy as Elizabeth.

But the possibility of recreating an independent and friendly Portugal was not the only issue at stake. At this moment the Spanish fleet was knocked out and the Spanish coast defenceless. In various Atlantic and Biscayan ports, in varying degrees of mutilation and unseaworthiness, were the remains of that fleet: galleons, great ships, carracks, armed merchantmen, galleasses, pataches, zabras. In spite of the havoc wrought off Gravelines and the disastrous wrecks off the Irish coast, a surprisingly large number of the great fleet had somehow drifted home: seven out of the ten galleons of Portugal, six of Recalde's Biscayan great ships, half of Pedro de Valdes's Andalusians, more than half of Diego Flores's Castilians, seven of Oquendo's, two of Bertendona's Levantines. These were the capital ships; no one could be sure how many of them could be repaired, or how quickly. But at the moment they were virtually defenceless in ill-defended seaports. Drake had demonstrated only eighteen months ago what he could do in

Cadiz. A bigger raid now – indeed something of a small armada in reverse – could wipe out these ships and so make absolutely complete the victory of last year. Drake put this to the Queen – in company with Sir John Norris, England's most accomplished and experienced soldier. It was all, for once, very much to Elizabeth's way of thinking, and she agreed in principle to the proposal within three weeks of its being put to her.

There was another idea too in the minds of the planners. It was to seize the Azores and establish a regular blockade of the treasure flota sailing to Spain from the Indies. Hawkins had put forward this proposal in December 1587 after Drake's successful raid on Cadiz; it had been impracticable then because of the existence of the Spanish fleet. Now, especially if it were preceded by the destruction of the remnants of that fleet, it was a very feasible proposition and, combined with his loss of control in the Netherlands, would be likely to force Philip to sue for peace. So it was agreed that the enterprise should be put in hand : another *empresa* but with much smaller resources and having three objectives instead of one.

It was floated as a joint stock company, with a capital of about £80,000. One quarter was to come from the Queen, one half from private adventurers, including merchants and nobility, one eighth in kind from the City of London and one eighth in kind from the Dutch. The Queen has come in for bitter condemnation from historians for allowing this to become a commercial enterprise, in which the aims became blurred; but in fact she had little choice.

As we have seen earlier in explaining if not excusing her neglect of her victorious sailors, she was on the verge of insolvency. By Christmas 1588 she had about £55,000 left. One half of what she could expect to receive in the following year from ordinary revenues she was pledged to pay towards helping her Dutch allies, under the treaty of 1585. Money was needed urgently in Ireland. James still expected his subsidy in Scotland. And if Henry of Navarre was to help Henry III to survive in France, he too was likely to need more financial help before the year was far gone. None of these calls on her purse was concerned with the ordinary expenses of English civil or military life. In 1588 Burghley had tried to borrow £50,000 abroad at 10 per cent interest. In early 1589 she tried and failed to raise £100,000 in Germany. By November of that year she was reduced to the straits of selling crown lands.

The Queen promised £20,000 towards the cost of the expedition to Portugal; it was the most she could do; and as a pledge of her intentions she advanced most of the money before the rest had been subscribed. London merchants, who had slid off into the country in 1588 in order to avoid paying the forced loans imposed then, now vied with each other in putting money into what so clearly was to be a profit-making venture. With the national hero, Drake, in command and 'Black' Norris at his side, one could hardly go wrong.

The assent and co-operation of the Dutch took longer to obtain. Parma, swinging his troops away from the invasion ports, had laid siege to Bergen-op-Zoom. Thanks largely to English help, the attempt to capture the town failed, but with Parma only hibernating for the winter months and clearly anxious to restore his lost credit in the eyes of Philip, it was not the most propitious time to ask the Dutch to release three thousand troops and six siege-guns with the necessary transports and ten hulks for carrying horses. They were seven weeks making up their minds, but eventually they agreed to send fifteen hundred of their own troops with ten warships, and they also agreed to the withdrawal of three thousand of the English troops to join the enterprise, provided that all their own men should be back by June.

Speed was of the essence, for winter had brought almost all the fighting in Europe to a standstill, and this was the moment when troops and money could best be spared. Unhappily a quarrel broke out with the Dutch, in which the English appear to have been to blame, about the number and manner of the withdrawal of the English troops. This was further aggravated by Lord Willoughby's jealousy of Norris and Drake and by a general reluctance of the English commanders to release trained veteran troops from their armies and have them replaced by raw country levies, so that other men should have the glory of leading them on a wildcat invasion of Portugal. One thinks of the Dardanelles.

So the expedition, instead of sailing for Portugal on the 1st February, did not reach Plymouth until the 19th March and was then held back by persistent south-westerly winds for another month. When it sailed it was in a much depleted condition compared to the original plan. Not one of the Dutch warships had arrived and only a few of their transports. The cavalry did not exist and the seasoned troops only numbered eighteen hundred. On the other hand the expedition was swollen by inexperienced volunteers who, flocking into Plymouth to follow Drake anywhere, increased the total number of soldiers from a planned ten thousand to around nineteen thousand. At the same time the long delay in Portsmouth consumed something like one-third of the total victuals laid on for the voyage.

At the last the Queen, who previously had been unwavering in her support of the expedition, began to have doubts about its success, for by now the winter was past and all the forecasts of the pessimists were coming true. Geertruidenberg, one of the key positions in the Netherlands, had fallen; Henry III's ineptitude in France put the Channel ports in peril, and he had sent a desperate appeal for a loan of £27,000 to hire an army of German mercenaries; while James of Scotland was asking for an extra subsidy to keep down his Catholic nobles. Elizabeth's attitude was also exasperated by the escape of young Essex who, having distinguished himself in the fighting in Holland, now disobeyed her express instructions to stay at court and rode down to Plymouth in time to sail in the company of the famous Welsh soldier, Sir Roger Williams. She dispatched message after message recalling him, and pinnaces to search the Channel. Eventually one of her darkest messages was sent winging in pursuit of Drake. 'Sir Roger Williams's offence,' she wrote, 'is in so high a degree that the same deserveth to be punished by death . . . If Essex be now come into the company of the fleet, we straightly charge you that you do forthwith cause him to be sent hither in safe manner. Which if you do not, you shall look to answer for the same at your own smart; for these be no childish actions . . . As we have authority to rule so we look to be obeyed.' (Happily for Essex's ambitions, this stern order did not reach the fleet until most of the land fighting was done.)

The English Armada which sailed with such high hopes and with so many diverse ambitions was, though much watered down from the original outline, still a considerable force. Its chief lack was siege-guns and cavalry, both of which had been included in the preliminary plan. For the first time, like the Spanish Armada, soldiers greatly outnumbered sailors, the numbers who finally embarked being approximately seventeen thousand of the former and four thousand of the latter, besides about fifteen hundred officers and gentlemen adventurers. Six royal galleons, sixty English armed merchantmen of displacements varying from four hundred tons to eighty tons, sixty tough little Dutch flyboats of around one hundred and fifty

149

to two hundred tons and a score or more of pinnaces. Nevertheless, even as a naval force, it was far from being an all-out effort, as Spain's had been. Most of the latest and finest of the royal ships were laid up at Chatham; Frobisher with three royal ships and three pinnaces was patrolling the Straits to prevent war material reaching Spain from the north; Sir George Beeston had a similar squadron in the North Sea protecting English sea trade with Germany; and the Earl of Cumberland was fitting out the *Victory* and six other ships at his own expense for raiding the Spanish sea routes.

Having learned the value of formation fighting from the Spanish, Drake had divided his fleet into five squadrons, each led by a Queen's ship: himself, again in the *Revenge*, in the first, Sir John Norris in *Nonpareil* in the second, Vice-Admiral Thomas Fenner in *Dreadnought* in the third, Sir Roger Williams (with the rebellious Essex) in *Swiftsure* in the fourth, and Sir Edward Norris in *Foresight* in the fifth. The first two were of five hundred tons each, the second two of four hundred tons, the fifth of three hundred.

Both Drake and Norris, much taken with Don Antonio and the thought of liberating Portugal, would have liked to attack Lisbon at once; but the 'Instructions' with which they were issued made the destruction of the Spanish fleet the first objective. This was a vital order of priorities; but unfortunately, although a few of the smaller Armada ships were sheltering in the west-facing Spanish and Portuguese ports, the majority, indeed more than fifty of the biggest ships, were in harbour in the northern ports: forty of them in Santander and twelve in San Sebastian. To attack these ships meant taking the whole fleet far to the leeward of the prevailing winds and alerting all Spain to the presence of the raiding force; and, once in this corner of Biscay, the fleet might find itself embayed.

Here was a strong conflict of interest: the national interest which dictated that the damaged galleons must be destroyed before anything else at all was attempted; and an interest which could be of great national advantage but which also promised much private profit for the investors. Two separate fleets could have attended to two such different objectives, but the existing fleet was not strong enough to divide.

Instead, as so often happens, a fatal compromise was attempted. Hearing that a large concentration of shipping was 'in the Groyne', they attacked Coruña instead. Here they found only one of the Armada galleons, the *San Juan* of one thousand and fifty tons, two greatships, two galleys and a hulk. Drake landed Norris to take the town, and after much confused fighting in the dark and the rain, which in those days rendered muskets useless, the lower town was taken with a minimum of loss. Young Admiral Martin de Bertendona, not long recovered from commanding the worst hit of all the Armada squadrons, had to set fire to the *San Juan* to save her from being captured. (Little wonder that two years later he enjoyed attacking the *Revenge*.) About five hundred Spaniards were caught and killed and Don Juan de Luna, the military commandant of the town, was taken prisoner. But part of the garrison contrived to retire into the higher town, from which they were able during the next few days to harass the English with gunfire.

The shipping burned, the scanty provisions of the fleet replenished, the remaining victuals in the town destroyed, there was nothing to keep the English fleet. But in the darkness and confusion of the first victory great wine barrels had been discovered, and most of the soldiers who had landed drank themselves into insensibility after sacking the town. Many of them were immediately ill, and dysentery was widespread. In the meantime an attempt was made to mine the fortress of the upper town, but this failed. Then an Italian came in with news that an army of eight thousand Spaniards was approaching to relieve the town.

Immediately Sir John Norris and his brother Sir Edward led nine regiments of pikemen and musketeers to intercept them. In the battle which followed, both Norrises behaved with that kind of mad, inspired gallantry which characterized the most successful generals of the sixteenth century, each in turn leading the way across a narrow two-hundred-yard-long bridge spanning a river, under a hail of musket-fire and into a barricade at the other end. Sir John did not even bother to put on his armour and escaped without a scratch; Sir Edward received a sword slash on his head. The Spanish were put to flight with about a thousand dead, and the country around was laid waste by the victorious infantry. The battle of El Burgo Bridge occurred not very far from where Sir John Moore, fighting for the Spanish, was to die two hundred and twenty years later.

By now the expeditionary force had been in Coruña two weeks and, apart from some not very valuable booty, they had little to show for the exploit. Their duty now lay, as it had always lain, two hundred and fifty miles west, where the bulk of the shattered Armada awaited them. But Sir John Norris now said he was doubtful of the ability to 'distress a fleet' while it was guarded by the guns of a town, and doubtful of his ability to take the town without the siege guns that he had been promised but notably lacked. Also the captains and shipmasters of the Queen's ships reiterated their opinion that with the prevailing westerly winds it was dangerous to take the fleet so far into the Bay.

There is no reason to doubt the sincerity of the second opinion, but the first, coming from, of all people, such men as Norris and Drake, sounds a trifle disingenuous. (Drake, with his notorious entry into Cadiz and a dozen other miraculous exploits; Norris with all his iron experience of campaigning in the Netherlands.) The truth is surely that they saw little prospect of profit in it for the investors. Also their clash with Spanish forces at El Burgo Bridge had convinced them that they could land where they chose in Spain and none to stop them. 'An army of 10,000 good soldiers may pass through the whole realm without great danger,' wrote the Queen's agent, Anthony Ashley, to the Council on the 7th May.

So, with full apologies and explanations sent hastening homewards, they deliberately disobeyed the Queen's instructions and sailed, as they had always wanted to, for Lisbon.

The Queen when she received the dispatches had no doubt in her mind as to what had happened. 'They go to places more for profit than for service,' she commented bleakly. The leaders of the fleet beating southwards towards Lisbon can hardly have been unaware that only a resounding success in Portugal could now make their homecoming a happy one.

Spanish spies, with unerring skill, had reported that when the English fleet arrived off Lisbon it was likely to land a force near Peniche, fifty miles north of the city; and this was what happened. Led by Sir Roger Williams, with Essex recklessly courageous beside him, several regiments succeeded in getting ashore through the surf, and after a brisk bloody encounter the defending forces retreated and the open town surrendered. The same night the castle overlooking the town surrendered to Don Antonio.

It was a propitious start. The rest of the fourteen regiments were landed safely, and the following day the two forces split: the army proposed to march to Lisbon overland while the whole countryside, one hoped, flocked to Don Antonio's standard; the fleet was to sail to Lisbon and intimidate the capital city from the sea.

That Lisbon was intimidated when it became known that *El Draque* was in the Tagus there can be no doubt. The little fortified town of Cascaes, sixteen miles from Lisbon at the mouth of the Tagus, surrendered precipitately, and there was a panic flight of the population from Lisbon despite all efforts of the Spanish governor, the young Cardinal Archduke Albert, to halt it.

But for once in his life Drake did not commit his ships to an all-out attack on the city. Perhaps the consciousness of having so flagrantly disobeyed the Queen hung heavy on him; perhaps he had been overborne by his military advisers to allow them first to attack from the land; certainly he overestimated the extent to which the Spanish, obviously warned of his coming, had been able to add to their garrison and fortify the town. There were in fact rather less than seven thousand troops in all available for the defence, and many of these were Portuguese with no stomach to fight on behalf of their conquerors. All that the Archduke Albert could do was initiate a reign of terror in the city, in which anyone suspected of having sympathy for the claims of Don Antonio was at once executed.

In 1580 when the Spanish took Portugal, Santa Cruz had landed the Duke of Alva with his seasoned Spanish veterans at Cascaes, and, while the troops marched on Lisbon, Santa Cruz had sailed his fleet up the Tagus, the two forces never losing contact with each other. Had this plan been followed now it would surely have succeeded again. Instead Drake waited for the Portuguese to rise and for news of Norris who, lacking cavalry or even enough horse for the transport of baggage, marched his troops in great heat across the peninsula. Many of the men were already sick from seaboard infections or from their excesses at Coruña.

Don Antonio, as well as being illegitimate, was half Jewish, and this did not endear him to some of the great Portuguese families; but he had always claimed that the general population would rise at his name. In Lisbon the Portuguese, intimidated by the Archduke's ruthlessness, could hardly have done more than wait and see. But in the countryside the response to the arrival of their 'rightful king' was dismally negative. Only about two hundred joined the English army, and those, according to Sir Roger Williams, were 'the greatest cowards that I ever saw'. Considering what they put at stake by joining at all, it seems an unfair description.

There was at first no fighting, for the Spanish withdrew before the advancing army, who by the 25th May were in the suburbs of Lisbon. Here, after firing the storehouses to prevent their falling into English hands, the Spanish launched a powerful counter-attack; but it was repulsed with heavy casualties and they then retreated within the walls of the city.

For three days Norris lay encamped outside the city, expecting Drake. Of his force of about nine thousand men more than three thousand were now too ill to be anything but a liability. He was running short of ammunition and he had no siege-guns. In this situation he could only wait for the Portuguese to rise, while in their situation the Portuguese could only wait for him to take the city. Had Drake come up the Tagus it might have turned the scales, but he, like Norris, was expecting the Portuguese revolt that did not come. One cannot imagine him being intimidated by the forty cannon of Fort St Julian which guarded the narrow entrance, though he claims this was a deterrent. Probably he was already turning his eyes on the third objective of the expedition, the treasure ships likely to be coming in from the Azores.

On the 28th Norris gave Don Antonio one more day in which to rally his supporters. When they did not come he struck camp and marched with his whole army to Cascaes. Because they had the Portuguese Prince with them, looting in the suburbs of Lisbon had been rigorously forbidden, otherwise, wrote Captain Richard Wingfield regretfully, 'we had been the richest army that ever went out of England'. Before they left Lisbon Essex, tall and splendid in his armour, walked up alone to one of the gates of the city and thrust his sword into the wood, crying in a carrying voice if any 'Spaniard mewed therein durst adventure forth in favour of my mistress to break a lance'. No Spaniard adventured forth.

When the army reached Cascaes, siege was already being laid to the castle there by Drake's men, and the arrival of the army settled the issue. But now there were repeated councils-of-war and mutual recriminations. Norris was not an easy man to get along with at the best of times, and here, justifiably, he had cause for complaint.

While they were in angry conference the only piece of luck of the expedition befell them. A fleet of Hanseatic ships sailed into the Tagus unsuspecting and, apart from a few escorting ships which made their escape, all were captured. The Hanseatic League, which was composed of the Baltic and north German cities, did not approve of the English blockade of their trade with Spain, and this fleet, carrying grain and valuable war commodities, had dodged both Sir Martin Frobisher's and Sir George Beeston's patrolling squadrons by sailing all round the north of Scotland, like the retreating Armada of the year before. Some of the ships were newly built and intended for Spanish use, and all were seized. It added sixty sail to the English fleet and new hope to their flagging spirits. At this stage the squadron of Dutch flyboats was given permission to return home.

Now supplies arrived from England – with that sulphurous letter from the Queen which hastened the departure of my Lord of Essex – and with news that Drake's vice-admiral and Ralegh's friend, Captain Robert Crosse, was off Cadiz with another squadron of supply ships. So the troops were re-embarked and the fleet abandoned Lisbon and sailed south. One spares a moment of sympathy for the broken hopes of Don Antonio, who had seen so much begun and then it all fail from the use of half measures.

After the juncture with Crosse they proceeded to try to accomplish the third object of their mission, or at least, in Drake's words, 'to find some comfortable little dew of Heaven', which would increase the profit of the venture. But now Heaven, or at any rate the weather, turned foul on them and they were beaten back to the Bayona Islands near Vigo. Here they again landed, one party led by Sir Roger Williams, the other by Drake in person, and captured and burned Vigo and laid waste the settlements and villages around. Here Rear-Admiral William Fenner, commanding the sixth Queen's ship, the *Aid*, died of wounds. By now there were scarcely two thousand fit men who could be mustered, and a number of the ships had been badly used by the storm, so it was clearly futile to attempt anything against the Azores in this condition. Drake therefore took the pick of the men and ships that were left – twenty ships in all – while Norris turned for home with the sick and the wounded.

But Drake's uncanny ability to conjure victory out of defeat, his knack of being in the right place to seize at least one rich prize, this time failed him. His luck would not turn for him, perhaps because for once he had hesitated to trust to it. A violent storm struck his ships and scattered them before

155

they could reach the Azores, and the *Revenge* sprang a dangerous leak that could not be repaired at sea. Robert Crosse and Thomas Fenner with a few other ships did in fact reach Madeira and landed at Puerto Santa and captured and plundered the port. But they missed the treasure fleet.

And Drake led the remnants of his own fleet home. The *Revenge*, nearly foundering, reached Plymouth just in time. The only prizes of substantial value gained out of the expedition were the sixty Hanseatic vessels and their contents seized in the Tagus, which later were sold for £30,000. Apart from this, like Norris, he only had excuses with which to attempt to placate Elizabeth.

11

The Loss of the Revenge

A comparison of the expedition of 1589 with the Spanish Armada of the previous year is hardly valid. The Lisbon expedition was never an all-out effort, and if every ship had sunk it would not have crippled the Queen's navy. In fact no ship was sunk. Yet, while no really reliable estimates exist as to the number of men who came home, it seems probable that about half of those who sailed were lost – a couple of thousand perhaps by enemy action, the rest victims of that other and more deadly and more thoroughly impartial enemy: General Disease. Ralegh, whose estimate is likely to be better than most, reckoned the total loss at eight thousand men.

By less demanding standards than those expected of it, the expedition could have been considered a modest success. It had landed in both Spain and Portugal and had marched with impunity about the countryside. It had diverted regiments intended for the Netherlands and caused the Spanish to recruit new ones. It had destroyed the granaries round Lisbon and had captured a whole fleet of grain and supply ships arriving to help the Spanish food and naval shortage. It had delayed the treasure ships, and a revolt in the Netherlands army in the following August for back pay can be traced to their late arrival. As Norris said: 'If the enemy had done so much upon us, his party would have made bonfires in most parts of Christendom.'

The narrowness of the margin by which they missed taking Lisbon is emphasized by historians who, unlike the commanders of the time, have the advantage of hindsight. But neither Norris nor Drake could have known by how much their attack on Lisbon, although long heralded, was a complete surprise when it occurred, by what a thin and disaffected garrison the city was held, and by what terrorist measures the Archduke Albert just prevented an uprising.

What reflects worst on the expedition is that they had no naval opposition to overcome. The Armada had to face a fleet as numerous if not as heavy as itself, much more mobile and fighting in home waters. One wonders what Medina Sidonia would have achieved if there had been no English fleet. Drake and Norris in 1589 sailed where they would and landed where they pleased, and made little enough of it.

Elizabeth, of course, with her usual grasp of essentials, knew exactly what had gone wrong, and she never forgave Drake. Pushed inch by reluctant inch and year by year into an out-right war with Spain which Philip at last had made unavoidable, she was well aware of the temporary advantage she held after the defeat of the Armada, and, having come to war, she was willing to wage war. Even as early as August 1588, while reports of the full extent of the Spanish disaster were by no means complete, she had personally initiated discussions on how best to capitalize on the victory. Never as enamoured as Drake and others of Don Antonio's chances of raising a full-scale revolt in Portugal, she had kept always before her the primary purpose for which an expedition must be launched: the destruction of what was left of the Spanish fleet.

These had been her instructions. If they had been followed, the loss of men could hardly have been greater than in the half-measure landings which were undertaken, and forty or fifty of Spain's remaining galleons lying in varying stages of repair and disrepair would have been destroyed – all those ships which had so narrowly got home from the disaster, all those ships which otherwise could be repaired to form the nucleus of a new fleet, all those ships which as soon as repaired would be at sea again to guard the treasure fleets. 'If,' wrote a correspondent from nearby St Jean de Luz, 'Sir Francis had gone to Santander as he went to the Groyne he had done such a service as never subject had done before, for with 12 ships he might have destroyed all the forces which the Spaniards had there, which was the whole strength of the country by sea. There they did ride all unrigged and their ordnance on the shore and some 20 men to a ship only to keep them.'

So Elizabeth's explicit instructions had been disobeyed, and perhaps more clearly than anyone at that time, unless it was Burghley, she saw that the one chance of ending the war quickly was lost. Of course she was only the principal share-holder in a joint stock company which was not this time

158

declaring a dividend. She made no public complaint about the outcome of the expedition; formally if icily she thanked her captains and men, as befitted a sovereign served loyally but inefficiently. Privately Drake and Norris were called upon to answer articles charging them with disobeying their instructions and other matters.

In the meantime England's correspondent in St Jean de Luz reported that in addition to the fifty-odd ships of the old Armada being repaired in the northern ports, nine new galleons were being built in Portugal, and twelve others designed on the English model – later to be known as the Twelve Apostles – had been laid down in various Biscayan ports. The hour of danger for Spain was passing.

A month after the return of Drake and Norris the face of Europe was convulsed by another event. A monk called Jacques Clément, encouraged by the Duchess of Montpensier, sister of the recently murdered Duc de Guise, gained an audience of Henry III and, while the king was reading his petition, drew a dagger and stabbed him in the belly. So, less than eight months after the assassination of Guise, and only seven after the death of the woman who had schemed and contrived all her life for the preservation and perpetuation of her line, the last of her sons passed from the scene. He was also the last of the house of Valois which had given thirteen kings to France in the space of two and a half centuries.

It is improbable that Elizabeth, whose great-great-grandmother was a Valois, shed any tears at the passing of the house.

The King did not die immediately, and to the many people crowding into his chamber in his last hours he left no doubt as to his will – that his cousin and brother-in-law and most recent ally, Henry of Navarre, should succeed to the throne of France. Thus the paradox emerged that the fanatic Clément had murdered a Catholic in order that he should be succeeded by a Huguenot.

But it was a murder as much of revenge as of religion. All the Guises went frantic with joy, and Catholic Paris set up tables in the streets and held midday banquets and midnight bonfires. Clément, who had been immediately killed by the King's attendants, was 'honoured in the pulpits, sung in the streets, invoked as a saint'. Pope Sixtus proclaimed him a new martyr.

The position of the new King, Henry of Navarre, was precarious in the extreme. Not only was the whole of the Spanish-dominated Catholic League against him, but half the supporters of the previous king were riven with religious scruples as to whether they could continue to serve a Protestant. Some continued to do so because they preferred a French King on the throne to a Spanish Infanta; and the Venetian Republic infuriated its co-religionists by immediately – and for the same reason – recognizing Henry. The Pope by his own famous Bull of Deprivation of September 1585 had declared Henry of Navarre forfeit of all his rights to the throne of France, so now, though as anxious as anyone that France should retain her independence, he could do no more than privately urge Henry to change his religion. Under much pressure from his French friends too, Henry could only reply that he had been born a Catholic, reared as a Calvinist by his mother, become converted to Catholicism to save his life at the St Bartholomew massacre and reverted to Protestantism as soon as he was free again. 'You require a change in me which would argue no sincerity either in one faith or the other.'

He appealed to Elizabeth for help, and Elizabeth, fearing once again for the safety of the Channel ports, was compelled to give it him. She was now drawn more and more into a military struggle in Europe, to the consequent neglect of her navy. As the years progressed, she found herself with troops dotted along the Channel coast or in adjacent regions supporting the Dutch and the French everywhere against the common enemy.

In March 1590 with a mixed army of French, English, German and Swiss, some of them quite unable to understand each other's languages, Henry of Navarre, now Henry IV, comprehensively defeated the Catholic Leagues under the Duc de Mayenne. This was at Ivry, now known as Ivry-la-Bataille, between Mantes and Dreux. It followed up his other two successes at Coutras and Arques, and had been confidently forecast by the incorrigible Pope Sixtus, who remarked that Henry of Navarre spent less time in bed than his opponents did at their food. The succession of victories marked Henry as a soldier of eminence, and there was a noticeable shift in general public opinion towards him. He had also that other gift of leadership, an ability for uttering the memorable sentence at the most suitable moment. It endeared him to his new subjects as much as Elizabeth's did to the English.

7. SIR FRANCIS DRAKE
(Detail from an oil painting by
Marcus Gheeraerts the Younger, 1594)

ÆTATIS SVÆ LVII
Año Dñi 1591

8. SIR JOHN HAWKINS
(16th century oil painting by Hieronymo Custodis)

AN° · DNĪ · 1571 ·
ÆTATIS · SVÆ
· 29 ·

ichard Granville, killed
ea-fight near the Azores.

9. SIR RICHARD GRENVILLE
(Oil painting by an unknown artist, 1571)

10. ROBERT DEVEREUX, 2nd Earl of Essex
(Oil painting by William Segar, 1590)

11. SIR WALTER RALEGH WITH HIS SON
(Oil painting by an unknown artist, 1602)

In May 1590 Henry laid siege to Paris, which remained re-
calcitrantly opposed to a Protestant King. It was a strange
siege, for Henry had thirteen thousand soldiers in all and the
city a quarter of a million inhabitants. But the young governor,
the Duke of Nemours, was overawed by the successes Henry
had achieved in the field and he did not trust the fifty thous-
and amateurs that he could command, so the city suffered
all the horrors of a three-month siege.

What was Philip to do? The unification of France under a
strong Huguenot king, the conquest of the pro-Spanish
Catholics, the complete collapse of his influence in the country
and the virtual isolation of his forces in the Netherlands:
could these be tolerated? Better to seize all France. And more
tempting. He still had far the most powerful army in Europe.
He wrote to Parma, instructing him to march to the relief of
Paris. Parma vehemently protested. Slowly, inexorably, he
was advancing again to squeeze the United Provinces into
surrender. To take off the pressure now might undo all the
dearly won victories of the last two years. The Armada had
failed but not Spanish military power. With the forces that
he now possessed, the Dutch, even with Elizabeth's aid, must
soon find their backs to the sea.

Philip's reply was peremptory: 'If Flanders is lost,' he wrote,
'it is mine to lose.' Parma must relieve Paris.

Parma was slow in moving, but this time he could not be
blamed for the delay. The English raid on Lisbon and the
Azores which had delayed the silver fleet from the Indies had
deprived Parma of the money to pay his long-deprived troops,
and there was a mutiny. He put it down as only he could,
but had to pledge his own jewellery as surety for his promises.

In Paris by August, with people dying in their tens of
thousands, there was great pressure within the city to surrender. This was chiefly resisted by the Archbishop of Lyons
and by Mendoza, the Spanish Ambassador. 'I am here serving
you as best I can,' old Mendoza wrote racily to Philip, 'but
wherever I am there is sure to be a storm, and I am running
under close-reefed topsails fore and aft.' When emissaries of
surrender were just about to leave the capital, news came that
Parma had joined the Duc de Mayenne at Meaux, only twenty-
five miles east of Paris. Henry raised the siege and faced the
relieving army, but Parma out-manœuvred and out-flanked
him, and the inconclusive clashes which occurred could not
hide the fact that Parma with an apparently inadequate army

of veterans was still master of the field wherever he chose to fight. Henry was driven from Paris, the city relieved and the pro-Spanish faction encouraged.

By the autumn a Spanish army three thousand strong, under Don Juan de Aguila, had landed on the coast of Brittany, to support the League there and to secure a base at the western end of the Channel. This gravely alarmed England, and the council sent Norris off with three thousand troops, half of them veterans, to oppose the landing. Henry contributed a small local force but nothing else, since Parma's presence was a menace to his whole kingdom. The situation in France at this stage posed as many dangers for England as those of the Armada year, because only Henry and his supporters stood between them and a Spanish occupation of the Channel coastline. Had France fallen then, it is unlikely that the Netherlands could have held out.

In November, however, Parma, conscious of a rapid deterioration of the situation in the Netherlands under his deputy, the Count of Mansfield, disengaged himself in France and, although harassed all the way by French cavalry under Henry, retreated in perfect order and without loss; another notable feat of arms, though it was not appreciated by Philip who wished him to stay and by his continuing presence assist the Spanish Infanta's claim, in defiance of Salic law, to the French throne. (She was of course the daughter of Henry III's sister.)

Information reaching Spain that Sixtus was willing to recognize Henry IV if only, or as soon as, he turned Catholic, led to a dramatic scene in the Vatican, where the new Spanish Ambassador, the Duke of Sesa, delivered a curt message from Philip declaring it intolerable that the Papacy should even be considering a reconciliation with a man who in Spain would have been 'burned a thousand times already' for his relapses; and stating that if Sixtus persisted in this conduct Philip would demand a National Council (at which Sixtus might be deposed). The Pope thereupon uttered words which were not far from anathema upon Philip and all Spaniards and strode from the room, leaving his Cardinals trembling. Sesa, white with anger himself, then turned to the Cardinals and told them that if they trifled with his master he 'would drop a brick on them', and he too stamped out.

Whether or not consumed by his own choler, the sagacious, eccentric Sixtus V died shortly after this, whereby Philip lost an enemy and the world an utterer of outrageous but brilliant *bons mots.* Philip declared himself '*muy contento*' with the Pope's death.

Thereafter followed a succession so rapid that the Papal chair might have been electric: Sixtus in August 1590, Urban VII in October 1590, Gregory XIV in 1591, Innocent IX in 1592, and Clement VIII thereafter. But none of them, willing or unwilling, could or would help Philip to marry his much loved daughter to the new Duc de Guise and put her on the French throne.

Henry IV, deprived of Paris, was encouraged by Elizabeth and Burghley to lay siege to Rouen. Almost all the great towns of northern France were staunchly Catholic, and without their revenues he was poverty stricken. In one year alone Elizabeth had to advance him £60,000 apart from material help, which consisted of an army in the field. For this latest continental adventure Elizabeth, after Essex had spent two hours on his knees before her on three separate occasions, was persuaded to let him lead the English army, which was to consist of four thousand foot soldiers and appropriate cavalry. Cautiously and hoping for the best, she appointed his old friend and mentor, Sir Roger Williams, to be his chief of staff. Williams, hard-bitten, scarred and worldly-wise, is thought to be the original of Shakespeare's Fluellen.

Essex was twenty-four, and, while conducting his part of the campaign on the best soldierly lines, yet contrived to give it all a flavour of twelfth-century chivalry. As soon as he landed he led a dangerous cavalry dash through enemy-held territory to link up with his hero, the French King; and the foot soldiers under Sir Roger Williams followed him, a notable march made without loss. A French writer describes Essex's arrival in Compiègne: 'Nothing more magnificent could possibly be seen. Six pages preceded him mounted on chargers and dressed in orange velvet all covered with jewels. His dress and the furniture of his horse alone were worth sixty thousand crowns. He had twelve tall body-squires and six trumpeters sounding before him.'

So the campaign for all its dour purpose took on a gayer air. At a dinner-party given by Essex the three Swiss colonels present could not stay the course and collapsed under the table, but Essex and his friends and the French officers present rode riotously out, shouting and singing right up to the gates of Rouen. When nearly there they met the Governor of Rouen out on a reconnaissance. Essex at once challenged him to a duel. The Governor's only reply was a volley of shot from his escort of musketeers.

Nevertheless the siege failed, and for the same reason as the siege of Paris. The campaign had dragged on all winter and Essex had returned to England, when Parma once again suddenly appeared with his army only ten miles from the city. Reluctantly, under orders from his King, he had again withdrawn from his campaign against Maurice of Nassau and marched his men through the spring muds of Flanders to relieve yet another Catholic city. But at Caudebec, on the Seine west of Rouen, he received a wound in the hand which was eventually to prove fatal. The greatest general of his age died in Arras in December of that year, not long before the letter arrived from Philip which was to relieve him of his command.

Parma's absence with part of his troops from the Netherlands had already opened the way to a Dutch revival. Though only twenty-four, Maurice of Nassau, William of Orange's son by his second wife, Anna of Saxony, had inherited his father's military talents, and in the space of five months he recaptured Breda, Zutphen, Deventer and three other vital forts, by the conquest of the last of which, Nijmegen, he was able to gain control of the whole of Gelderland. Surviving the customary attempts at assassination, he reorganized the army of the Netherlands, instituting a high level of training and discipline which matched the Spanish, and introducing many new ideas, such as arming his cavalry with carbines instead of with swords. Behind the army Jan Oldenbarneveldt was organizing the rebel provinces into a unit of great economic strength. Indeed the contrast between the southern provinces, which, under Spanish rule, were declining into poverty and banditry, and those northern provinces comprising the Union of Utrecht, which prospered in conditions of war, was yearly more marked. Antwerp, occupied and blockaded, lost its great position as the trading centre of Europe. Amsterdam, free and thriving, took its place.

Nor by sacrificing such advantages as his great general had gained in the Low Countries did Philip advance his cause in France. The Duc de Mayenne permitted twelve hundred Spanish troops to be garrisoned in Paris; but the Spaniard had by now become more unpopular in France even than the

Englishman. If Spain sent money the French accepted it but derided the Spanish for sending it; if they sent troops it was a greater offence. It is not an unfamiliar pattern.

In January 1593, Mayenne summoned the States General and received the Spanish Ambassador with regal honours. The Count de Feria reminded the French of all the favours they had received and the six million gold ducats Philip had spent. He urged the assembly not to disperse until they had elected a truly Catholic King – or preferably Queen.

But even this gun was in process of being spiked. Convinced at last by the Spanish armies of Parma and the obduracy of his own people that there could never be peace in France with a Protestant on the throne, Henry IV changed his religion for the last time. In his famous words, he had decided that 'Paris was worth a Mass'. Elizabeth, shocked and indignant, sent him several strongly worded letters on the theme of 'what shall it profit a man'. Henry replied that his change of religion would not affect his friendship towards England. Nor did it. As François Guizot later wrote: 'He became a Catholic of France without ceasing to be the prop of the Protestants in Europe.' But for many earnest Protestants in England and elsewhere it was a bitter disappointment.

In consequence of his apostasy Henry was able to enter Paris without a shot fired and, from a window in the Port St Denis, to watch the Spanish garrison marching out. 'Commend me to your master,' he said, 'but do not return.'

If Philip had been giving ground on the military front he had been recouping it on the naval. By 1590 there had been a complete reorganization of the defences in the Caribbean. All the ports, such as St Domingo and Cartagena, and those in the Canaries and Azores too, had been greatly strengthened to resist surprise attack, and at most of these places frigates and other small but fast warships were now stationed to be on hand if the Flotas were attacked. A system of communication had been established by means of pinnaces which could make the passage across the Atlantic in twenty-eight days and carry advance news of hostile squadrons approaching. More important, Pero Menendez Marquez in Havana developed a new type of warship of about two hundred tons burden which he called galleyzabras – on the same principle as the galleass but of quite different proportions and seaworthiness. Built like galleys but mainly propelled by sail, they were sufficiently heavily armed to outfight anything of their own size and too fast to be caught by anything bigger. (One thinks of Admiral Fisher's dicta in the First World War, of the birth of the battle-cruiser, and, later, of the German pocket-battleships.)

But these ships were not just for war: they were to take over the carrying of the silver bullion and other treasure from the old conventional slow-moving carracks. Merchants were compelled to unload at Havana and have their valuables re-freighted in the galleyzabras. There were not really enough of these ships yet to take over from the East India carracks, and they for the time being still had to take their chance. Towards the end of 1589 both the Earl of Cumberland and Sir Martin Frobisher seized prizes of great value on the trade routes; but this sort of raid was to become more difficult with each year that passed.

Hawkins had a more methodical plan, which was the establishment of a regular blockade off the Azores, maintained by a squadron of English warships four months at a stretch, each squadron to be relieved by another, so that at no time throughout the year would the treasure-ships be free to sail through. It was a plan he had advocated before the Armada, but then the menace to England was too great to see it implemented. The year 1590 was the big opportunity, and although like most such schemes of the time it failed to be efficient for the half measures employed to furnish it, the fact of its presence, plus the remarkable depredations of a leading city merchant, Alderman John Watt, and other privateers in the Caribbean, caused Philip to send word that the treasure-ships were not to risk the Atlantic crossing that year.

As soon as this was learned in England it was resolved to fit out a squadron of warships to intercept the treasure-fleet in the spring of 1591. Drake remained in eclipse, though busying himself reorganizing the defences of Plymouth; neither Hawkins nor Frobisher had particularly distinguished himself in the Queen's eyes in last year's blockade – that is they had brought nothing of value home; Lord Admiral Howard's was rather too big a name to command this light compact squadron. So Elizabeth chose Lord Thomas Howard, the Lord Admiral's young cousin, with Sir Walter Ralegh as second-in-command. Lord Thomas Howard, who was thirty, had commanded the *Golden Lion* against the Armada and had handled his ship like a master; but his other sea experience was slight.

Ralegh, now thirty-nine, had had a lifetime's experience of soldiering but relatively little naval experience, though as an empire builder he had already set down one colony of settlers in Virginia.

However, at the last moment the Queen, who seldom liked her favourites to stray far from court – and just then Ralegh was back in favour – forbade him to go. She may also have realized that the Howards as a family no more liked Ralegh than he liked them. They looked on him as an arrogant upstart living on the Queen's favour. He looked on them as his mental inferiors, which, not unnaturally, they were.

Probably on Ralegh's initiative, the Queen appointed his cousin, Sir Richard Grenville, to sail in his place. The outcome is both history and legend. The squadron that sailed was small but well found. Howard in the *Defiance*, Grenville in the *Revenge*, were accompanied by two comparable Queen's ships, the *Bonaventure* (Captain, Robert Crosse) and the *Nonpareil*, Sir Edward Denny, of around five hundred tons each, with crews of two hundred and fifty and about forty guns. The *Crane*, a ship of half that size, a half dozen well-armed London merchantmen, and about eight pinnaces, made up the fleet. Before they had been at sea more than a month news reached London that a Spanish fleet of remarkable size and power was abroad: about fifty sail, of which thirty were galleons, including six of the new 'Apostles' of fifteen hundred tons each. They were under the command of Don Alonso de Bazan, younger brother of the dead Santa Cruz; and immediately this news reached Ralegh he sent off a fast pinnace to warn the English. At the same time strenuous efforts were made to reinforce Howard's fleet. Thomas Vavasour in the *Foresight* and George Fenner in the *Lion*, with seven more armed merchantmen, were hurried off towards the rendezvous that Howard had appointed, an area a little to the west of the island of Flores.

In mid-August the Spanish fleet reached Terceira, the main naval base in the Azores, and shortly afterwards news of the English took them to Flores. By this time the English squadron had been at sea nearly four months, had captured little and were heartily tired of waiting for the treasure-fleet. As usual they were beset by sickness, and when Captain Middleton, who had been dispatched by the Earl of Cumberland, arrived in a pinnace to warn them of the approach of a Spanish fleet, most of the ships' companies were ashore. Ralegh in his famous *Report* writes: 'Some were providing ballast for their ships; others filling of water and refreshing themselves from the land with such things as they could either for money or by force recover . . . one half part of the men of every ship were sick . . . in the *Revenge* there were ninety diseased.'

The Spanish admiral had so divided his fleet that the English would be surrounded and attacked from all sides; and, but for Cumberland's warning pinnace, the plan would have been entirely successful. As it was, Howard had less than an hour in which to recover his crews from the land before, at around four in the afternoon, the first squadron of the Spanish fleet under Marcos de Arumburu – that Paymaster of the Castilean galleons who was so nearly wrecked off the Blasket Islands – came round the corner of the island and was upon him. So close was it that several of the English ships had to slip their cables in order to be away in time; and then it was touch and go whether they could gain the weather gage and so make out to sea. One indeed, the *Revenge*, did not.

Sir Richard Grenville is one of the strangest, fiercest, most heroic figures of all that fierce, heroic age. Obstinate, of an inflammable temper, a man of action, always at war either on land or sea and a natural leader, his reputation in Spain was nothing like Drake's, but it was a darker one. '*Ricardo de Campo Verde gran cossario.*' A great pirate. He took a pride in his grim reputation. The legend was current at the time, and for long after his death, that when Grenville took prisoners he would have them to dine and would chew and swallow glass till the blood ran from his mouth. Returning from Virginia in 1585 he had come on a Spanish ship containing treasure and, having no small boat to board her, had used an old ship's chest which floated him and his men across and sank as they sprang aboard the Spaniard. Not a man to turn his back on the enemy however much common sense demanded it.

By turning tail and running back before the wind the *Revenge* almost certainly could have got clear. Instead, while Arumburu and Howard exchanged broadsides, Grenville decided to force his way right through the Spanish fleet, obliging the big galleons of Seville to give way before him. Naturally they did no such thing. The *San Felipe* first got a grappling-line aboard, but this parted, being of rope, and the *Revenge* 'discharged her lower tier loaded with cross-bar shot and forced her to fall away and stop her leaks'. But so big was the *San Felipe* beside the *Revenge* that she becalmed the sails of the

English ship, and after a succession of further broadsides Martin de Bertendona, thirsting to repay all the defeats he had suffered, came up on the other side in the *San Barnabas*, and was able to grapple more securely.

'The Spanish ships,' says Ralegh, who got it all direct from survivors, 'were filled with companies of soldiers, in some two hundred besides the mariners . . . In ours there was none at all beside the mariners but the servants of the commanders and some few voluntary gentlemen. After many interchanged volleys of great ordnance and small shot, the Spaniards deliberated to enter the *Revenge*, and make divers attempts, hoping to force her by the multitudes of their armed soldiers and musketeers, but were still repulsed again and again, and at all times beaten back, into their own ships or into the seas.'

One English ship only turned back to help, the *George Noble*, an armed London victualler of one hundred and fifty tons, which sailed recklessly into the fighting zone and put herself under Grenville's command. Grenville's order was to save herself before she was shot to pieces.

In the meantime Arumburu had crashed into the poop of the *Revenge* and got some men aboard, who fought their way as far as the mainmast and captured the ship's ensign; but Arumburu had so damaged his own galleon in the collison that she had to disengage and request aid from others of the fleet. His place was immediately taken by Don Pedro Manrique in the *Ascension* and behind him came Don Luis Cuitiño who put his flagship alongside the *Ascension* and ran his men across her decks. Then the *San Andrea* forced her way in near the bows.

By now night had fallen, but the fight went on in the dark unabated. Grenville was everywhere, furiously encouraging his men and directing them, and somehow he bore a charmed life in all the slaughter about him. The *Revenge*'s upper works were torn to pieces and many of the crew who had taken to the tops for better aim had died. At eleven Grenville at last was seriously wounded in the side, and had to retire behind a splintered bulwark while his surgeon attempted to dress the wound. While fastening the bandages the surgeon was shot dead and Grenville again wounded, this time in the head.

The commander of the Spanish fleet, Alonso de Bazan, having very narrowly missed catching and boarding Howard and having lost the other English in the dark, returned and circled helplessly round this bitter and bloody battle in which one lone Queen's ship was locked inextricably with fifteen of his own, like a fox among a pack of hounds. About three in the morning the galleon *Ascension* went to the bottom, Don Luis Cuitiña's flagship was found to be fatally holed, and this too was abandoned, to sink soon after dawn. Two others were so damaged that they foundered later. But there were always more eager for the kill. And Bertendona's *San Barnabas* was still locked to the *Revenge*'s larboard side in a grip that could only end in death.

At dawn the fighting almost stopped. No Spaniard lived on the decks of the *Revenge*, but few English either. All the upper works had been shot away down to the main deck. Not a mast or a spar was standing. English and Spanish dead and dying lay heaped together in the scuppers. Not a pike remained unbroken. All powder was spent. The Spaniards surrounded her still, but they had fired something like eight hundred rounds of heavy shot, had lost nearly four hundred men killed, including two captains, and they waited for her surrender to save more bloodshed. Out of the morning mists another English ship, the *Pilgrim*, under Captain Whiddon of Plymouth, having hovered in the area all night listening to the battle, put in a brief appearance, but a dozen Spanish ships closed on her and she slipped hastily away.

Meanwhile Grenville, dying in his cabin, gave orders to the master gunner to split and sink the *Revenge* so that she should not fall into enemy hands. The gunner and others were willing but were stayed by Captain Langhorne and the Master, who argued that the *Revenge* was already so badly holed that if surrendered now it was unlikely anyone would ever get her safe to port, and it was not dishonourable to save themselves and those others not mortally wounded to fight another day.

While some pleaded with Grenville, the Master, who had 'at least ten or twelve wounds in his head or on his body,' – and was to die of them later – hastened to be conveyed aboard the *San Pablo* where he met Don Alonso de Bazan and demanded generous terms if they were to yield. The terms were willingly granted, and the great fight was over. 'When the answer was returned and that safety of life was promised, the common sort being now at the end of their peril, the most drew back from Sir Richard and the master gunner, it being no hard matter to dissuade men from death to life. The master-gunner, finding himself and Sir Richard thus prevented and mastered by the greater number, would have slain himself with a sword, had he not been by force withheld and locked in his cabin . . . Sir Richard thus overmatched, was sent unto by Alonso Bazan to remove out of the *Revenge*, the ship being marvellous unsavoury, filled with blood and the bodies of dead and wounded men like a slaughter-house.'

Sir Richard Grenville died two days later on board the *San Pablo*. Shortly afterwards a storm of hurricane force from the west and north-west scattered and sank many of the Spanish ships. With them went the *Revenge*. So many ships were wrecked and so many thousands of bodies were cast up on the islands that, according to a Dutch merchant called Van Linschoten, the islanders began to doubt the power of God. 'So soon as they had thrown overboard the dead body of Vice-Admiral Sir Richard Grenville, they verily thought that, as he had a devilish faith and religion and therefore the devils loved him, so he presently sank into the bottom of the sea and down into hell, where he raised up all the devils to the revenge of his death. Such and the like blasphemies against God they ceased not openly to utter, without being reproved by any man.'

Lord Thomas Howard was much criticized at the time for leaving the *Revenge* to her fate, rather as Medina Sidonia was for leaving Pedro de Valdes in the *Rosario*. Although the behaviour of the two captains thus left behind is so opposite as to belong to different worlds, the action of the admirals has a similarity in that it was dictated by larger considerations than the safety of one ship. Medina Sidonia by staying with the *Rosario* would have split his Armada. Howard by returning to fight alongside the obstinate commander of the *Revenge* would probably have lost his squadron. Also to stay to grapple or be grappled would have been contrary to all the precepts of the Armada battle. It was precisely this that the Spaniards wanted, precisely this that the English had learned to avoid.

But Howard, it is argued, might have stayed near, harrying and biting at the edges of the Spanish fleet and distracting them from their attack on the *Revenge*. This presupposes that the English ships were still much faster and more manœuvrable than the Spanish. But the Spanish ships, or the majority of them, had been built in the last four years on lessons learned in the Armada battle; the English were the same ones and had been at sea four months. It is doubtful if Howard could

171

have harried the Spanish ships and yet maintained his distance. Indeed the Spaniards claimed that had night not fallen, they would have overtaken several of the English ships, certainly the *Defiance*, which was the slowest of the royal vessels.

The news of the capture of the *Revenge* and the scattering of the English fleet was brought in to Lisbon by one of the Apostle galleons, the *San Andrea*, which had been in the thick of the fight, with all her flags and banners flying. This was the first and only English capital ship captured throughout the war, and efforts were made in Spain to make the most of it and to hide the cost in Spanish ships and the disaster of the gale which followed. In England the defeat and death of Grenville was accompanied by wild rumours which only the publication of Ralegh's *Report* helped to stifle. The Queen privately was upset and offended by the manner of Grenville's death. The ultimate realist, she saw no point in sacrificing a valuable and famous warship and a valuable and brave commander and crew for the sake of an immortal gesture. Pedro de Valdes, safe in comfortable captivity in England, would no doubt have agreed with her.

But the last fight of the *Revenge* has become a legend in men's minds that defies rational assessment. In Froude's memorable words: 'As the most glorious actions, set like jewels in the history of mankind, are weighed one against the other in the balance, hardly will those three hundred Spartans who in the summer morning sat combing their long hair for death in the passes of Thermopylae have earned a more lofty estimate for themselves than this one crew of modern Englishmen.'

In 1590 the Earl of Essex married Frances, the widow of Sir Philip Sidney. Her Majesty was furious but quickly forgave him. Late in 1591 Sir Walter Ralegh secretly married Elizabeth Throckmorton, one of her ladies-in-waiting, and when it was all discovered the following year they found themselves both in the Tower – in separate cells, as Ralegh's numerous enemies were amused to point out. Even when released, Sir Walter was banished from court, and it took him years to regain a partial return to favour.

Elizabeth was as conscious as most of her court that she alone had raised Ralegh to great eminence. Essex, on the other hand, had royal blood in his veins. Through Thomas of Woodstock, Duke of Gloucester, he traced his ancestry from Edward

III. An ancestor, Eleanor de Bohun, had been the sister of Mary, wife of Henry IV. Another, Anne Woodville, had been the sister of Elizabeth, wife of Edward IV. His grandmother had been Anne Boleyn's sister. There was almost too much royal blood in his veins, as Elizabeth was to decide later. But for the moment it counted in his favour. And his choice, though perhaps it aligned him too closely with the Walsingham faction, was otherwise a highly respectable one. Whereas Ralegh had married one of her ladies-in-waiting – this was the unforgivable sin: a breach of his oath as Captain of the Guard, and of the girl's oath too. It was a direct affront to the Queen; and even when it was discovered there seems to have been no full submission or apology.

When it came to recovering the Queen's favour, Essex had the additional advantage of being thirteen years younger – and so handsome and chivalrous and so much the popular hero. And it may have been that for all Ralegh's loyalty – and this never wavered towards the Queen, terribly to his detriment in the last two years of her life – the dark, haughty brilliance of his mind was a challenge to hers, as other men's were not, and that, although at first fascinated, almost hypnotized by it, she later, when the spell began to wear off, unconsciously resented the challenge.

Just before his disgrace, Ralegh had the mortification once again of mounting a naval expedition in which he was to play the leading part, this time in company with Sir John Borough, and once again of being recalled to court, while Sir Martin Frobisher was appointed in his place. But neither Borough nor Robert Crosse, Ralegh's vice-admiral, would serve under Frobisher; so the expedition broke up and went its several ways, Frobisher to sail to Cape St Vincent, only to feel the full weight of Spain's new naval power and be forced to run for cover. Borough and Crosse, however, succeeded in capturing the seven-deck, two-thousand-ton *Madre de Dois*, the richest prize of all the war, and bringing her into Dartmouth. Here scenes of pillage and looting took place which were so uncontrollable that Elizabeth, who had only just consigned Ralegh to the Tower, was forced much against her will to release him in company with a gaoler to try to restore order. This he quickly did, since he was as popular with his sailors and Devonshire country folk as he was unpopular with the courtiers of Westminster and the citizens of London.

For a time these and smaller raiding successes, which helped to disrupt the Spanish trade routes, disguised the lack of purpose in English naval policy. It looked for a time as if Philip did not intend another Armada, but planned instead to establish a naval base somewhere along the Channel coast so as to harass English shipping at its source. So England's chief energies were still directed to helping Henry IV in France and Maurice of Nassau in the Netherlands. Between 1589 and 1595 Elizabeth sent five armies to France in support of Henry, and by the latter year Henry could call himself King in more than name, in spite of individual pockets of League resistance and in spite of an attempt on his life by a Jesuit youth. Guise was made governor of Provence in an attempt to heal the schism, and Henry, to fulfil his obligations to his chief ally, declared war on Spain in January 1595. By the Edict of Nantes full rights, religious and civil, were granted to Protestants and Catholics alike.

In the Netherlands a new English commander, Sir Francis Vere, proved to be the most successful ever sent, both as a soldier and as a friend of the Dutch. And for the first time the two nations fought together and worked together in harmony. Parma's successor in the Low Countries, the Count of Fuentes, a Portuguese of noble birth, was another very able commander who, taking over after a brief interim period, soon brought the Spanish troops up to their old level of efficiency and discipline and was a combatant to be respected by both Maurice of Nassau and Henry of France. Indeed, he besieged and took Doullens, only forty miles from the French coast south of Boulogne, and then swung east and took Cambrai too. In the meantime the Spanish penetration of the Brittany peninsula went on – indeed it sometimes seemed that Henry, preoccupied with emergencies nearer his capital, left the defence of Brittany entirely to Elizabeth – and in 1594 the Spaniards, having been able to land strong support for their troops at Blavet, opposite Lorient, marched across country and seized and fortified Crozon, a rocky promontory overlooking Brest harbour. Quite clearly their next move would be to take the city and so obtain a near-Channel port.

This was not to be tolerated, so a joint expedition under the two veterans, Sir John Norris and Sir Martin Frobisher, was launched with a substantial army and a fleet of eighty sail, and after weeks of sporadic but bitter fighting the Crozon fort was captured and the remains of its garrison put to the sword. Leading his sailors up a ladder over a wall, Frobisher was shot in the thigh. So close was the gun discharged that wadding entered the wound. It was allowed to remain and caused blood poisoning, from which the tough, quarrelsome, courageous old sailor died.

So went the first, if the least, of the great triumvirate of sea captains and strategists who had fought against Medina Sidonia in 1588. In England at this time the other two were making ambitious plans which were to lead to their own end.

12

Ralegh at Cadiz

By 1592 Philip II was sixty-five, and he was ageing quickly. Gout and arthritis plagued him, and he had withdrawn more and more into the monastic life of the Escorial. When in that year there was an insurrection in Aragon he made the long and difficult journey across the mountains to Segovia, Valladolid, Burgos, Logrono and Tarazona, where the Cortes was waiting for him, and received its expressions of loyalty and a grant of six hundred thousand ducats towards his expenses of war. On his return to Madrid he was thought to be a dying man. The doctors warned him that unless he reduced the amount of work and took more regular and prolonged rest he could not hope to survive.

The famous *Junta de Noche* had been in existence since 1588, whereby a few intimate counsellors worked far into the night with the King, formulating policy and carrying out his secret instructions; but from 1592 it became still more exclusive, the King's closest advisers being Don Cristoval de Moura, who was a Portuguese, and Don Juan de Idiaquez, a Basque; and it was seldom that directives were not signed by Idiaquez on behalf of the King. Philip also recalled the Cardinal Archduke Albert from Portugal to act as Regent if he were to die while Philip, his sole surviving son, was only fifteen. The thirty-three-year-old Albert was the son of the late Maximilian II, the enlightened ruler of Austria and Germany, and therefore Philip's second cousin. He was also Philip's nephew and brother-in-law, and, in the almost incestuous way of the time, was in a few years to become his son-in-law, when he married the Infanta Isabella, Philip's beloved daughter. In order to do this Albert received a Papal dispensation to renounce his holy orders.

The following year the King's health improved again, and he was able to bend all his considerable energies once more to the prosecution of the war. Setbacks in the Netherlands and in France, induced at least partly by English support, convinced him that his only hope of military success was by way of naval supremacy. His spies reported that Drake was emerging from the eclipse he had suffered and was much at court now; and there were rumours that he would soon be let loose again. In the Parliament which met in February 1593 both Drake and Ralegh had argued for a new and aggressive naval policy against Spain. Ralegh had also been active in planning a new adventure to Guiana, and in 1594 sent out his emissary, a Devonshire captain called Whiddon, on a reconnaissance to the Orinoco. All this trespassed on the King's domains.

Where, however, when it was assembled, should the next Armada be directed to land? Ireland was, as always, in a state of smouldering rebellion, and a landing there with several thousand troops could set the country aflame. Then a bargain might be struck that Spain would only withdraw from Ireland if the English agreed to withdraw from the Continent. Or another descent on the Isle of Wight, this time to capture it and possibly to parley with Elizabeth from there. To attempt any ferrying of troops from the Netherlands was clearly impracticable without a French port. But Philip as always was reluctant to land in support of the Irish; and in any event an occurrence in 1595 had the effect of turning his attention elsewhere.

In July of that year the aristocratic Don Carlos de Amesquita, commanding a squadron of four Spanish galleys with their accompanying small craft on a routine cruise, raided a fishing-village in Brittany and then was blown by adverse winds across towards the Scillies. Running short of water, he decided to put in on the Cornish coast and get water and to see what was to be found. It was not of course unusual for Spanish warships to be about in those waters. In May of that year a shallop from Blavet had captured a St Keverne fishing-boat in Falmouth Bay and taken its crew prisoner; a month later there had been galleys close in to the savage cliffs of St Eval on the north coast; following that there were twenty enemy sail sighted off the Manacles. The English coastal towns, particularly the west-country towns, lived ever on the *qui vive*. What was exceptional about this was that the Spanish captain dared to land. But Captain Amesquita had aboard with him at the time a noted English renegade called Captain Richard Burley, who knew the coast well and no doubt directed the landing at Mousehole.

It was a startling success. The population fled in panic and

Amesquita landed two hundred men, pikes and musketeers, and burned the village, then sent pickets up the hill and they burned Paul Church and several hamlets around. Sir Francis Godolphin rushed an urgent message to Plymouth for help, supposing this to be the opening move of a full-scale invasion; but the Spaniards returned to their ships, rowed two miles across Mount's Bay and landed again at Penzance, which they fired also. Godolphin tried to rally opposition here, but apart from his servants none would stay with him, and the Spaniards, four hundred of them now, celebrated Mass on the western hill and took an oath to build a friary on the spot after they had conquered England. Then, learning of the nearness of a fleet under Drake and Hawkins, they took advantage of a favourable wind and made off for Brittany.

It was the first time Spanish soldiers had landed on English soil, and the weakness of the opposition was something that Philip was not to forget.

If the galleys had not left when they did they would have been trapped by Drake, who at last had received a commission to go to sea again. It was tardy and reluctant when it came, and the Queen, no longer sure of her old hero, appointed the even older Hawkins to sail with him as joint commander. No doubt she felt that in sudden crisis or emergency the sager counsels of Hawkins would keep Drake in check. Hawkins was by now sixty-three, a tired man who had spent much of his life in the service of his country, who was unwell and had no desire to go to sea again; but he accepted the commission as an order from the Queen. Drake was only just turned fifty and was itching to resume his role as England's greatest sailor. But neither of them quite appreciated the change in sea power which had taken place in the six years of their retirement.

In any event the shared command soon proved to be a grave error — as shared commands always do. Their fleet, though small, was well found, with six of the Queen's ships and twenty-one other warships of varying sizes. It carried as colonel-general of the army, Sir Francis Baskerville, another of the new officers, who had so distinguished himself against Parma that, in a brief period of truce, Parma had embraced him and told him that there was no braver soldier alive.

Four days out of Plymouth Hawkins discovered that Drake

was carrying three hundred men more than he had provisions for – they had so flocked in he had not had the heart to turn them away – and proposed to raid the Canaries first to levy a ransom of new supplies. There was a quarrel between the two captains which Baskerville attempted to heal by appealing to Hawkins's good nature. In the end this early diversion was agreed to.

Partly because of these dissensions, they just missed a fleet of thirty carracks carrying something like ten million ducats' worth of treasure. Drake was bitter about this, but had they met them they would also have encountered twelve of Spain's best galleons which sailed as escort, so the misfortune might have cut both ways. Then when they reached Las Palmas they found the fortifications of the town so strong and newly developed that they had to call off the attack and sail for the Indies, having watered on the other side of the island but without further provisions.

It was the end of October before they reached Guadeloupe, and there they lost one of their smaller ships, the *Francis*, which had been lagging behind and was captured by five of the new fast and well-armed galleyzabras. News of Drake's coming therefore preceded him to Porto Rico, where an attempt to land failed with the loss of many men and several of his best officers. At the same time Sir John Hawkins, who had been a sad man and failing throughout the voyage, died; and this cast a deep gloom over an expedition which was as thoroughly pursued by bad luck as so many of Drake's earlier enterprises had been by good.

Leaving Porto Rico, the fleet now made a succession of other raids on the way to Panama; some modestly successful, some repulsed by the new defences. Where they were not repulsed, a scorched earth policy deprived them of the booty. Unimpeded by any Spanish fleet attack, for his name was still dreaded everywhere, Drake at last reached Nombre de Dios, where the fort was taken, the town burned and the shipping seized. Baskerville was sent overland with seven hundred and fifty men on the old Panama road, but after three days in constant wet weather, which ruined his supplies and rendered his muskets useless, he came on hills and a ravine heavily defended by Spanish troops and knew his march to be useless. He could only retire to the ships, which he did by the 2nd January and so ended yet one more of Drake's hopes.

There was nothing now to do but go on and try to find

some treasure somewhere to carry home, but at Escuda de Veraqua, an island near the coast, so many of the crews were ill with dysentery that barely enough were left to man the ships. Then Drake took it, and, in order to find healthier air, the defeated fleet again put to sea. At sea on the night of the 27th January 1596, Sir Francis Drake died. He was buried three miles off the town of Puerto Bello, and so many others were sick or dead that his prizes and two of his own ships had to be sunk over his grave so that enough sailors were left to man the rest home.

It is probably true that Elizabeth never fully forgave Drake for his failure to destroy the remnants of the first Armada in Santander in 1589, for, although she allowed him to go on this final raiding venture and provided him with some of her excellent smaller ships, she did not reserve him to lead or assist in the much bigger venture which was being planned for 1596. This had not, of course, been approved when Drake sailed. In typical Elizabeth fashion it was not approved until the last minute, though it had been in the air long enough and indeed in preparation.

What brought it to sudden implementation was the turn of events in France. Henry IV was now king in more than name, and his war against Spain had prospered to the extent that only in Brittany and Picardy and parts of Normandy were the Spanish still established. But there were endless disagreements between the Allies, and the French people were impoverished and heartily sick of war. There was talk of the Pope mediating and negotiating a separate peace between France and Spain. Into this situation came the Archduke Albert, fresh from Philip's council and the strongest man in Spain. Injecting new life into the Spanish army of the Netherlands, he began to move towards the Channel ports. This caused alarm both in France and in England; but in reply to Henry's urgent request for more English help, Elizabeth said that she could only do this if in return the French would give Calais into English keeping. It was an answer which bitterly annoyed Henry. 'I would as lief be bitten by a dog as scratched by a cat,' he observed.

As indeed he was, for while both countries were hanging back waiting for the other, quietly confident anyway that Calais was in no immediate danger, the Archduke switched his direction and sent a flying column north under de Rosne. Calais was quite unprepared for the attack, its fortifications almost in ruins and its garrison inadequate. By the 17th April the Spanish were in the city, and a week later they took the citadel and massacred its defenders. Later they fanned out south, taking Ardres and Guisnes. This brilliant coup struck dismay into all three of the allies, but particularly into England; for Spain at last had its Channel port available for a future Armada.

At first it seemed probable that the projected fleet being made ready to attack Spain on her own coasts would be cancelled; but on the 24th May, Elizabeth signed a new treaty with Henry, and from then on, saving the customary vacillation, there was no pause until the fleet sailed.

This was another 'joint' command, the Lord Admiral Howard himself sharing it with Lord Essex. There was a slight but wise division of responsibility in that the former was given precedence at sea and the latter on land. The fleet consisted of forty-eight fighting vessels, including some of the finest warships, and eighty transports and victuallers. It was divided into five squadrons: the first under Howard, again in the *Ark Royal* of eight hundred tons; the second under Essex, in the *Due Repulse*; the third under Lord Thomas Howard in the *Mere Honour* of nine hundred tons; the fourth under Sir Walter Ralegh in the *Warspite*; the fifth, a Dutch squadron under Admiral Van Duyvenvoord, Lord of Warmond, in the *Neptune*. It will be noticed that the names of ships built since the Armada were beginning to appear on the English side too. Both *Due Repulse* and *Warspite* were new ships, launched only that year and the last to be laid down in Elizabeth's day. The tonnage of the *Due Repulse* was seven hundred and seventy-seven and of the *Warspite* six hundred and forty-eight. About six thousand five hundred troops sailed under Sir Francis Vere, two thousand of them veterans from the Netherlands. There were nearly a thousand gentlemen adventurers, many of them titled youths seeking fame more than fortune.

Just before the expedition was due to leave, Sir Francis Baskerville arrived off the Scillies with the remnants of Drake and Hawkins's fleet, having fought a successful engagement on the way home with the fleet sent out by Spain to intercept him. Barely four hundred of his men were left alive. Thrilling rumours of Drake's successes had been reaching England over the last few months, and this crushing news of the total failure of the voyage, coupled with the death of both Drake and Hawkins, was a terrible blow to English morale. This later and stronger expedition had been partly organized to cover Drake's return.

News of Drake's death had been greeted in Spain with overwhelming joy. Lope de Vega, who had sailed and suffered with the First Armada, wrote a poem of praise and thanksgiving; and to many a devout Spaniard it seemed that the sins they had had to expiate were now at last forgiven them. But the news had the mistaken effect of persuading the Spanish that any proposed English raid on their coasts would certainly now be cancelled, what with the death of their two greatest seamen and the threat of a Spanish-occupied Calais.

By the united persuasions of Essex, the Howards and Ralegh, and by that of Maurice of Nassau, who had a true conception of the strategy of war, Elizabeth did not change her mind, and the fleet left England on the 3rd June and in just over two weeks was off Cadiz.

It was a moment of pent-up passion for the English leaders. The triumph of 1588 was eight years behind them – already a part of history. Since then, apart from numerous successful minor ventures, the picture had been a dismal one. The utter failure of the Lisbon expedition to fulfil its primary purpose. Grenville's death and the capture of the *Revenge*. Howard's flight. Drake's defeat and death. Hawkins's defeat and death. A Spanish garrison seven leagues from Dover. Another one in Brittany. Spanish galleys off the Cornish coast landing with impunity and burning villages and churches and saying Mass. Another Armada partly built.

At daybreak on the brilliantly clear morning of the 18th June, while the fleet was thirty miles off Cadiz, Howard captured an Irish barque bound for Waterford and learned that in the harbour were twenty galleys and sixty ships, among them four of the Apostle galleons, the *San Andrea*, the *San Felipe*, the *San Tomas* and the *San Mateo*. It was an opportunity not to be missed.

The reconciliation between Essex and Ralegh, fresh from his tremendous adventure in search of El Dorado, had been begun last year, and this year it had warmed to friendship. It was fortunate that this was so, for the exigencies of the next hours were to put a strain upon tact and understanding. On the Friday Ralegh, much against his own wishes, was ordered away to try to cut off a fleet of ten ships which the Waterford captain reported had just left Cadiz for Lisbon laden with a rich cargo. He returned on Monday, having run one of his quarry aground but lost the rest in fog, to find that he had not as he feared missed the attempt on Cadiz, but that it was about to begin, in a way which offended all his best tactical instincts.

Lacking the genius and the splendid arrogance of Drake, Howard and Essex had held a number of councils at which differing views had successively prevailed; then the weather had turned adverse; and now Essex was committing himself to a frontal attack with soldiers on the sea side of Cadiz where a creek called the Caleta ran into the sea. With the surf rough, all advantage of surprise lost, and four galleys drawn up inshore to oppose the landing, this was an attempt bound to result in enormous casualties among the landing troops – they were in full armour and when spilled into the sea sank like stones; and Ralegh rushed aboard the *Due Repulse* to try to stop the landing before the assault troops were too far committed.

It was a difficult meeting, at which Ralegh did not mince his words, and Essex at first haughtily refused to alter his dispositions, declaring it was all the fault of the Lord Admiral for refusing to force the bay until Cadiz was taken. Eventually however the vehement arguments of the older man took effect, and Essex agreed to call off the assault if Howard would admit the error of his own arguments. At once Ralegh swung down into his pinnace and was rowed across to the *Ark Royal* where Howard standing stiffly at the taffrail awaited him.

We do not know what charm Ralegh used on the essentially reasonable old admiral, but presently Howard agreed to a complete reversal of the order of assault, and Ralegh was back in his pinnace calling to Essex as he slid past 'Entramos! Entramos! we're going in!' Essex threw his hat in the air, and a burst of cheering broke out along the bulwarks of the *Due Repulse*, to be caught up by sailors on all the nearby ships. They were going in as Drake had gone in. What had been done before could be done again.

But reorganization of the ships, and re-embarking of the soldiers already in the boats, took several hours; and they missed the tide. Ralegh, having saved the precipitate and foolhardy landing, now counselled caution; there could be no surprise; then let all be got ready for the following dawn.

At ten that night in the great cabin of the *Ark Royal*, with the yellow lanterns gently swaying, and all the captains, generals and admirals present in their gold braid and rich velvets, Ralegh put forward his plan of attack, as if he had quietly insinuated himself into a position of supreme command. And when all had agreed his plan, the position of honour, the privilege of leading the attack, was accorded him in the *Warspite*.

So at first light of dawn next morning the attack began. During the night the Spanish galleons, which had been drawn up in defensive formation opposite Fort St Philip, had retired a mile or so more into the neck of the inner harbour, with the intention of blocking the entry at its narrowest point where the two pincers of land were less than a mile apart. To reach the Spanish ships the English therefore had to run the gauntlet of shore fire from Fort St Philip and from the town. The *Rainbow*, under Sir Francis Vere, trying to catch the wind nearer the Cadiz shore and so steal ahead of her larger rivals, was the first to come under fire, and she had her sails shot to ribbons. *Warspite* was the next to receive attention, but the range was greater and she suffered no hurt. Ralegh ordered his trumpeters to blow a triumphant blast on their trumpets every time the batteries fired.

It would be satisfactory to record that some of the naval discipline reluctantly adopted by the English captains during the later stages of the Armada fight remained with them in 1596; but in fact each captain was so eager to get at the enemy that he looked on every other captain with a sort of angry rivalry. These were huntsmen, leaping every fence, taking every risk, and jostling each other dangerously to be in at the kill.

The fair channel at its narrowest point between Puntal and Matagorda was almost blocked by the four Apostle galleons, anchored head to stern across the passage, and behind these were two Portuguese galleons, three Italian armed merchant ships and a group of Levanters. Three of the galleyzabras – out of their element in a battle in such a confined space – were in the shallower water of St Mary Port, and a group of galleys lurked under the protection of Fort St Philip. Into this defensive formation the whole weight of the English fleet crashed: Ralegh in the lead by half a ship's length in *Warspite* from

Lord Thomas now in *Nonpareil*, Sir George Carew in *Mary Rose*, Sir Robert Southwell in the *Lion* and Sir Conyers Clifford in the *Dreadnought*. Ralegh made first for the *San Felipe*, 'being resolved as he wrote later, 'to be revenged for the *Revenge* or to second her with mine own life.'

Like the others, Ralegh had been forbidden to hazard a Queen's ship by boarding – this was to be left to fly-boats later – but after a heavy exchange of broadsides lasting two hours Ralegh rushed across to see Essex, demanding that this prohibition should be lifted. Essex agreed and said he would go in with him. But in the twenty minutes Ralegh had been away his rivals had stolen up on him. Vere, coming up in the tattered *Rainbow*, had slid around ahead of the *Warspite*; also Lord Thomas Howard in *Nonpareil*. So Ralegh ordered Captain Oakes to up anchor and seize the initiative again, even at the risk of going aground and losing his ship. Then *Due Repulse*, forcing a way in, collided with *Dreadnought*, and both ships were out of the fight for half an hour. In the confusion Ralegh dropped his anchors again so that he swung athwart the tide and so sheltered the others from the fight, but *Rainbow* and *Nonpareil* threw lines aboard him and warped themselves into the front line again. 'The shooting of the ordnance was great,' wrote Vere, 'and they held us good talk by reason their ships lay athwart with their broadsides towards us, and most of us right ahead, so that we could use but our chasing pieces.'

In the three-hour battle *Warspite* suffered the most of the English ships, but the Spanish were in much worse shape. All had been holed repeatedly and many of their guns fell silent, either put out of action or for lack of crews. As the English edged nearer, the Spanish galleons at last slipped their cables and began to drift further inshore. Within a matter of minutes both the *San Felipe* and the *San Mateo* had grounded, 'tumbling into the sea heaps of soldiers,' wrote Ralegh, 'so thick as if coals had been poured out of a sack in many portholes at once; some drowned and some sticking in the mud.' Both these fine galleons were fired by their captains to avoid capture, and presently blew up: '. . . many Spanish drowned themselves; many, half burnt, leapt into the water; very many hanging by the ropes' ends by the ships' sides, under the water, even to the lips; many swimming with grievous wounds, stricken under water and put out of their pain, and withal so huge a fire and such tearing of the ordnance in the Great

Philip . . . if any man had a desire to see Hell itself, it was there most lively figured.'

This was virtually the end of the sea fight, but in the last minutes of it Ralegh was wounded in his leg, which was 'interlaced and deformed with splinters'—and would limp from it for the rest of his life—so he took no part in the storming of the city of Cadiz: a wonderful but bloody exploit in which Essex, Vere, Bagnal, Savage, Morgan and others performed prodigies of valour. Sir John Wingfield, one of the most daring of the leaders, was killed as the last of the resistance was collapsing. But many of the inhabitants fought bitterly from house to house—one of the most destructive of all forms of warfare. One enormous Franciscan friar killed nine Englishmen before being overwhelmed. Orders had been given by Essex that there was to be no burning of the city, and although a few soldiers got out of hand on the first night, this was brought under control, and two men were hanged for molesting a woman. Priests and churches were spared and fifteen hundred nuns were permitted to leave—even politely assisted to. 'Such a gentleman,' said Philip when he heard, 'has not been seen before among heretics.'

On the night of the conquest Ralegh had himself conveyed by his men into the city. All along he alone of the commanders was concerned with the treasure-fleet, which had retreated into the Port Royal basin. He tried to find Howard to convince him of the necessity of seizing the ships at once, but Howard would not split his forces, and since there was no way out of the harbour except past the narrow entrance where the English ships and the Spanish wrecks lay, he felt they could wait. While the flota was being bargained for on the following day the Spaniards fired the fleet. Thirty-six vessels were destroyed and treasure valued at twelve million ducats was lost. The loot of Cadiz, enormous though that was, was trifling compared to this. It was a tragic loss to England, a supreme sacrifice on Spain's part. The King approved it but the merchants concerned were bitterly antagonized: they would rather have paid the ransom.

The English remained in full possession of Cadiz for two weeks, debating whether to stay in permanent occupation or to go. They buried Sir John Wingfield with full military honours in the cathedral, while the whole fleet fired guns and dipped flags in salute. John Donne, who was with the expedition, wrote a poem on Wingfield's gallant death. The following day they held a state banquet in the Friary of St Francis, and in Stow's words: 'After dinner they made a great many knights, even all almost that did deserve it or affect it or not neglect or refuse it (as some did).' In all sixty-four officers were knighted. In the Armada Howard had knighted only five. Essex's prodigality in honouring his friends was a continuous source of irritation to Elizabeth.

In the end the invaders left Cadiz, for disease was spreading again and they had great quantities of booty to carry away. At the last, through a misunderstanding, most of the churches were fired and the city left in ruin. It was a fitting overplus revenge for the burning of one small church in Cornwall. On the way home the English landed at Faro, sacked the town and made off with the library belonging to Bishop Osorius. This became part of the Bodleian Library at Oxford.

They missed, however, by a matter of two days the great West Indian convoys which reached Lisbon safely in late July.

The shock to Spanish pride and Spanish finance by this invasion was enormous. Drake's raid in 1587 was puny by comparison. They had lost the whole of the treasure-flota, plus one hundred and twenty thousand ducats in ransom money; four of the fine new Apostles (*San Felipe* and *San Tomas* sunk, the *San Andrea* and the *San Mateo* captured and taken to England), five Biscayans, four Levanters, two galleasses, three galleyzabras, and three Italian ships laden with stores and artillery for the Low Countries, plus a host of small ships. It was an Armada in itself. As a result of this defeat and the financial loss entailed, Philip had to default on the payment of the whole of the bills of the Archduke Albert in the Netherlands: about one and a half million ducats; and on his own loans he offered only 45 per cent payment. Banks and commercial houses went into liquidation and there was a panic on the exchanges.

But its effect on the King's health was remarkable. He had been seriously ill again at Easter, but the news of the shattering defeat at Cadiz was like a shower of cold water on him. He began to move more quickly, his red-rimmed eyes grew bright and alert, his capacity for work returned.

In his reaction to the loss of Cadiz, as in so much, he reflected the feelings of the Spanish people. They were tired of war, lethargic, financially impoverished, disunited; but the events of Cadiz galvanized them and brought them together again with one common purpose. Money flowed in from the

Church, from the Cortes, even from the provincial towns. The court, the petty noblemen who proliferated throughout Spain, the clergy, the peasants, all were demanding that now, at whatever cost, the Second Armada must sail. Whatever the cost in money and lives, Cadiz must be avenged.

13

The Second Armada

The man chosen to command the new Armada was Don Martin de Padilla Manrique, Adelantado Mayor of Castile, Count of Santa Gadea and Knight of the Order of Alcantara; in fact the man the Duke of Medina Sidonia had suggested should take his place in 1588.

At least ten years older than Medina Sidonia, Padilla had had a long and continuous experience of war, having received his baptism as a junior officer at St Quentin in 1557. Nine years later he was made commander of four galleys of Sicily, and the next year led eight hundred sailors against the Moors of Granada. In the great battle of Lepanto in 1571 – 'the new Salamis' – he sank four Turkish ships. In 1585 he was Captain General of the galleys of Spain, but did not take part in the Armada of '88, possibly for the reasons already stated. In 1589 he was concerned in the defence of Lisbon against Drake and Norris. In 1591 he captured three English and twenty Dutch vessels in the Gulf of Almeria, east of Malaga, and had generally been the scourge of Anglo-Dutch trade in the Mediterranean.

This hardy and experienced fighter, now about fifty-six, was appointed *Primer General de la Armada del Oceano* and instructed to lead a fleet against England that year. He protested – as most admirals appointed by Philip seemed doomed to protest – for the fleet was far from ready and the great blow struck at Cadiz had seriously weakened its fighting power. Nor can it have been easy to have followed in Medina Sidonia's wake, knowing in full the disaster of '88 and the obloquy heaped on the Duke's head. Any captain facing the same enemy in the same waters would be doubly concerned to avoid a similar catastrophe.

Of course in some ways circumstances had altered much for the better. The Spanish galleon was a greatly improved fighting vessel; many of them were recently built and most of their captains were of a new generation and spoiling for a chance to wipe out the stain of their predecessors' defeat. Nor, with Blavet and Calais in Spanish hands at either end of the Channel, was there risk of a similar kind of disaster. True, Archduke Albert, between the two fires of a resurgent Netherlands and a hostile France, could hardly commit his army to an invasion of England as Parma could have done. But although Philip knew that Henry had entered into an agreement with Elizabeth that neither should make peace with Spain without the other, there was signs that Henry was wavering. If he could be detached . . .

And England itself still appeared to be militarily undefended – just as she had been in 1588: militia, trained bands, raw farmhands brandishing pikes, gentlemen on horseback with swords. The professional regiments of England were quite different; no one could fail to respect them; the reports of Parma, Mansfield, Fuentes, and Albert were plain to read, and Philip was not so foolish as to disregard them. But nearly all England's professional soldiers were in the Netherlands or Brittany. England lay unguarded except for her navy. For instance Falmouth: as fine a natural harbour as you could find in the world, yet little better defended than Penzance where Don Carlos de Amesquita had landed with such success. The renegade, Richard Burley, reported to the King that for the defence of Pendennis Castle at the entrance to Falmouth harbour the Captain, John Killigrew, had only himself, a deputy captain, a master gunner, two other gunners and a porter, and the 'trained' bands of Budock to call on in need. And, by way of arms, some old cannon, two lasts of powder and forty muskets.

It was a great temptation; but all through 1596 Philip had been beset by letters from Hugh O'Neill, Earl of Tyrone, appealing for his help in saving Catholic Ireland from the English. Tyrone was a master of diplomatic intrigue and quite brilliant at playing friend to both sides; but in 1595 he was forced into open rebellion, and by 1596 his need of Spanish help was urgent. Not only had he and O'Donnell and Maguire and MacWilliam Burke written repeatedly and separately to Philip begging for an army to help them to preserve the Catholic faith; but when none came Tyrone and O'Donnell sent a joint letter to Prince Philip asking him to intercede on their behalf with his father. They asked that the King might be persuaded to help 'this most excellent and just cause, that of assisting Catholic liberty and of freeing the country from the rod of tyrannical evil, and that, with the help of the Divine Majesty, he may win for Christ an infinite number of souls, snatching them from the jaws of hell, and may wholly destroy or compel to return to reason the ministers of satanic fury and the impious disturbers of the Christian state.'

It was an appeal that was difficult to ignore. Two Spanish officers had brought back a precise statement of what Tyrone wanted. He had men, already far more than the English; but most were untrained and nearly all lacked arms. A stiffening of Spanish troops would set the country aflame.

One can picture the long sessions of the night during which this matter was debated by the *Junta de Noche* in Philip's simple study in the Escorial. The flickering candles, the windows open to the soft September night, the old King crouched behind his desk fingering his crucifix, one foot up on the stool to ease his gout; his close advisers seated in stiff wooden armchairs around the desk, two or three personal secretaries hovering in the shadows, the crackle of parchment, the scratch of quill, the dry murmur of responsible voices, a shaft or two of moonlight, colder than the candles, falling on the blue Talavera tiles.

In that room, after much weighing of the risks and opportunities, the decision was made that this time the Second Armada should indeed sail to Ireland. It was not an unwise decision, if the Armada had to sail that year at all; for the maximum embarrassment would be caused to the Protestant cause at the minimum risk. It was unlikely that there would be a fleet action of any sort, so if the fleet sailed in an incomplete condition the consequences need not be so serious. Troops and supplies the Irish wanted. A single voyage of the fleet to Sligo or Galway would carry a sufficient army with all provisions for a campaign and land it on friendly soil. The Armada would then return to Spain, and during the winter regular supplies could be ferried up from Coruña and Blavet. By the summer of '97 another armada could be got ready to invade England.

So with remarkable speed for those days a scratch armada was assembled in San Lucar and in Lisbon and made ready to sail in October. It was to consist of over one hundred ships, with some thirty galleons including the remaining eight 'Apostles'; and picked regiments of soldiers were withdrawn from Flanders and Spain to man it. The number sailing was nine thousand Spanish and three thousand Portuguese, and it was arranged that more soldiers should join it from Brittany. New galleons were being built in most of the Biscay ports, but these would not be ready in time. Pedro de Valdes, newly released from his long exile in England, where he said there was much war-weariness and desire for peace, requested that he might go as vice-admiral, but this post, not unnaturally, was refused him. Only de Bertendona and Arumburu of the former officers were given important commands.

Even for this, the smallest of the three main armadas, the preparations were immense, the provisioning a mountainous achievement of the Spanish commissariat. A list of provisions shipped – published by the Spanish Ministry in October – includes 12,837 barrels of biscuits, 696 skins of wine, 1,498 barrels of salt pork, 1,031 barrels of fish, 6,082 barrels of cheese, 2,858 barrels of vegetables, 2,900 barrels of oil, 850 barrels of vinegar, 2,274 barrels of water, 631 barrels of rice; this apart from the requirements of war such as 1,200 barrels of powder, 30,000 cannon balls, 1,300 bullets, 700 cables, 200 wheels, and 50 wagons.

In England, which had as excellent a spy system as Spain, news of the coming reprisal was soon received. For all the striking success of the capture of Cadiz, the financial gain to England – as against the loss to Spain – had been small, and Elizabeth had been bitterly disappointed, for she too desperately needed the money for survival. So, for economy, the fleet had once again been laid up at Chatham, the soldiers disbanded; Vere had been sent back to the Netherlands with the crack regiments, and England again lay relatively undefended. Nor were Pedro de Valdes's reports of war-weariness so wide of the mark. From 1594 onwards had been years of great rainfall in England, with corn rotting in the fields and grain at famine prices. 'Our July is like to February,' people said. In Devon in midsummer 1596 wheat was nine shillings a bushel, which one might multiply forty times to arrive at a modern equivalent. Although there was undiminished loyalty to the Queen and great pride in such adventures as that at Cadiz, this was matched by wide discontent throughout the country over the conditions of day-to-day living, with dispossessed farmers, ruined smallholders, and crime and vagabondage everywhere. Areas of the country were becoming waste land for lack of cultivation, villages were emptying and falling into ruin, beggars were crowding into the coastal towns. Justices of the Peace were urged to go back and live in their country houses and to care for the poor of their own parishes; but they themselves were hard hit by the double subsidies imposed by parliament, by having to pay for the musters and trained bands of their parishes, by trying to enforce unenforceable laws in dealing with desperate and starving men.

But once more the cumbersome and hideously expensive processes of mobilization had to be gone through to try to avert the threatened invasion. Two thousand veteran soldiers bound for Picardy under Sir Thomas Baskerville were halted at Dover, Sir Samuel Bagnal was posted to defend the Isle of Wight, Ralegh hastened down to Cornwall, ten of the best of the bigger warships were recommissioned, and relays of dispatch boats were kept at sea to give warning of the enemy's approach.

The problem was, as in 1588, that no one knew where the blow would fall. At a council-of-war summoned by the Queen, Essex said he expected the Spaniards once again to attempt the Isle of Wight or the Margate coast. Lord Burghley thought they would attack Falmouth. Willoughby thought it would be Ireland, Lord North thought the Isle of Wight, Sir William Knollys said Plymouth, Ralegh said the Thames, Carew agreed with Essex. So all through a wild November the country was on the alert. The weather at times was so bad that even the screen of scouting vessels could not get out of port, and they the most weatherly of ships.

In fact by then, though no one knew it, the danger for that year was past. On the 24th October the Adelantado had set sail from Lisbon with his unfinished but still formidable Armada. In vain he had protested to the King that the season was already too late: no ships in those days, not even the English, made war in November. It was inviting disaster. But the King would brook no delays so the fleet sailed, and four days out disaster duly struck. Off the north Portuguese coast a storm, violent even for that month of storms, blew in from the west. It was worse than anything dreamed of in 1588, and in a matter of days the Armada was destroyed. Seven galleons were wrecked between Finisterre and Santander, and twenty-five armed merchant ships and forty other vessels. Three thousand men were drowned, among them many Irish, Catholic English, friars and Jesuit priests.

It was the end of the King's hopes, of Spain's hopes, and

indeed of Tyrone's hopes, for another year. The Protestant God was still looking after the heretics.

As 1597 dawned it became clear that both countries, though weary and impoverished by the long war, were building up for a final trial of strength. The destruction of the Second Armada had not in any way weakened Philip's resolution, nor, for that matter, that of his ministers and intimates. The Adelantado himself saw this year as the one in which the errors and short-comings of last year should be repaired. In the spring the Third Armada would begin to assemble in Lisbon and in Coruña and this time it would all be ordered differently. Early in the year an expert pilot was dispatched in a vessel trading under the French flag to make a new and full survey of the English coast. When completed the report filled eighteen sheets of parchment and covered all the most useful harbours from Liverpool in the north-west, through Chester, Milford Haven and Bristol, right round the coast to Scarborough, Newcastle and Berwick in the north-east.

Liverpool is described as 'a good harbour after entering within, broad and deep, but the entry is dangerous and to be approached by soundings; it is encircled by sand banks. There are many Catholics in this region . . . The mouth of the harbour at low water has six fathoms and four within. There is room for 300 ships. The land is inhabited but there is no fortress there. There is water, meat, bread, an abundant countryside and everything is priced cheaply.'

North of Milford Haven 'is a bad coastline, and on this account every year many of those fishing for herring are lost. Milford is the finest port in England; sixteen fathoms at the mouth and within there are seven or eight fathoms . . . There is no fortress and but one tower at the entrance. On the right side it usually has two pieces of artillery, but these cannot prevent an entry. It is six leagues to the head of the river. There is an open village, with water, meat and grain in abundance. There are many Catholics and the people are the natural enemies of the English and do not speak their language.'

The document was sent to Philip, who consulted with his ministers but for the present kept his own counsel. He had ideas for the Third Armada as definite as for the First, for he had not forgotten the outstanding success of the galleys at

Mousehole and Penzance. So that part of the pilots' report which privately he must have studied most closely ran as follows:

> From Cape Lizard to Falmouth is eight leagues. At the fourth league care must be paid to the rocks which are called Manacles, which are on the shore side.
>
> On the left side before entering Falmouth there is a harbour called Helford. At low water there is six foot at the mouth and at high tide twenty-four feet; within at low water there is four fathoms. The harbour has room for 200 ships. The port is a haven for the corsairs and robbers of England, for there is not any fortress to restrain them.
>
> In the middle of Falmouth harbour there is a rock named Falmouth which can be passed on one side or the other. There are four fathoms at the mouth at low water, and, within, it is eighteen fathoms. It will hold any number of ships. At the two points of the harbour there are two castles, one at each shore, with much artillery. On the right side it is flat, but both reach to the middle of the channel. Care must be had of some shoals on the right side after passing the isle. Almost all the artillery is emplaced outside of the two castles together with their gabions. They can be taken by land with a small party of men. There is a large population, but it is not warlike. There is water, meat and grain.

Queen Elizabeth was now sixty-four – and a vigorous and healthy sixty-four at that. Paul Hentzer, a foreign traveller in England, writes of a visit he paid to her that year at Greenwich. He was met at the door of the hall by a gentleman 'dressed in velvet, with a gold chain, whose office was to introduce people to the Queen'. In the hall were a large number of people, including the Archbishop of Canterbury, the Bishop of London, most of the Privy Counsellors, and officers of the Crown and other gentlemen. When the Queen came in she was attended by 'Barons, Earls, Knights of the Garter, all richly dressed and bareheaded, followed by the Lord High Chancellor of England with two other gentlemen, one carrying the royal sceptre, the other the sword of state in a red scabbard studded with fleur-de-lys'. The Queen, he says, was 'very majestic, her face oblong, fair but wrinkled, her eyes small, jet black and pleasant, her nose a little hooked, her lips narrow, her teeth black'. She had two pearls in her ears, an auburn wig set with a small crown, her bosom was uncovered, as was the English fashion with all ladies until they married, she was of medium height, her hands slender, her fingers long. She was 'dressed in white silk bordered with pearls the size of beans, with a mantle of black silk shot with silver threads, her train was long and borne by a marchioness'. She spoke very graciously as she went along, in English, French and Italian. 'Whoever she speaks to is kneeling, unless she raises them up. Sometimes she pulls off her glove as a special favour for her hand to be kissed; then it is seen to be sparkling with rings and jewels.' Wherever she turned her face they fell on their knees, saying: 'God save the Queen!' To which she replied: 'I thank you, my good people.'

At dinner that afternoon – the Queen now having retired – a gentleman came in bearing a rod, and another carried a tablecloth and spread this upon the table with great veneration and then retreated. Two others followed, one again with a rod, the other with a salt-cellar and plate and bread. Then 'a beautiful young lady (a countess) and another older woman' came with a tasting fork and rubbed the plates with bread and salt with 'as much reverence as if the Queen were there'. Then the Yeomen of the Guard came in, a hundred of the biggest men in England, bearing at each turn a course of twenty-four dishes, served on silver-gilt. These were received by one of the first gentlemen and put on the table, where 'a Lady tastes a mouthful of each dish that he brought, for fear of poison. During all this, twelve trumpets and two kettle-drums make the hall ring for half an hour'. At the end of this a number of the Ladies in Waiting appeared to convey the food to the Queen's inner chamber for her to make her choice. The rest of the food went to the ladies of the court. 'The Queen dines alone with very few attendants.'

Round the Queen at this time, among her counsellors, an unusual and unexpected harmony prevailed, particularly with regard to England's foreign policy. Burghley and his second son, Robert Cecil – recently created Secretary of State – though seeing peace with Spain as their ultimate objective, sided for once with the two fire-eaters: Essex, soon to be Earl Marshal of England, and Ralegh, just restored to his old post as Captain of the Queen's guard. The latter two wanted to defeat Spain; the first two thought that one more blow now would bring a reconciliation nearer.

It is also possible that the quietly calculating Robert Cecil knew that naval adventurers abroad involved not only physical hazard for the leaders but also – if they failed – damaged prestige. His position close to the Queen could hardly fail to become closer while her two favourites were off fighting the country's wars.

So unanimity of counsel persuaded the Queen to sanction another expedition similar to last year's. But its destination this year must be Ferrol, where the bulk of the new armada was assembling. After that the intention was to seize Terceira in the Azores and cut off the year's treasure-flota. When this was planned it was also intended that a strategic reserve of some of the most powerful warships should be kept ready at Chatham, as in 1588, as a second guard against the Armada; but sheer lack of money and supplies prevented these ships from being commissioned. Indeed, a request made to the City of London – usually the most willing of donors – for a squadron to augment the royal fleet was met with an apologetic excuse and a plea of complete impoverishment.

This time, the Lord Admiral Howard pleading his age not to go, the expedition was to be led by Essex in undivided command, with Lord Thomas Howard as Vice-Admiral, Ralegh as Rear-Admiral and Admiral Van Duyvenvoord again leading a Dutch squadron. Although Sir Francis Vere went as Marshal, the military command was given, much to Vere's chagrin, to Lord Mountjoy, one of Elizabeth's younger favourites.

In France in March the Spanish under Archduke Albert took Amiens, and Henry IV's position was materially weakened. Then the Spanish turned and threatened Boulogne. There was a partial mobilization in England to meet the new threat, and for a time it seemed that the old familiar counterstresses of the long war would prevent the naval expedition from sailing. But as in the previous year the English refused to be diverted and the fleet preparations went ahead. Seventeen royal warships – of which two were the Spanish 'Apostles' captured at Cadiz and modified to meet English ideas – twenty-four Dutch warships, a similar number of transports and supply ships and various ancillary vessels, made a total of ninety-eight, carrying six thousand soldiers and five thousand sailors.

It was the objective of both Philip and Elizabeth to be the first to strike; and news of the assembling fleet reached Coruña in May where the Adelantado was struggling to get the Third Armada into shape. But the Groyne, though an admirable harbour, was too distant from the centres of Spanish administration, and the accumulation of supplies went on with desperate slowness, for as soon as they were assembled they were consumed. Sailors deserted even faster than they did in England, and too many already lived in too confined a space, so that disease was epidemic. About the bare hillsides the soldiers camped in tents, talking in a half dozen languages and dialects, spending their leisure dicing or sleeping, swearing or drinking or whoring, while the priests kept their temporary chapels open for Mass all day long, the militia patrolled, and the white dust settled over all.

The harbour of Ferrol, which is twelve miles from Coruña, is approached through a narrow channel that can be guarded from the rocks on either side, and it is even more defensible than Cadiz. When the news reached Padilla that the English fleet would be ready well before his own, he put out a screen of guard-boats, manned mainly by Ragusans – for he was desperately short of good Spanish sailors – and stationed four of his oldest and biggest merchant-ships ready to block the harbour entrance in case of surprise.

Ferrol was not of course to provide the fleet, but it was to be the assembly point and the nucleus. The galleys of Genoa were to make their way there under Prince Andrea Doria; also a strong Andalusian squadron under Don Marcos de Arumburu, with smaller contingents from Naples, Guipuzcoa, Vizcaya and Vigo. In the meantime the main fleet, under the supreme direction of the Adelantado, was to be led by Don Diego Brochero, Knight of the Order of St John of Jerusalem, and a man who in vigour and experience matched the Recalde of 1588. About forty-eight at this time, he had had a chequered career, having at one time served a prison sentence for privateering with his own galleon in the Mediterranean. An energetic advocate of reform in the Spanish navy, he was known as a leader of great courage and resource.

Below him, after Bertendona, were the new men : Urquiola, Oliste, Villaviciosa and Zubiaur. The last of these, a hardy and adventurous Basque of fifty-five, had been at sea since he was sixteen, but had interspersed his maritime life with periods spent in England. Coming first in 1580, as 'a merchant of Seville', overtly to negotiate the restoration of, or compensation for, some of the plunder brought to England by Drake, Zubiaur in fact had remained as a spy, reporting direct to Philip and by-passing Mendoza, the then Spanish Ambassador.

Implicated in one of the unsuccessful attempts to assassinate William of Orange, he had been in and out of English prisons during the next few years, and in 1585 had been sent to the Tower for being involved in a plot to seize Flushing (from the early days a centre of Dutch resistance) and other activities directed against the state. After two years, during which he was tortured, he had been exchanged for English prisoners, and at the time of the First Armada was in Flanders. After he made his way home, and after the Spanish landing in Brittany, he had been put in charge of the Biscayan galleys which with notable success had for five years ferried supplies and reinforcements up to Blavet from the Spanish ports.

And behind the scenes of the Third Armada was the influential Captain Pedro Lopez de Soto, the newly appointed Secretary to the Adelantado, a fanatic to get to sea and a man in constant personal touch with the King. Indeed, such were his activities, that he might be looked on as approximating to the dark-suited man in the modern police state sitting behind the commander to see that he keeps up to scratch and toes the party line. In his confidential letters to the King de Soto frequently remarks that the Adelantado's complaints about lack of supplies and the unreadiness of the fleet are exaggerated and defeatist and should be ignored.

In the first week of July the English fleet, which had been pinned in Dover and Chatham by contrary and violent winds for nearly a month, at last managed to get as far as Weymouth, where it picked up reinforcements and supplies before moving on to Plymouth. It left Plymouth for Spain on the Sunday afternoon of the 10th July, but almost immediately was scattered by a short but violent storm, and each squadron became separated from the others. There was a brief interval of good weather and then a worse gale than ever blew up from the south-west and almost destroyed the English fleet. John Donne, who had again sailed hoping to find his fortune, found instead scope for his descriptive pen.

> Then note they the ship's sicknesses, the mast
> Shaked with this ague, and the hold and waste
> With a salt dropsy clogged, and all our tacklings
> Snapping, like too high stretched treble strings;
> And from our tattered sails, rags drop down so
> As from one hanged in chains a year ago.

Ralegh was blown back into Plymouth, trying successfully to save the two ex-Spanish galleons which stood the gale even less well than the English ships. Essex, after a contest lasting a day longer, put into Falmouth with his *Merhonour* sinking under him. Van Duyvenvoord lost touch with his own squadron trying to keep company with the damaged *Merhonour*, and returned to port with Essex. Thomas Howard and his squadron missed the absolute worst of the storm and arrived off Ferrol as arranged; he cruised up and down for several days, putting the Spanish defences into a panic, before despairing of his comrades and returning to England.

This storm, which seemed to suggest that after all God might be impartial, was a signal respite to the Spanish, for several of the English ships needed extensive repairs – the *Merhonour* in particular – before they could be considered seaworthy again; and the raw 'pressed' English seamen ran through the fingers like sand, as Ralegh put it. Many of the gentlemen adventurers went home too.

Howard's parade off Ferrol also lulled the English into a false sense of security. If the Adelantado could not come out to fight a half dozen English warships challenging him on his own doorstep – and this in July – there seemed little chance of his being ready to do anything offensive this year at all. So the leaders began to think less seriously of their original mission of attacking the assembling Armada, and more of capturing the treasure fleet again, or even of a West Indies raid in the old style of Drake. Even the news that the now famous Captain Pedro de Zubiaur had moved out of Ferrol and sailed along the Biscay coast to Blavet with seven galleys, some supply ships, and two thousand veteran soldiers did not seem to disturb them greatly, though the west country defences were strengthened against the possibility of another galley raid like last year's.

When the English fleet at last got to sea again in mid-August it was much more a naval adventure than the month previous; but Elizabeth had left her commanders in no doubt that they were still expected to attempt Ferrol before they went off on any adventures· in search of treasure fleets. She also insisted that Essex must not hazard his life in attacking the port, a prohibition which meant that Essex immediately lost interest in the attempt; and when transports were not ready to accompany the fleet, and there was a favourable wind, he insisted on sailing without them. It seems clear that despite the lack of success which had attended Drake's Lisbon voyage of 1589, the leaders were bent on following in his footsteps, and if at all possible they intended to find an excuse to disobey the Queen.

Again the weather was unseasonably violent and the fleet was scattered. Ralegh's *Warspite* lost a mainyard, the *Repulse*, with Essex in her now, was leaking badly, and the two ex-Spanish galleons were so damaged that they were only saved from wreck by taking refuge in La Rochelle. Then while the scattered ships were reassembling off Finisterre the wind set strongly east, making an attempt to beat back to Ferrol a long and difficult process. This was the excuse Essex needed, and after a brief consultation he followed Ralegh and Howard to Lisbon.

Cruising off there, attempting to catch one of the small Lisbon carvels to pick up information, they stopped instead an English barque which told them that Ferrol was in fact empty of their prey and that the Adelantado and most of the Armada were in the Azores to cover the return of the treasure-fleet. Whether the captain of the barque was misinformed or whether he was one of the renegades such as Burley and Elliot, deliberately sent out to spread false news, it is impossible to tell. But the news so exactly suited the commanders of the English fleet that they immediately and gladly acted on it. By the time the various units reached the Azores and assembled there it was the 18th September.

14

The Third Armada

It did not seem to occur to anyone in the English fleet that the reason the Adelantado did not respond to Lord Thomas Howard's challenge was that he would not hazard some of his ships in a small an' indecisive action off his own coast, nor did he wish to betray his strength or preparedness – or lack of it – to a scouting squadron of the enemy. The English assumed his weakness – and later his absence.

And the English at home felt equally secure, waiting for news of some feat of arms from their own fleet, not at all worried, as they had been last year, about a possible visit from the Spanish. Sir Henry Palmer, in charge of a small Channel squadron – the only defensive squadron at sea – was ill, and his place had been taken by Sir John Gilbert. The rest of the Queen's ships were out of commission at Chatham. The military defences of the country, though in a far better state of organization than in 1588, were not on the alert.

In 1588 every Englishman knew that the great Spanish *Empresa* was coming to attack them. It was common knowledge throughout Europe, and everyone in England was at the stretch to meet the threat. Bonfires were tended and beacons manned day and night. The whole English fleet was either mobilized or on the verge of mobilization. In 1597 no one suspected or feared an imminent attack. If surprise is half the battle, then the Adelantado had a battle half won.

But in spite of an urgent command from Philip, who saw the possibilities plain, Padilla took his time. He still did not know his destination. No one in the fleet did – it was a matter on which even de Soto bitterly complained to the King. But intensive preparations were still going ahead. Every ship had been issued with an English flag, and all carried English-speaking personnel. The Proclamation still exists which was printed for the Adelantado for distribution and exhibition when he landed in England. It is the first printing ever done in Portugal in the English language, and the text was obtained some time later by a Cornishman, one John Billett, master of a trading vessel, who called in at Coruña and brought the paper away hidden in his shoe. The Proclamation promises freedom and fair treatment for Catholics and for all who turn Catholic and calls on them to rally to the support of the Spanish invaders.

The reason for the Adelantado's delay in sailing in September is one of the most vital questions of the whole Anglo-Spanish war, and no absolute or single explanation can be given. For instance on the 4th July de Soto, writing one of his private letters to the King, says the fleet should be ready to sail by the middle of August with an effective landing in England on the 8th September. He gives the details of the ships available then: twenty-three large galleons, twenty-five smaller galleons, twenty-six supply boats, a number of galleyzabras and about seventy pinnaces to land soldiers rapidly – the force to consist of twenty thousand soldiers and four thousand sailors. And de Soto was on the spot in the midst of all the preparations, not writing airily from Madrid.

Yet in mid-September, when the greatest opportunity of the war presented itself, the fleet still remained in port. The reasons for the delay can only be speculatively listed: (1) The Adelantado was not only dealing with pressed men, as the English were, but with impounded ships and pressed captains. Whatever the hard core of Spanish fighting ships wanted to do, the Flemish and German hulks, the Italian and Ragusan supply ships, were not at all anxious to sail into those enemy waters where others of their kin had perished nine years ago. It is not easy to get a mixed fleet ready to sail as a unit when considerable parts of the unit are seeking cause for delay. (2) After a sudden and astounding return to health during the summer, when he went hunting and had a wild boar turned loose for his entertainment, the seventy-year-old Philip was taken ill in early September; and as always happens when one hand alone holds the power, the reins fell loose at a crucial stage. (3) The appearance of the English fleet off Lisbon had put Portugal in a panic, and at least until news was confirmed that the English had actually been decoyed to the Azores, Arumburu and his Andalusian squadron of eleven fine galleons dared not leave Lisbon undefended. Then contrary winds kept them embayed. (4) Rumours were widespread in Spain that England had sent ambassadors to Turkey attempting to form an alliance against Spain (a heretic banding with an infidel against the true faith), and in August it became known that thirty-four ships under Mami Pasha had left Constantinople and were cruising in the Mediterranean. This menace, combined with a sudden attack of French Protestants, who had advanced across the eastern Pyrenees into Catalonia, caused Prince Andrea Doria with his squadron of ships and three whole *tercios* of Italian veteran soldiers to halt at Lisbon and come no farther; and presently he returned to the Mediterranean.

The Adelantado, not unnaturally at first, waited for his expected reinforcements to come up: it is not in many admirals to want to sail with two-thirds of a fleet. But Philip, as soon as he recovered, sent an urgent messenger spurring across the dusty Sierras and the mountains of Galicia to instruct Padilla not to delay a moment longer but to leave at once. So embarkation began on the 25th September.

This took two days, and it was late in the morning of the 27th before the first galleon was able to make sail and be under way out of the narrow jaws of the harbour. The fleet had orders to assemble in Betanzos Bay, fifteen miles from Ferrol, and this took another thirty hours to complete in gusty and none too favourable weather. But there they at last were assembled in six lines, each line consisting of ten galleons of varying sizes and fourteen other ships, hulks, transports and flyboats; and there they were inspected by the Adelantado from a decorated barge rowed by twenty-four crimson-clad oarsmen. His own personal standard, a swallow-tailed flag in green silk, fluttered and dipped from the maintop of the *San Pablo* of twelve hundred tons. The whole fleet was dressed with flags and standards, and the men lined the decks and cheered and guns were fired as the supreme commander passed. According to Agostino Nani, the Venetian Ambassador, the fleet consisted of forty-four Royal galleons, sixteen private galleons and fifty-two urcas or hulks, of a total tonnage of thirty-five thousand. In addition there were seventy-six smaller ships, and the complement was four thousand sailors and eight thousand six hundred and thirty-four soldiers, besides three hundred horses, together with mules, carts, mills, field artillery and siege material. Some historians put the final muster even higher than this. In Cheyney's words, it was 'scarcely less in strength than the Armada of 1588'.

Even then there was a hesitation before sailing, for the weather was poor and the winds threatening, and they awaited

204

a flyboat from the Azores confirming the position of the English fleet. This arrived on the same day as a further message from Philip, now recovered. He promised that Arumburu and his Andalusian squadron would follow the Armada within a few days, but ordered that in the meantime the Adelantado must brook no further delay, and any captain who created difficulties was to be hanged from his own yard-arm.

Man proposes, but in the days of sail even a threatened admiral could not defy the winds, and that night a gale blew up that pinned the fleet within Betanzos Bay for six more days, and it was the 9th October before at last the weather set fair and they were able to get away.

And at last the Adelantado was permitted to open his sealed orders.

He was to proceed to Falmouth and land his troops there. It was perhaps the best kept secret of the sixteenth century, and only four men apart from Philip knew what was in the sealed letter before it was opened. Once he had gained possession of Falmouth and left eight thousand troops in occupation of the peninsula, Padilla was to return to the Scillies and catch the English fleet on its way home, since he was enormously more powerful than they. But he was given freedom of action in this, depending on weather conditions, the success of the landing at Falmouth and what naval opposition, if any, he encountered in the Channel.

The fleet went on its way now with high hopes and in fine favourable weather. The first squadron was led by Don Martin de Padilla himself flying his green cleft pennant; the second by his vice-admiral, Don Diego Brochero in the *San Pedro*, of one thousand tons, with a yellow flag; the third by Don Martin de Bertendona, with a scarlet flag, in the new *San Mateo*, of twelve hundred tons, just launched from the shipyards of Renteria to replace the one taken by the English at Cadiz. Orders were given that at sunset all ships of the fleet were to pass by the admiral's ship and to shout three times and sound their trumpets. Each ship as it passed was to ask the watchword for the night and what course to steer, and then to drop astern into its allotted position. The evening hymn to Our Lady, with her image held high, was to be followed by all lights out except those in the cabins of gentlemen, who had their lamps trimmed with water covered with oil to combat the lurching of the ship; but no candles were permitted for fear of fire. At the stern of the *San Pablo* a cresset with flaming combustibles was to burn so that everyone knew the Adelantado's ship and could follow. When the wind was too strong for the cresset, a large lantern with four lamps in it was to be used instead. Each sunrise there was a fanfare of trumpets, and the ships came up to salute again, the *San Pablo* keeping under sail until this was done. Then a *Missa Sicca* (dry Mass without consecration) was celebrated before the Armada proceeded on its way.

Fine weather and favourable winds took the fleet quickly to Blavet, where Captain Zubiaur was waiting with his seven galleys, his extra supply ships and his two thousand picked infantry. In easterly winds the fleet then made for the Scillies, and after assembling there and a final council-of-war, Don Diego Brochero led his squadron as the advance guard against Falmouth. With him was the eager Captain de Soto in command of the *Espiritu Santo*, one of the new galleyzabras of three hundred and fifty tons, three other galleons, three of the Zubiaur galleys, twelve flyboats and a half dozen supply ships.

Nobody in England knew anything about a Spanish Armada being out and almost on their coasts. The Lord Admiral Howard was about to be created Earl of Nottingham in reward for his distinguished services against the First Armada of 1588 and Cadiz last year. Parliament was meeting in leisurely session, and one of the subjects up for discussion was defence measures to be taken in the event of a Spanish attack the following year.

The security of that autumn in England is, as has been said, in the strangest contrast with the almost constant *qui vive* in which the country had lived for more than a decade. Only the year before there had been the partial mobilization and a recommissioning of the fleet against the Second Armada. All through 1598 there was acute apprehension; and in 1599 came the famous and most complete mobilization of all, when, as it turned out, no fleet of any sort sailed against England. On every other occasion throughout the long war Spanish preparations had been carefully observed and prepared against. Spies had brought news, fly-boats had scurried home. Drake was waiting on the Hoe playing his immortal game of bowls. The fine ships built by Hawkins were waiting to warp out into the Channel to attack the oncoming enemy.

Not so this time. Sir Ferdinando Gorges was in command at Plymouth, but he had no warships at all to send out to battle. Those that were not laid up in Chatham were, apart from the small squadron patrolling off North Foreland, far out with Essex in the Atlantic returning from the Azores after yet one more unsuccessful attempt on the treasure-flota.

But after all the Protestant winds came just in time to save the country. The weather steadily worsened during the last day of the Armada's advance from the Scillies, and, when only twenty miles off the Lizard, a violent north-easterly storm broke in the Channel and the flagship of the advance guard, the *San Pedro*, was so badly damaged that she had to drop out of station and run before the wind. This at once robbed the enterprise of its most aggressive admiral; though Brochero, as soon as his ship was in a Biscay port, put to sea again in a flyboat to try to rejoin the Armada. At the same time the Adelantado, half a day behind with the main fleet, tried to ride out the storm. But the storm would not relent. It blew unabated from the worst possible quarter for three days, and one by one the Spanish galleons however hard they fought were broken and had to give up the unequal struggle. The Adelantado hung on and refused to give way until of all his great fleet only four other ships remained with him; then he had no recourse but to return to Spain empty-handed, as he had the year before, defeated not by the enemy but by the autumnal storms.

A few of the advance squadron, however, rendezvoused off Falmouth, as they had been instructed to do if scattered, and the appearance of these ships was the first notification the English had of the peril in which they stood. At least two of the contemporary foreign accounts say that the Spanish landed seven hundred soldiers near Falmouth, and these threw up defences, held them for a day or so; then when the rest of their fleet did not come they withdrew again. No English account mentions this, and it seems very improbable that there would not be some record of it if it had occurred. It is possible that some Spanish troops may have briefly landed at Helford, that 'haven of corsairs and robbers', as the Spanish pilot calls it. There are also stories of a landing on the north Devon coast.

Whatever the case, panic prevailed in England. Parliament was prorogued, all English troops in France were recalled, mobilization of the western countries was decreed and the Lord Chamberlain, the second Lord Hunsdon, posted down to organize the levies there; the big warships in Chatham were ordered into commission, Sir Robert Crosse rushed to take command of the Channel squadron. It was a tremendous shock, a tremendous blow to confidence, that this emergency should occur when the whole of the commissioned English fleet was at sea and England daily expecting news of some great and glorious exploit of the Azores. It was exactly what Elizabeth had feared when listening to Drake's 'forward' policy in 1587 and 1588.

It is interesting to speculate what might have happened if, instead of the bitter and seemingly endless gale, there had been a couple of weeks of golden autumnal weather to aid the Adelantado in his plans. Certainly he would have landed at Falmouth and thrown ashore six or eight thousand troops with minimal or no loss. The captain of Pendennis Castle at the time, John Killigrew, though of a staunchly Protestant family, had lived a rake's progress for twelve years, getting even deeper in debt than his father, similarly bent, had left him. As the *Salisbury MS.* puts it:

Having brought himself into desperate case, he lived chiefly by oppressing his tenants, being a landlord in name only, by robbery of strangers in harbour there, by cosening his friends and neighbours, by selling her Majesty's provision of the Castle, by receiving of stolen goods, by consorting with pirates and abuse of his place and command.

The same MS. accuses him of treacherously conniving with the Spanish, a charge which, not unnaturally, he denies. In an MS. written some years after his death he is referred to as the man 'who sold his castle to the King of Spain'. Certainly the Spaniards looked on him as a friend; but, since his loyalty was never put to the final test, there is no proof of what his choice would have been. No charge was preferred against him in England, but as soon as the emergency was over he was called to London and imprisoned for the rest of his life, ostensibly for debt. In May 1598 he was writing that he had now been three months in the Gatehouse 'without knowing my offence'.

Whatever John Killigrew's choice, it could not have affected more than temporarily the Spanish landing, and, although the local population would no doubt have resisted where they could, there was no force in the west remotely capable of withstanding veteran troops skilfully deployed. In the meantime the English fleet was returning from the Azores with, apart from a feat of arms by Ralegh in capturing Fayal, nothing to show for its long and arduous voyage. The commanders were by now at odds with each other; the ships were making for home anyhow, as best they could, in ones and twos and in haphazard groups; sickness was rampant among the crews after so long at sea, and many ships were short-handed. Most of the battleships had stowed away their big guns in the hold to ease the strained timbers after all the storms. Certainly the straggling, disorderly squadrons were in no condition to fight a fleet action.

That English command of the narrow seas would have been quite soon re-established there seems no doubt. With the Channel squadron reinforced by the great ships hastily recommissioning at Chatham, and a Dutch squadron to assist, the Spanish fleet could hardly have maintained its temporary supremacy. But how soon the Spanish in Cornwall could have been dislodged is an open question. It would have been no more difficult to supply the forces in Cornwall by sea than it was those in the Low Countries; and the Genoese, Frederico Spinola, was to demonstrate in 1599 how that could be achieved by his masterly use of that outdated warship, the galley.

Conceivably the Spanish would have been content with a short occupation of a piece of England in retaliation for the seizure of Cadiz. Conceivably they would have attempted to hold it permanently as a forward base for the harassment of English trade. Or they might have used it as a bargaining counter to force an English withdrawal from the Continent. At the best they were still hoping, of course, for a Catholic rising which would put all England in their hands. But most English Catholics had made their choice in 1588, and the militant Romanists – those who would actually have taken up arms to fight for a foreign power – were few. In fact England in the last two decades had become rapidly more Protestant in thought and sympathy. Those with Heaven to gain combined with those with property to lose, and the union had been fused in the heat and peril of the Spanish war.

But the value to England of the storms which wrote off so many of the already defeated Armada of 1588 was as nothing compared to the great north-easterly gale of October 1597, which in fact sank only one galleon, the *San Bartolomeo*, but which alone protected the West Country from the horrors of a full-scale Spanish invasion.

The returning English fleet came back by instalments at the height of the scare. They had entirely missed contact with the Spanish in the wild waters of the Channel. Mountjoy was the first to come in at Plymouth on a change of wind with four of the Queen's galleons. They were all hardly used and the crews in a poor way, but their appearance caused an acute alarm. Soldiers rushed to the fortifications, people began to barricade their houses and prepared to fight as the Spanish had done at Cadiz. Not even the English flags fluttering at the mastheads could at first reassure them. On hearing of the emergency Mountjoy ordered the four ships to turn about and ride in the Hamoaze, to be able to put to sea again at once to meet the Adelantado if he came in. Essex, arriving the following day, sailed incautiously right up the Catwater, so was caught and could not get out again. Ralegh with part of his squadron put in at St Ives on the opposite coast; and on hearing of the emergency he landed and galloped overland to take charge of the defences of Cornwall. Lord Thomas Howard arrived at Plymouth, and other ships of the returning fleet were blown in at various south coast ports. Here and there a Spanish ship appeared, giving fight to small English coasters or themselves surrendering.

Essex was in his usual fever of impatience to be at the enemy's throat, and wrote an emotional letter to the Queen in which he offered to eat ropes' ends and drink nothing but rainwater until they were at sea again and able to destroy the Armada that threatened them. The Queen was not assuaged. Indeed she was bitterly angry, for all that she had so often feared had happened – she had been right and her blundering war-advisers had been wrong. The English fleet had cost an enormous amount to fit out, and it had achieved nothing, nothing. What was infinitely worse, its absence had deeply imperilled the kingdom. She swore to old Burghley that she would never again let a fleet out of home waters, and she did not.

She wrote to Essex: 'Seeing already by your late leaving the coast upon an uncertain probability that no army would come forth from Ferrol until March, you have given the enemy leisure and courage to attempt us.' She then charged him not to leave the coasts again on any pretext, 'whereby our own kingdom may lie open to serious dangers; but that you do proceed in this great affair according to the rules of advised deliberation as well as affection of zeal and diligence. For treasure, for victual, and what may be fit for us to send, you shall find that you serve a prince neither void of care nor judgment what to do that is fit in cases of this consequence.'

It was a dignified letter worthy of a great Queen, and when Essex posted up to court to explain his actions and to enumerate his needs he was greeted with an icy disapproval, which upset him deeply. After the emergency was seen to be fully past, he withdrew to nurse his injured dignity at Wanstead. It was the beginning of another break between them; each one cut deeper than the last and left a more memorable scar. Essex was growing out of the brilliant and impulsive boy, handsome, charmingly wayward, ineffably brave and gallant, the idol of the unthinking crowd; middle age was turning his impulsiveness into obstinacy, his high spirits into arrogance; his popularity with the crowd gave him delusions of greatness beyond even his attainment. The Queen was as astute as ever beneath her feminine fads, as clear-sighted as she had been when she came to the throne; but in her last years there were hints of that sombre unpredictability of mood with which her father had made his courtiers tremble for their lives half a century ago. Less than ever now was she a woman to be trifled with, and in Essex's underestimation of her – as he underestimated everybody but himself – lay the seeds of his eventual downfall.

15

The Fourth Armada

In February 1598 Martin de Bertendona, the most successful of all the Spanish admirals in their war against England, sailed up the Channel with twenty-eight ships of varying size and power and a complement of four thousand troops. They were destined for Calais, and they reached there unchallenged and for most of the voyage as unannounced as the Adelantado's great Armada of the previous October. When news of this fleet reached England there was another emergency. Essex and Ralegh went hurriedly down to the south coast. The Earl of Cumberland, who was just off on a privateering raid with a small but sturdy squadron, was ordered to reinforce the Channel Guard.

But a landing was not attempted. The troops were intended as a reinforcement not only of the Calais garrison but of the bargaining power of Philip in his new negotiations with Henry of France – a show of the iron hand still available if Henry were not amenable to the velvet glove. And, like the escape of the German warships, the *Goeben* and the *Breslau*, into Turkish waters in 1914, the success of the stroke served to upset the whole delicate balance of power. France was half seduced, half intimidated into signing a peace treaty with her old enemy. Cecil, who had been about to sail to bolster up the weakening resolves of Henry with more promises of English and Dutch support, and was delayed by the advent of Bertendona, arrived in Paris too late to prevent the collapse of the old alliance. The Peace of Vervins was signed in late April.

When Elizabeth heard of it she called Henry, whom she had supported for so many years, 'the Antichrist of Ingratitude'.

But at Vervins in 1598 Henry gained almost as much by changing friends as in 1593 he had gained by changing religions. Both were primarily political moves to gain great objectives – they would have been betrayals of principle only in a more

212

principled man. In 1596 Henry wrote: 'I have hardly a horse on which I can fight. My doublets have holes at the elbows and my pot is often empty.' A contemporary estimated that in the twenty years up to 1598 nearly a million French had died in wars and massacres; nine cities had been completely destroyed, two hundred and fifty villages burned, one hundred and fifty thousand houses reduced to rubble. It was a situation which Henry was determined to redeem or perish. By the Edict of Nantes he had already granted a large measure of tolerance and freedom to both religions in France, thereby reducing the likelihood of a return to the bloody civil wars. Now by the Treaty of Vervins the Spanish agreed to evacuate Picardy and Calais, to leave Brittany, to give up Blavet, to recognize Henry as legitimate King of France; and received in return only a recognition of their own rights in Burgundy, which, however, they promised not to assert by force of arms. For Spain it was a great strategic withdrawal, partly balanced by a diplomatic success. For France it was a major victory on all counts.

It removed from England the most obvious danger of a fourth Spanish Armada, but it deprived England for ever of the return of Calais, something dear to the hearts of most sixteenth-century Englishmen; and it marked the re-emergence of a strong and no longer necessarily friendly France. In justice to Henry it must be said that he had made some half-hearted efforts to include his old allies, but Spanish terms for the Dutch provinces were still unacceptable to the Dutch and England would not desert the Netherlands.

Nor now would the Netherlands desert England. In the last few years, so rapid had been the expansion, commercially and militarily, of the United Provinces that an Anglo-Dutch alliance, instead of being the greater supporting the weaker, was becoming an association of equals. Within months of the Franco-Spanish peace, the English and the Dutch signed a new treaty whereby the Dutch agreed to repay the Queen by large instalments all the money loaned them and also all the expenses incurred in their defence over the years. If the Spanish fleet were to attack England the Dutch undertook to supply forty warships for its defence, and, if the Spanish landed, five thousand infantry and five hundred cavalry, all at Holland's own expense. Moreover, if the Queen wished to send another expedition against Spain the Netherlands promised to contribute an equal number of ships and men. It was a striking proclamation of the growth of Dutch power, which in the next century was to make Holland one of the most prosperous countries in the world and was to see the founding of the Dutch East India Company and the establishment of the great empire in the Netherlands Indies.

On the 4th August Lord Burghley, Elizabeth's oldest and most trusted counsellor, died at the age of seventy-eight. Her Spirit, she had always called him; and at the last, trying to rally him, she fed him with her own hand. With old adversaries and old friends dying about her, the Queen must have felt more than ever her lonely eminence. It was not now just a regal eminence but one which comes to all who live beyond their generation. So many had gone from around her: her beloved Robert Leicester, embittering the triumph of the Armada year; then Walsingham and Warwick, Frobisher and Drake and Hawkins, Hatton and Shrewsbury and the elder Hunsdon. Now Burghley. All about her were younger people, eager, thrusting, loyal, but *younger*, belonging inevitably to another world, without her *memories*. Who but she could remember her father, his later wives, her brother, her sister? There was none she could talk to in the old way, except Lady Warwick and old Lady Nottingham, the Lord Admiral's wife. Before this sort of loneliness even the disaster of war loses its importance.

Yet the responsibilities of kingship must go on, so long as life lasted, and she was giving up none of them. In her grief she found time to write James of Scotland a stinging letter rebuking him for having had the impertinence to send envoys to Europe asserting his reversionary rights. Let him beware, or the English crown could still be snatched from his feeble grasp. Then, only ten days after Burghley's death, news reached the English court of a defeat in Ireland, one of the gravest ever suffered. Sir Henry Bagnal, marching with four thousand men to the relief of a besieged fort on the Blackwater, had been utterly defeated by Tyrone in a pitched battle, with the resulting death of Bagnal himself, thirteen other officers and about fiften hundred men. With this victory resounding through Ireland a rebellion at once broke out, and, according to the *Annals of the Four Masters*, within seventeen days 'there was not an Anglo-Saxon left alive in all the Desmond domains'.

It was a situation which must be redeemed as quickly as possible by the dispatch of fresh troops; for such open rebellion as now existed was the perfect opportunity for Spanish intervention. (Just as Elizabeth had intervened in the Netherlands in 1585.)

Philip did in fact send a hearty message of congratulation to the triumphant Tyrone; even the Pope sent a crown of peacock's feathers; but unfortunately for the Irish earl Philip II was at last dying.

He had spent the winter in Madrid, still, with the help of his few intimates, holding tight to the reins of his empire. He had had the Adelantado before him to make a full report on the failure of the Third Armada and to receive instructions for the preparation of a fourth, to sail in the coming summer. But when spring came he was so ill that his doctors would not allow him to return to the Escorial. At the end of June he defied them and announced his intention of going there to die, 'to lay my bones in my own house'.

So he was carried on a litter in great pain, it taking six days to cover the thirty-one miles. He now had four suppurating sores on the fingers of his right hand, another on his foot and an abscess on his right knee, from which could be pressed great quantities of foul smelling matter 'as thick as plaster of Paris'. He could not sleep or eat and his stomach was distended with dropsy. In this condition he remained for fifty-three days. After a while it became impossible to change the bed-clothes or his night-robe, and, following the purges given by his doctors, he lay for the last days in his own excrement, surrounded by swarms of flies and overrun with vermin, his eyes fixed on the high altar in the great church, thanking God for the pain and the humiliations. 'Look at me,' he said to his son. 'This is what the world and all kingdoms amount to in the end.' Dr Affaro who attended him, and the thirty-year-old Infanta, about to marry the Archduke Albert, were both taken ill from the insufferable stench in the sick-room. He died, holding a crucifix firmly in his hands, at dawn on the 13th September 1598.

So died the first of the two great monarchs who had confronted each other across a war-torn Europe for exactly forty years, and who for the last ten had themselves been in open conflict. It is impossible to summarize the character of Philip. To the Protestant world he was a monster of evil, cold-blooded, vengeful, cruel, spinning his intolerable webs, a symbol of the Inquisition and the *Auto-da-Fé*, the 'Spanish fury' and the iron hand of oppression. In the Catholic world outside his own country he had always been unpopular, representing the slow-moving but irresistible colossus, the enemy of small freedoms as well as large, the military dictator, the religious bigot who yet used religion for the aggrandizement of his own state.

Nevertheless in Spain itself he was esteemed and popular and held in warm affection by his subjects. He represented so much that the Spanish people revered and prized, and under his rule they remained a united nation proud of their eminence as the masters of Europe. Yet even in his own country his reign was riddled with contradictions. When he came to the throne his father was already heavily in debt, so he put up titles for sale at five thousand ducats a head and in this way added a thousand petty new noblemen to the many who had already existed. The building of the Escorial cost three million five hundred thousand ducats over two decades; in it he assembled one of the finest libraries and one of the greatest art collections in the world. Under him poetry, literature, music and art flourished, and the golden age of Spanish painting began. Yet, although he commissioned Titian to paint a series of religious masterpieces for the Escorial, Titian complained to the end of his long life that he had not been fully paid for them. And when Titian's favourite pupil, the Cretan Domenicos Theotocopoulos, moved to Spain and settled in Toledo, there to become known simply as The Greek, or El Greco, Philip first commissioned him to paint exclusively for the Escorial, and then, not liking the first two paintings, cold-shouldered him and gave the work to a relative nonentity.

Philip converted Madrid, an old fortified town standing on a spur of rising ground at the foot of the Guadarrama Mountains high above the sea, into his new capital city, and rebuilt it. He fought an interminable war, lost his battles against the Protestants, unified the Iberian peninsula, saved the Mediterranean countries from the Turk. He gave his name to the Philippine Islands, where the Spanish conquest and rule was unusually mild and beneficient. He devotedly loved his children; yet when his eldest son began to show signs of the family insanity, he had him shut up in a room from which the young man never emerged alive.

Personally fastidious, quiet and modest, by turns kindly and cruel, forgiving and revengeful, he would not allow anyone to write his biography because he thought this an evidence of worldly vanity. Yet in the midst of all his war expenditure, when Spain was twice bankrupt, it never occurred to him to cut down on the vast cost of his own household, which absorbed over seven per cent of the total income of the nation and comprised more than fifteen hundred persons. Under his parental rule for forty-three years Spain suffered no serious invasion, no rebellions – except one Moorish one – within its own frontiers, no religious schisms. Yet everyone in the country groaned under taxes or the results of taxes; men went overseas to fight or for conquest and the fields they left behind grew rank and untended. The King planted twenty thousand trees, but they were intended only for timber for his galleons. During his reign the population fell from ten million to eight million. The condition of the countryside is not exaggerated in *Don Quixote*. Although the monasteries and convents prospered, the inns were in ruin, so that travellers could hardly find a bed to rest in; roads, such as there had been, became rutted tracks, rivers were silted up.

A lover of flowers and music and dancing, Philip lived much of his life in a gloomy austerity that could hardly have failed to satisfy the most convinced Calvinist. A personal renunciation of the world within his palace doors went hand in hand with a rigid, fanatical determination to continue to control every aspect of the world outside. In his later years in particular, he lived in absolute piety, and once, it is said, spent three consecutive days making his confession. He died full of self-contrition for his sins against God but without a trace of self-doubt about any sin against man. It was a source of genuine remorse to him that he had frequently not carried out God's will with sufficient fervour. It did not occur to him ever to wonder if sometimes he might be confusing God's will with his own.

The war did not end with Philip. Elizabeth said of his son: 'I am not afraid of a King of Spain who has been up to the age of twelve learning his alphabet', but, after an initial period of irresolution, reports began to come in of a new vigour being injected into Spain's military and naval plans by Philip III's advisers. Indeed, the Adelantado, who had suffered a great deal of frustration and intimidation from the old king, remarked that the world would now see what Spaniards could do when they were no longer subject to a ruler who thought he knew everything and treated everyone else as a blockhead.

In England efforts were being made to retrieve the situation in Ireland. By the end of March 1599 Essex, chosen after much ill-tempered discussion and intrigue to lead the relief troops, was in Dublin with the largest expeditionary force ever to leave England in Elizabeth's lifetime: seventeen thousand infantry and thirteen hundred cavalry. Part of the fleet, ten of its largest ships, were commissioned to protect the transportation of so important an army; but it was not used, for the Dutch informed Elizabeth that they were sending a separate fleet of seventy ships against Spain to attack Coruña. This was partly provoked by new measures in Spain putting an end to the commercial trade between Spain and the Netherlands which Philip II had wisely tolerated; but the fact that Holland could now mount such a naval offensive was a mark of her rapid emergence as a power in her own right. The attack on Coruña was a failure, but the English rightly reasoned that with the Dutch fleet at sea Spain would be too busy to launch another armada against England.

So Essex transported his troops in safety and misused them so badly that by September he was back in England, to be cast into prison in the penultimate act of his life's tragedy. And his friend Mountjoy took his place and was as startlingly successful as Essex – and many others before him – had been a failure.

By July 1599 the Adelantado under his new master had concentrated once again a force of ships and armoury at Coruña. Thirty-eight galleons and great ships, fifty supply vessels, eight thousand troops, twenty-three galleys, again commanded by the seasoned admirals of the '96 and '97 Armadas: Brochero, Zubiaur, Bertendona, Villaviciosa and Oliste. News of these intensive preparations reached England at the same time as word of the complete failure of the Dutch fleet to damage the port, and in the middle of the month Captain George Fenner, perhaps the most distinguished seaman England had left, sailing in the *Dreadnought*, with Captain Matthew Bredgate in the *Swiftsure*, returned to Plymouth from a cruise in Biscayan waters with the news that the Adelantado was about to sail. His numbers were exaggerated to one hundred warships, seventy galleys and fifteen thousand troops.

The English council ordered instant mobilization, and panic ran through the country. By the first week in August much of the English fleet was ready for sea and troops were pouring into the old Armada camp at Tilbury. On the rumour that the

Spanish had already landed, chains were strung across the streets in London and coast towns, men barricaded their houses, levies rushed to their stations. Ralegh and Howard, Carew and Grenville worked night and day to bring the country to a state of preparedness, and thirty thousand troops were concentrated on London; the whole of the south of England was on its feet. It was said that Philip III had himself sailed with his Armada and that he had vowed that he would 'make his finger heavier for England than his father's whole body'.

Rumour and counter-rumour flew, and Howard put to sea with twelve of the Queen's largest warships, fourteen of the new smaller vessels called 'crompsters', and a dozen armed merchantmen. In the Downs he was joined by the Channel squadron under Sir Richard Leveson and by a Dutch squadron of twelve ships with a promise of sixteen more under Justin of Nassau. It was nevertheless a puny force to pit against the reported fleet which had set out from Spain.

But the Armada never came; nor did it ever approach the Channel. Six Spanish galleys only appeared; but it was the returning Dutch fleet – worn out with months at sea and decimated by disease – which, seen through the Channel mists, gave rise to the rumour that the Spanish had already arrived. In fact the Dutch, although they had failed at Coruña, had succeeded in diverting the Spaniards by sailing on to the Canaries and capturing Las Palmas. From there it was likely that they would attempt the Azores and the treasure-fleets, so the Adelantado, ready to sail for England, at the last moment had his orders countermanded and was directed to the Azores instead.

It seems certain that the excessive sensitiveness of the English in 1599 was caused by the near miss of the 1597 Armada – they must never, they knew, be so caught again. It was an enormous expense to counter a false alarm, and people murmured and bitterly complained; but at least it was a full-dress rehearsal if the play were ever to be put on, and it did prove not only to themselves but to Spain and all Europe how vastly the organization for mobilizing England's strength had improved since 1588.

The six galleys which appeared in the Channel were no part of the Adelantado's fleet at all but were commanded by the young Genoese Frederico Spinola, who had fitted out the galleys at his own expense and during the next few years was to light up the last days of those outdated warships with a startling brilliance. The twenty-eight-year-old Spinola, Duke of Santa Severina, who had served his apprenticeship with his fellow Italian Parma in the Netherlands, had proposed to Philip II shortly before he died that by establishing a squadron of galleys in one of the Spanish-held ports on the North Sea it would be possible to help break the stranglehold on Spanish relief supplies to Flanders and at the same time interrupt the Dutch maritime trade on which they depended for so much of their growing wealth. Philip, now thoroughly disillusioned with the value of galleys as against sailing-ships, especially in northern seas, had given a grudging and qualified approval so long as it cost him nothing; and on this Spinola had acted.

Now, just as Bertendona had done the year before, the Genoese began to work his way up the coast, from Santander to Conquet near Brest, from Conquet to Le Havre, from Le Havre to Dunkirk. Unfortunately, unlike Bertendona, who had the good fortune to make his passage unobserved, Spinola's progress was spotted early on, and English and Dutch warships were sent out to destroy him. At each port where he put in officers deserted him, preferring to face possible charges rather than the certain death he offered. However, by stratagems, using his oars to better the winds, with clever seamanship and great courage, he outwitted the warships sent to intercept him. He arrived in Dunkirk, his ships laden with treasure to finance the Archduke Albert's armies, and full of shipwrights and industrious Italian workers, who proceeded to dig out the harbour so that it was suitable for galleys to use, and built there, right under the noses of the enemy, new galleys and several small warships to harass their shipping. Spinola had only been in harbour a day before he slid out with two galleys and captured a Dutch ship and brought her in as a prize.

It was an augury of things to come. For three and a half years he maintained his position against the united attempts of both enemies to dislodge him, and continued to menace and raid English and Dutch shipping – indeed to take on their warships when the odds were not too great. So impressive were his successes that both the English and the Dutch were constrained to put the clock back and lay down galleys in an attempt to beat him at his own game – an extraordinary backward step in naval development which should have made Drake turn over in his West Indian sea-grave. Four were actually built by England, two being completed in 1600 and two in 1601. Meanwhile the Dutch built three: the 'Black

Galley' of Dordrecht, which was to spend most of its time watching for Spinola to come out – 'a great ship to lie like a bulwark in the channel before Sluys' – and two lighter galleys for patrol work.

It was an expensive resort for the northern allies, for they had to pay their galley 'slaves'. Spinola ran through hundreds a year from combat or disease, but he always succeeded in getting more from Spain.

Archduke Albert, now married to the Infanta and recently created independent sovereign of the loyal provinces of the Netherlands, opened peace negotiations with England and the rebel states on behalf of the young King of Spain; but these progressed no further than what we should now call discussions for the agenda before they broke down. Yet for the time being active combat between the two sides died away. Epidemics were decimating the Spanish sea towns and dockyards. The Dutch, using their new-found strength, were taking care of the Narrow Seas and trying to contain Spinola and the Dunkirk pirates. England was preoccupied with the Irish problem.

Kings are notoriously bad at picking favourites: history is littered with the debris of their extravagances and their mistakes. But Elizabeth, even with her favourites, had a pretty shrewd eye for a man's worth under his gallant manner and handsome face. Essex was her worst error, yet even he, before he developed delusions of semi-kingship, was a tireless and fearless soldier with a splendid gift for leadership. As for the others: Leicester, Ralegh, Hatton, Mountjoy and the rest, they were all men of parts.

Charles Blount, Lord Mountjoy, came of an old but impoverished family, and had intended to study law; but an appearance at court and a marked talent in the tilt-yard brought him into prominence and an entirely unmerited command over his elders and betters in the Azores expedition of 1597. Since then, and before then, being refused permission to leave the court and get himself killed 'like that inconsiderate fellow Sidney', he had spent most of his spare time studying the art of war. When he reached Ireland after his friend's disastrous failure he proceeded to put his book learning into practice.

By the judicious combination of sea and land power, and with Sir George Carew as his experienced right-hand man, he so overcame the Irish that by the beginning of 1601 Desmond was a fugitive, McCarty was trying to change sides, and many of Tyrone's followers were giving up the struggle.

Now, too late by a couple of years for the most favourable circumstances, Spain chose to intervene. It was known all through the spring and early summer that yet another Armada was assembling in Lisbon in spite of lack of money, discouragement and rampant disease. Don Diego Brochero and Pedro de Zubiaur were to command it, and, though by early standards it was small, it still consisted of about twenty galleons and twenty other ships, carrying four thousand five hundred of Spain's best soldiers, a quantity of siege equipment and a mass of military stores.

As always (except in 1597) the English were well alerted to its approach, but as always, being on the defensive, they had no certainty as to the objective in mind. Ireland was certainly considered, but an attack on the West Country could not be ruled out. Nor, in spite of a lack now of Channel ports, could there be ruled out a possible attempt to link up with the Archduke Albert, who was at present laying siege to Ostend. The English commissioned a new squadron under Sir Henry Palmer to meet the threat, but in September news reached Plymouth that the Spanish fleet of some forty or fifty ships had been seen on a northerly course clearly bound for Ireland.

The Spanish fleet carried with it as commander of the military the sturdy Don Juan de Aguila who had been landed in Brittany in 1590, had remained there in spite of all Anglo-French efforts to drive him out, and had only been compelled to relinquish his position there under the terms of the peace treaty of Vervins. Now it was the Spanish intention to inject him and his *tercios* into Ireland, where they could, if successful, remain like an unassailable foreign body in possession of a part of the coast where they could be most nuisance to the English. It was not the intention of the Spanish to keep a fleet in being off Ireland; their aim was to land troops and from time to time furnish it with supplies and more troops, just as Zubiaur had so successfully done for so many years in Brittany.

Inevitably the weather intervened in these plans. A storm struck the Armada and it was split into three parts. Zubiaur was driven back into Coruña. With him nine ships, eight hundred of the soldiers and most of the stores. A large transport in distress was captured by an English privateer. Three ships under the command of Don Alonso del Campo reached and seized Baltimore on the southern coast of Ireland. The main fleet under Brochero arrived off the mouth of Cork harbour and were about to attempt to take the town when the wind changed, making their entry up the river impossible. They therefore sailed west and took Kinsale instead – another fine harbour but a less important base. Here they encountered no resistance; the people opened the gates of the little walled town and welcomed them in as friends and deliverers. Brochero, not wanting to stay in harbour a moment longer than he need – for if the wind changed he might find himself pinned there until an English fleet arrived – disembarked his three thousand army veterans, their equipment and supplies, and put out to sea again.

Aguila knew that most of the Irish rebels were far in the north, so he set about making the place as defensible as possible to await their arrival. He put a garrison in Castle Park on the Bandon River and another on the opposite bank in Rincurren. There were, however, no horses to be found in the vicinity of Kinsale, and this greatly reduced the Spanish mobility.

With the troops was Mathew de Oviedo, the Spanish-appointed Archbishop of Dublin, and he issued a proclamation stating that Queen Elizabeth had been dethroned by the Pope and therefore Irishmen were relieved of their allegiance, and to fight for Spain was to fight for the Pope and the only true religion. The proclamation fell flat, for there was an unexpected English army just arrived near Cork, and the ordinary folk of the district did not yet feel like committing themselves.

As soon as the news reached him that the Spaniards were coming to Ireland, Carew was convinced they would try to take Cork; he had moved quickly south and there he had been joined by Mountjoy, who had ridden down from Dublin with only one hundred men as escort. The presence of the Lord Deputy in their midst had a steadying effect in Munster, but neither English or Spanish were yet in sufficient force to risk a major encounter. Mountjoy had sent urgent messages to England for reinforcements and awaited them and the rest of his troops from Dublin. Aguila waited the arrival of Tyrone and O'Donnell.

Weather and problems of organization caused delays on all fronts, but by the end of October Mountjoy had built up a force of about six thousand infantry and six hundred horse, and with these he moved in to invest Kinsale. On the 1st November, after a bitter struggle during which Aguila tried repeatedly to relieve them, the hundred and fifty Spaniards in Rincurren surrendered.

In the wild north-west the Irish earls were also, though more slowly, on the move. O'Donnell, Lord of Tirconnel, gathered together an army of three thousand men in Sligo, ferried them across the upper reaches of the Shannon and then stayed three weeks in Tipperary waiting for Tyrone. While waiting he ravaged and plundered the countryside for miles around, even though the victims were Irish Catholics like himself – presumably on the excuse that those who were not for him were against him. On hearing of his approach, Mountjoy decided to take the risk of splitting his own army, and sent Carew north with twelve hundred foot soldiers and two hundred and fifty cavalry to intercept O'Donnell before he could join forces or co-ordinate with the Spanish.

As Tyrone had still not arrived, O'Donnell eventually moved on again and came upon Carew's army straddling the only road south. It was an impasse. O'Donnell did not want a trial of strength against regulars who had the choice of position. Carew did not want to attack an army which could melt at will into the bogs and the forests. Then occurred that extreme rarity in Ireland, a sharp November frost. Immediately and successfully O'Donnell led his army across the temporarily frozen quagmire of the Slievefelim Mountains and so gave Carew the slip. By dawn Carew knew what had happened and turned about and led his troops back by forced marches, hoping to rejoin Mountjoy in Kinsale in time.

He succeeded, for O'Donnell, having come to within thirty miles of Kinsale, once again sat down and waited for Tyrone. In the meantime Aguila inside Kinsale had not been idle, and Mountjoy with his depleted force had had several bloody encounters with the Spanish. At this stage the army investing Kinsale was fewer in number than the army defending it.

But now the forces began to build up on both sides. Zubiaur, back in Coruña, had forced repairs through and quantities of provisions and powder and shot. With him sailed the secretary to the Adelantado, Pedro Lopez de Soto – two fire-eaters together – and although the usual storm split the squadron, they arrived in Castlehaven – near Roaring Water Bay and thirty miles west of Kinsale – with seven of their ships and proceeded to land men and stores there.

News of their arrival was a welcome fillip to the spirits of the Spaniards beleaguered in Kinsale, and this, together with the rumoured approach of Tyrone, gave rise to the first dangerous signs in Munster of Irish support for the invaders. The castle at Castlehaven and two overlooking the entrance to Baltimore were handed over without a shot being fired, as a few days later was the important castle of Dunboy, which has a valuable small harbour overlooking Bantry Bay. All these strategic points were quickly garrisoned by Spaniards, and soon they joined forces with O'Donnell and with the Spanish in Baltimore. It was an explosive situation.

In the meantime the Earl of Thomond arrived in Kinsale Harbour with English reinforcements of sixteen hundred men and one hundred horse, and three days later Sir Richard Leveson put in at last with his strong fleet of *Warspite*, *Garland*, *Defiance*, *Swiftsure*, *Crane* and *Refusal*, together with seven supporting ships and two thousand very raw, very seasick troops, whom he proceeded to land. The stage was all set and waiting only for Tyrone.

Leveson, on landing his men, learned of the arrival of Zubiaur in Castlehaven, and at once split his force and warped his part of it laboriously out of the harbour in the teeth of the wind to try to attack Zubiaur before he could establish himself. He took with him *Warspite*, *Defiance*, *Swiftsure*, *Crane* and three supporting ships and by the following morning was off Castlehaven.

Zubiaur had already firmly established himself, not only in the castle but in entrenchments along the beach, now manned by musketeers; and eight guns were just being hauled up to cover the narrow entrance of the harbour. Leveson did not pause for a council-of-war but, like Drake at Cadiz fourteen years before, burst straight in. Zubiaur had two galleons of about five hundred tons each, as against the heavily armed *Warspite* of six hundred and fifty tons and the lesser English warships (the other Spanish ships were transports); but with the guns and soldiers ashore the prospects of an attack could hardly have been less favourable. But in a battle lasting five hours Leveson sank Zubiaur's flagship and three other ships and left a fifth burning.

In spite of this signal victory he could not hope to dislodge the Spanish soldiers from the shore and now, again like Drake at Cadiz, he found himself unable to retreat, for the wind was adverse. He stayed there two more days waiting a change that would let him out, and in the meantime was the target of Spanish gunnery. It is said that the *Warspite* was hit three hundred times by shot. When he was finally able to leave, he was soon followed out of the harbour by Zubiaur, who took the remnants of his battered fleet back to Spain. Pedro Lopez de Soto remained behind to command the Spanish infantry.

Now at last the slow-moving Tyrone was almost on the scene – not without his own record of burning and pillaging on the way; but at the sound of his name all Munster, which had hardly lifted a finger for the Spaniards, was ready to rise. He made contact with the Spaniards at Castlehaven, and a contingent of two hundred of them joined him. Then he linked up with O'Donnell and advanced on Kinsale. Between them the Irish alone had about seven thousand men.

It was a nasty position for the English. Mountjoy with all his reinforcements from England had at one time commanded twelve thousand troops; but, thanks to the problems of bringing raw recruits from England, some of whom died on the way, the enormous number of desertions which followed (hundreds at a time), and the long siege of Kinsale with its routine casualties from disease and warfare, his active force was now down to about six thousand. All were on short rations, the horses were starving, and he had none too much powder and shot. Although he was officially investing Kinsale, he was now in fact between two armies whose total force was fifty per cent greater than his own. The Spanish were veterans. And Tyrone had shown what he could do to the English on the Blackwater.

It was a suitable moment to lift the siege and evacuate his army as best he could – by ship to Cork, since he was cut off by land. Instead he remained obstinately where he was and continued to bombard Kinsale in the hope that it would provoke an attack. The Spaniards within the walls were in none too good a state either, being reduced to eating rice and stale biscuits, and Aguila wrote in some irritation to Tyrone proposing an immediate joint assault upon the English from front and rear. Tyrone, whose policy of masterly inactivity had been producing desirable results, was reluctantly persuaded by O'Donnell to agree, and the time of the attack was fixed for dawn on Christmas Eve.

Betrayals through the centuries have taken many peculiar shapes, but few perhaps have been quite so bizarre as that of

Brian MacHugh Oge MacMahon on the 23rd December 1601. One of the chiefs close to Tyrone, he found himself short of whiskey. There was none in the camp, nor was any to be obtained in the villages round. It was an acute crisis; so, very thirsty, and friendly as you please, he sent off a boy to the English camp to ask Sir George Carew if he could possibly be letting him have a bottle for the old times' sake. (MacMahon's son had once been a page to Carew.) The Englishman, not to be outdone in the courtesies, sent him a bottle. MacMahon could well have sent the boy back with a note of thanks. Instead he sent, along with his love, a warning to Carew to be on his guard against a surprise attack on the following day at dawn, with details of the dispositions.

People betray for money, for power, for religion, for vengeance. Surely only an Irishman could betray out of sheer goodness of heart.

The battle began in a thunderstorm just before daybreak and lasted for three hours. Warned in advance, the English, though outnumbered, could concentrate their best troops in the most threatened places. The Irish advanced in three main armies: Tyrone and his men from Tyrone and Londonderry, O'Donnell leading the regiments of Tyrconnell and Connaught; while the third army consisted of some of the best troops in Ireland under Tyrrell, a mixture of Munster volunteers and the small Spanish contingent under Alonso del Campo himself. These last were on the Irish right and their task was to establish contact with the beleaguered Spanish in Kinsale.

But no sooner did they probe forward than they met strongly posted English forces barring the way. As day broke del Campo, seeing the thin lines of the English slowly advancing to meet the Irish main armies, pressed Tyrone to attack them at once; but instead Tyrone, fresh from a quarrel with O'Donnell over precedence, ordered a retreat. His aim was to immobilize the English cavalry by retreating behind a bog; but the partly untrained Irish did not know how to retreat in good order and Mountjoy, seizing the moment while it was there, ordered a general attack. Sir Edward Wingfield with two hundred and fifty cavalry charged a force of eighteen hundred pikemen, who stood firm and repulsed him. But then, reinforced by regiments under Sir Henry Danvers, he swung off to the right and attacked the Irish cavalry. These were no match for the English and scattered widely; and the Irish pikemen, seeing their own people fleeing towards them, parted ranks to let them through and could not reassemble in time to keep out the English cavalry.

So a rout began. Brian MacHugh Oge MacMahon, fighting valiantly be it noted, was severely wounded in the fight. In a short time the only Irish standing firm were Tyrrell's vanguard, which resisted for a while and then also fled, leaving del Campo and his Spanish contingent standing alone. Though now hopelessly outnumbered the Spaniards fought on, giving no ground, until of the original two hundred only del Campo, two other officers and forty-seven soldiers were left alive. Then they surrendered. The Irish loss in the battle was perhaps twelve hundred, though on their return northwards many hundreds more were set upon and killed by the other Irish they had despoiled on the way south. A favourite way of killing them was throwing them into a bog and then treading them down.

Having never received the prearranged signal from del Campo, Aguila and the Kinsale garrison did not make a sally until the fighting was virtually over, and then they were sharply rebuffed.

Through the next week they continued to make sorties but to no avail. It was a stalemate, for an English attempt to take the fortress would have been a desperate and bloody business. Then on the 31st December Aguila offered to parley. Mountjoy gratefully accepted the invitation and sent his Cornish friend Sir William Godolphin to open negotiations. The bargaining was hard on both sides, but, since Mountjoy only had six days food left for his troops and most of his guns were out of action, he felt justified in agreeing generous terms.

So presently English and Spanish officers were dining amicably together, and even Captain Robert Harvey, who was sent to Castlehaven to accept its surrender under the terms of the general agreement, was greeted and entertained to dinner by Pedro Lopez de Soto. Indeed de Soto, arch apostle all his life of the war against England, as he became friendly with Harvey during the next weeks, allowed it to be seen that his mind was changing. Why could there not be peace between England and Spain? he asked. Who was benefiting from this dreary and bloodthirsty war?

16
Last Skirmishes

Aguila, de Soto, del Campo and three thousand six hundred Spanish officers and men were repatriated to Spain, without ransoms, without massacre. This was of course contained in the terms of the agreement; all the same it speaks a new spirit.

For the failure to exploit the last Armada, the Spaniards blamed the Irish, the Irish blamed the Spaniards. Feeling was very bitter. Aguila said that when Satan showed Christ all the kingdoms of the earth he withheld Ireland as being fit only for himself.

The Spanish had a lot to complain of, for they had landed as promised with a large contingent of troops, had subsisted there for nearly three months without any help at all, when they had been promised assistance 'within days'. Then when the Irish army did come it had 'been broken by a handful of men and blown asunder'. They had done their share and been abysmally let down.

This was true enough; but lack of judgment, or lack of local knowledge, had been shown by the places at which they landed. Munster was peaceful: no chief or earl raised his standard of rebellion there. If the Spanish had sailed to Sligo it would have been different. As it was, the two great northern earls had had to make a trek of more than two hundred miles across wild and mountainous country, with all the difficulties of ordnance and supply that that entailed. To help a rebellion in Lisbon, would you land troops in Coruña?

The man who came out of it with an enormously heightened reputation was of course Mountjoy. Throughout the emergency he had contrived to do the right thing at the right time. Always with inadequate forces and poor supplies, he had deployed his resources notably and had achieved one of the outstanding tactical victories of the sixteenth century.

Almost as important as his defeat of the Irish armies was his creation of conditions around Kinsale such as to induce

Aguila to parley. It had been very much the intention of the Spanish to retain Kinsale permanently and to use it as a forward base against England. A considerable fleet could lie at anchor there. It could be a place from which it was possible to harry enemy shipping with far greater impunity than Spinola could employ from Sluys. Whatever the initial failure to rouse them, it would gradually have become a focal point for the rebellious Irish, who would be sure of sanctuary there. And as Spanish-Irish power grew, it could spread along the coast and take a firmer grip inland. It would lock up or pre-occupy a sizable proportion of Elizabeth's army and navy.

Don Martin de Bertendona had been about to sail with more troops and supplies when news reached Madrid of Aguila's surrender. When Aguila reached Spain he was placed under house arrest; but before he could answer the charges against him he was taken ill and died. One of his last acts was to send off a crate of wine and oranges and lemons to his late captor, Sir George Carew.

So the long war was petering out at last – partly from exhaustion, partly from a growing mutual respect.

Of course there were still some flickers of the flame. The Spaniards, keeping to their terms of surrender, gave up Dunboy Castle, but it was at once seized by O'Sullivan Bere who owned the castle, who claimed descent from the Spanish and who now proposed to hold it in the name of King Philip III. It was a difficult place for the English to tackle, and so it remained as a thorn in the English flesh. O'Donnell of Tirconnell after his defeat went to Spain and there was received at court with every honour; so Dunboy would prove to be a most useful harbour if Bertendona came out with his fleet, as he seemed disposed to do. .

At the same time the active Frederico Spinola had been back in Madrid pressing the young King for reinforcements to improve on his recent successes. His brother, the Marquis of Spinola, was willing to raise five thousand infantry and one thousand cavalry in Italy if Philip would match it with eight more galleys and two thousand Spanish veterans. Then they would sail back to Dunkirk and have a force there ready to disrupt Channel shipping and even seize an English port. Young Philip, beset by failure elsewhere, agreed.

In England Elizabeth's veto on large overseas expeditions

still remained, but the sore memories of 1597 were now five years old. Leveson, though elevated in the first place through marriage and not merit, had now established himself as one of the outstanding admirals of the day; and he was permitted to take a fleet of eight galleons on a tour of the Spanish coast to see what mischief they could wreak. He took with him, apart from a few auxiliaries, the *Repulse, Warspite, Defiance, Nonpareil, Mary Rose, Dreadnought, Garland* and *Adventure*; and as his vice-admiral he was given the thirty-three-year-old Sir William Monson, who as a young lieutenant of seventeen had fought against the first Armada in the frigate *Charles*, had commanded the *Repulse* at the taking of Cadiz and been knighted in the general euphoria following that event. He had made three voyages with the Earl of Cumberland, and in 1591 had been taken prisoner by the Spaniards while manning a recaptured prize and had served some time as a galley slave, so he had old scores to settle.

It was a fleet big enough to disrupt trade but not big enough to try conclusions with a Spanish fleet, as Leveson found to his cost when, sailing some days ahead of Monson with four of his ships, he intercepted the Spanish treasure-fleet – the failed dream of so many of his distinguished predecessors. He took one prize and then found his small squadron surrounded by thirty-eight Spanish ships-of-war. He could have died like Grenville but preferred to live like Leveson, and, abandoning his prize, he found a gap in the closing fleet just in time.

Thereafter, joined by Monson, he cruised up and down the Spanish coast for several weeks with nothing to report but the usual decay of his crews. Then in early June, off Lisbon, he learned that one of the great Portuguese carracks, laden as always with the treasure of the Indies, was sheltering just inside the mouth of the Tagus under the guns of Cezimbra castle. She had been two years on the voyage, her crew of six hundred reduced to thirty by sickness and privation, and she had made the shelter of the river at her last gasp.

Already help for her was on its way from Lisbon. The governor had sent out four hundred men to supplement the exhausted crew, and Spinola, just ready with his eight new galleys and one thousand trained soldiers to begin his dash north, was diverted to protect the carrack. Three other galleys under the new Marquis of Santa Cruz kept him company. By the time Leveson looked in it was a formidable sight, for he faced the guns of the fort, the big forward-firing guns of the galleys, and cannon and infantry camped on the hillsides. Riding at anchor towered the great carrack with her seven decks, being rapidly unloaded. Leveson and Monson had five warships with them, but the captains of all the ships protested that to go in meant suicide, and it took the two commanders all their persuasion and authority to force them to attack.

Thereafter followed five hours of battle during which in spite of their choice of stations the galleys suffered the more. Indeed Santa Cruz and his three Lisbon galleys had had enough by noon and would have fled, but Spinola held his ground and the others would not be shamed into admitting defeat before he did. However by two p.m. Santa Cruz had been seriously wounded and his crews decimated and Spinola's fine new galleys were all badly damaged. Monson wrote later of 'watching the slaves forsaking them and everything in confusion amongst them'. Two galleys surrendered – one, to Monson's understandable glee, the galley in which he had been chained – and in the end even Spinola had to make off to save what was left of his fleet.

Then, after long parleying, the carrack itself surrendered, the Portuguese captain and officers were entertained to dinner and music aboard the *Garland* before being set ashore, and next morning the English sailed away with their enormous capture while thousands of Spanish and Portuguese soldiers watched helplessly from the shore.

It was an epic worthy of Drake and deserves more honour than it has received in English naval annals.

The indefatigable Spinola was not yet beaten. With his usual consuming energy he set about repairing his battered flotilla, and within two months was ready for sea again. He sailed direct for Santander with fifteen hundred slaves as motive power and one thousand troops. His own galleys had five slaves to an oar instead of the usual four, to give him extra speed when necessary. Monson, who was on the prowl again, this time with flag command, missed him altogether; but the Dutch were able to send a warning, so by mid-September all possible dispositions had been made to welcome Spinola in the Channel.

The English Channel Guard at this time consisted of three ships only under Sir Robert Mansell, the *Hope*, the *Adventurer* and the *Answer*, but it was supplemented by four Dutch warships under Admiral Cant; and of course there were the two usual Dutch blockading squadrons outside Dunkirk and Sluys, making it almost impossible to enter or leave the ports. Spinola decided this time he would change his tactics and hug the English coast instead of the French; but Anglo-Dutch reasoning had anticipated this, and Spinola and his galleys were first spotted by two Dutch fly-boats as he was running before a stiff south-westerly breeze off Dungeness. They gave chase.

He kept his distance well throughout the night, but at dawn he found he was being carefully headed towards the English flagship, which lay waiting for him. It was not his purpose at present to try conclusions with a warship of the size of the *Hope*, so he struck sail and took to the oars, heading back athwart the wind. So began, during most of a fine September day, a battle of manœuvre between three sailing-ships and six depending on sail and oar. Not once during it did the Anglo-Dutch squadron come within firing distance of the galleys, and the day's end saw the galleys slip through a gap their brilliant navigation had created and make off up Channel with their opponents crowding on sail to try to keep them in sight.

But Mansell was not done yet, for the north-easterly course the Spaniards were taking would bring them close by the South Foreland and almost into the waiting arms of the rest of his squadron headed by Admiral Jan Cant in the *Moon*. Mansell therefore veered east-north-east, away from Spinola in anticipation that, when the Italian saw his way blocked by Cant, he would swing his squadron south-east and make directly for Dunkirk: then Mansell would be between him and his home ports.

It happened as Mansell foresaw. So close did Spinola come to the coast that people ran along the cliff watching him, and Dover Castle sounded an alarm gun. The sight of the white cliffs was too much for three English slaves and they jumped overboard and swam ashore at St Margaret's Bay.

Mansell kept the galleys just in sight, but well to the south of them, shepherding them towards the Goodwin Sands. Then just as dusk fell the leading galley saw three warships in their path. It was the *Moon*, the *Sampson* and the *Answer*, completely blocking the way ahead. Behind Spinola were the two Dutch frigates, and on his starboard quarter but on the seaward side of the Goodwins, Mansell waited in the *Hope*. It looked like a fair capture.

Spinola, of course, had chosen a moonless night, but now

fortunately for him cloud came up too, blotting out the stars, and for an hour after dusk the wind dropped. So it was a game of blind man's buff with only the galleys capable of movement and the dangerous Goodwins never far away. Spinola had turned about as soon as darkness fell and had made for the southern end of the Goodwins; but as he reached them the breeze sprang up again, this time from the north-east.

Mansell for the second time had guessed right and suddenly loomed up among the galleys. There was an explosion of broadsides and sixty-pounders. In a violent ten minutes of blind fighting one of the galleys was severely damaged, and then Mansell himself hauled away in the freshening breeze. With galleys all around him he was enormously outnumbered and might have been boarded and quickly overrun. So Spinola once more continued on his way, with apparently only the Dutch blockading squadron now between himself and safety.

But he was still pursued by the six Anglo-Dutch vessels he had eluded, and his rowers after twelve hours of stroke and counter-stroke were near the end of their endurance. Also one of his galleys was partly disabled and Spinola would not desert her. So as the wind freshened on that last thirty endless miles from the Goodwins to Gravelines the sailing warships began to catch up.

Mansell, at last guessing wrong, made for Sluys and took Captain Bredgate in the *Answer* and Captain Jonas in the *Advantage* with him. The Dutch held on for Dunkirk, and it was they who began to overhaul the galleys in the dark of the night. First the damaged galley was caught and raked with broadsides until she was a wreck; then Captain Sael in the *Sampson* rammed another and bombarded her until she sank, forty only of a complement of four hundred and fifty being picked up. Then Vice-Admiral Cant overran a third in the dark and shot her to pieces, so that eventually she drifted upon Calais beach and was wrecked.

The cannonade had attracted a swarm of blockaders, who, having already been forewarned, were out in extra strength, and the three remaining galleys could not avoid running into them. In the ensuing fight two of the galleys were badly damaged and captured, the third with Spinola on board and its extra turn of speed, reached the shoals of Dunkirk beach. Here, pursued only by boats of the shallowest draught, he had everything possible flung overboard to lighten his craft, and promised the galley slaves freedom if they made the harbour.

Somehow he avoided taking the ground and entered Dunkirk with his own ship and his treasure intact.

One would have thought that the lessons of Lisbon and the Channel would have convinced even the bravest of men. Or the most obstinate. Spinola continued undeterred, and throughout the winter his galley and those he commanded were a continuing menace to shipping in the vicinity of Dunkirk. But like Grenville and others in that strange heroic century, he seemed to have a death wish, or at least a wish to triumph over quite insuperable odds. By May 1603 there were dissensions among the Archduke and the officers he commanded, and Spinola had angry exchanges with the Governor of Sluys who he thought was impeding him at every turn. Gathering his eight remaining galleys and four frigates, he sailed out of the harbour to attack the island of Walcheren, and so deliberately challenged the blockading squadron of four ships under Vice-Admiral Joost de Moor. The battle began at daybreak and went on all through the morning until Spinola had his right arm blown off by gunfire. He died an hour later, and the galleys, damaged and outgunned, retreated into Sluys harbour, never to emerge again.

Spinola was twenty-eight, and had he lived might have matched his elder brother's later military fame with an equal or greater renown at sea.

17

The Setting of the Sun

In the last year of her life Queen Elizabeth finished her translation of Horace's *Art of Poetry*. She entranced the Commons with two of the finest speeches from the throne to be heard even in her reign. She welcomed the Venetian Envoy in fluent Italian and told him it was a pity the Republic had waited forty-five years before venturing to appoint a full diplomatic representative. She made another of her 'progresses', and once or twice rode horseback to the chase and to the other field-sports. Sometimes the palace at Westminster still rang with her hearty laughter.

But these were flickers of a flame that burned low. Luckier than her Spanish brother-in-law, she did not suffer from diabetic gangrene – nor indeed from any other apparently incurable complaint. It was just age bearing her down: old age, fatigue, loneliness and a sad heart. Most old people not weeded out by one of the killer diseases suffer the same way, and it is as much a matter of mental stamina as of physical how long they survive.

Elizabeth's stamina was notorious, but seventy was a great age in the sixteenth century, and she never had the same spirits after Essex had gone to the block. 'She disregardeth every costly dish that cometh to the table,' Harington wrote, 'and taketh little but manchet and succory pottage. Every new message from the City doth disturb her, and she frowns on all the ladies.' When he tried to entertain her by reading her some of his witty verses she said: 'When thou dost feel creeping age at thy gate, these fooleries will please thee less.' Harington thought her 'in a most pitiable state'.

She had made a new favourite of the young Earl of Clanricarde, but sometimes his marked resemblance to Essex distressed her as much as it pleased her. She told the new French Ambassador, Count Harlay de Beaumont, that she 'was tired of life, for nothing new contenteth my spirit or giveth me any

236

enjoyment'. Her days became as substantially peopled by ghosts as by the faces and figures of the middle-aged courtiers around her who had not been born when she came to the throne. Even her old friend Lady Nottingham had just passed away and so had moved over the far side of the arras where lurked the whispering faces and forms of all the other dead.

Just after Christmas the Queen was well enough to attend several state banquets, but at one of these she caught cold, and so shortly moved to Richmond, where the air was less dank from river mists. There she began to fail more rapidly, and she sat for long hours in silence 'with the dulness and frowardness familiar to old age'. She had always had a distaste for the ministrations of her doctors, a fact which had contributed materially to the length of her life; but now she would not let them even come near her; nor after a while would she eat or drink. Feeling the end approaching, she rose from her chair and stood beside it, refusing now even to sit lest she should never rise again. So she stood for fifteen hours while her court watched from the shadows and waited in awe for the end.

Many of her courtiers posted back to Whitehall, preparing for the change. Orders were issued to transport to Holland all vagrants and unknown persons found in London or Westminster; numerous gentlemen who it was thought were likely to cause trouble were arrested and put in the Tower, to be on the safe side. Arms and ammunition were supplied to the court, an armed guard put on the exchequer. The fleet was ordered to sea. All that could be put in readiness was put in readiness.

At last the Queen was forced to sink back upon some cushions, which had been spread around her, and there lay unspeaking for four more days, her finger in her mouth. Music was played for her, and this seemed to bring a little pleasure to the old eyes. More than did Archbishop Whitgift's prayers, though he prayed unceasingly at her side. Unlike Philip, religion had never been a dominating influence in her life; this had enabled her to rise above the prevailing passions; now it provided her with small succour at the end.

From her only relative of near contemporary age, the old Lord Admiral Howard, now Lord Nottingham, she accepted one bowl of soup. To him she complained that she was tied with an iron collar about her neck. He tried to reassure her but she said: 'No, I am tied, and the case is altered with me.'

To the last she would not name her successor, though those about her thought she nodded once at the King of Scotland's name. Towards the evening of the 23rd she allowed the Archbishop to examine her in her faith; she replied only by nods or a raising of the hand. Then he prayed at her bedside until late in the night, when she fell asleep. At three o'clock in the morning the courtiers remaining around her couch noticed a change in her and saw that she was dead. She had passed away 'as the most resplendent sun setteth at last in a western cloud'.

Fate sometimes has a way of staging the sorry anti-climax, and one scarcely more painful could have been arranged than the succession of King James. In place of the dead Queen with her great authority, with the aura of forty-five years as a monarch, with her talent for majestic eloquence, her wit, her coarse dynamic vitality, her legendary prestige, there came a thin-shanked, pot-bellied little man, wearing a bonnet awry upon his head and clothes so thickly padded to protect him from possible dagger thrusts that he looked like Humpty Dumpty; a man who could only sit a horse if it were saddled like an armchair, whose fingers were ever fumbling with his codpiece, whose tongue was too large for his mouth, whose eyes were large and watery and his beard thin and straggling. It is extraordinary that two such handsome creatures as Mary and Darnley could ever have produced so unhandsome a son.

But underneath his shambling, drooling exterior he had a good deal of shrewd wisdom and a clear eye for the practical realities of a situation. And the situation regarding Spain was to him perfectly straightforward. As King of Scotland he never *had* been at war with Spain; why should he now be in his larger domain? He saw himself as the Peacemaker, and on the whole his new subjects were ready enough to accept his point of view. France was already at peace with Spain. Holland was virtually independent. It was time for England to come to terms with her old enemy.

This James did on England's behalf very quickly, and by 1604 peace was formally signed. The terms of the peace were unsatisfactory to the adventurous and burgeoning spirit of maritime England, and could only lead – as they did – to a renewal of the struggle later in the century; but for the time the treaty sufficed. It sufficed too to see the end of the great Spanish fleets built regularly in the Atlantic ports to be launched against a heretic England. Though religious divisions were to remain as acute for another hundred years, it was the end of Spanish hegemony in Europe and Spanish monopoly in the Caribbean. Though frequently at war with England, or near war with England, Spain never again considered, or was in a position to consider, conquest. It was never again between the two countries a war *à outrance*.

The last of the Spanish Armadas had sailed. For two centuries England was to be free from the threat of invasion.

Tudor and Stuart Succession

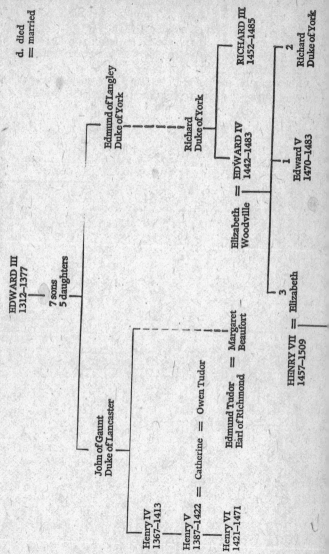

d. died
= married

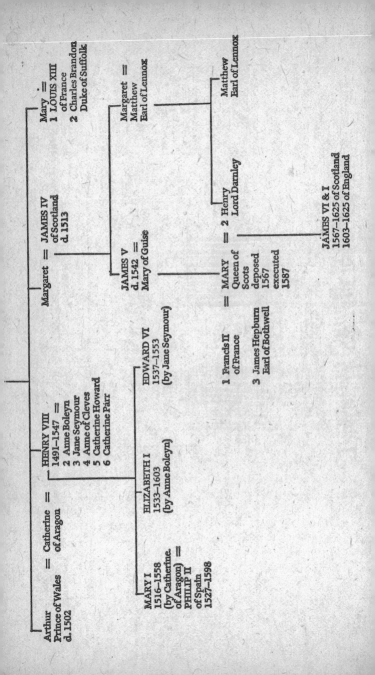

The Spanish Hapsburgs to Philip III

d. died
= married

FERDINAND II of Aragon 1452–1516 = ISABELLA of Castile 1451–1504

Isabel = MANUEL the Fortunate of Portugal

Juan = Margaret of Austria, daughter of MAXIMILIAN I

Joanna the Mad = PHILIP I son of MAXIMILIAN I

Maria = MANUEL the Fortunate of Portugal

Catherine of Aragon = 1 Arthur, Prince of Wales 2 HENRY VIII of England 1491–1547

Alfonso

Miguel

JUAN III of Portugal

Isabel

Luis

Don Antonio of Crato (illegitimate) claimant to Portuguese crown

MARY I of England 1516–1558 = PHILIP II of Spain 1527–1598

Leonore = MANUEL the Fortunate of Portugal

CHARLES V 1500–1558 = Isabel of Portugal

Isabel = Christian II of Denmark, Norway, and Sweden

FERDINAND of Bohemia = Anna of Hungary

Maria = Louis II of Hungary

Catherine = JUAN III of Portugal

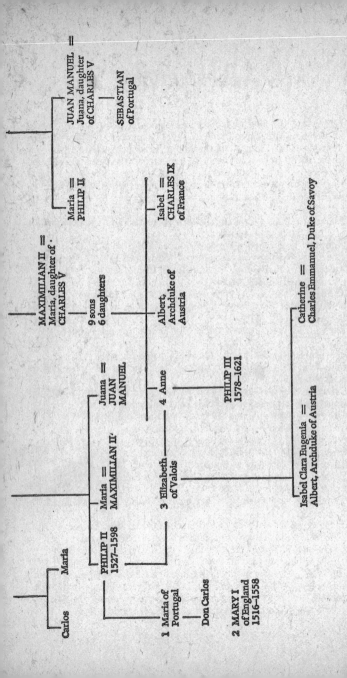

Bibliography

This is not the kind of book in which source notes at the bottom of the page are appropriate. A full bibliography is therefore the more essential. Clearly all the books listed here are not of equal importance; from some only a few facts have been gleaned, to others my debt is considerable. Yet for the student who wishes to go to source material it is probably more helpful to list the lot, so that he may pick and choose as he wishes.

Allingham, Hugh. *Captain Cuellar's Adventures in Connaught and Ulster, 1588.* London, 1897.

Andrews, K. R. *Drake's Voyages.* London, 1967.

Aramburu, Marcos de, account of (translated by W. Spotswood-Green), in *Proceedings of the Royal Irish Academy*, Vol. XXVII. Dublin and London, 1908-9.

Artiñano, G. de. *La Arquitectura Naval Española.* Madrid, 1920.

Aubrey, John. *Brief Lives.* Edited by Oliver Lawson Dick. London, 1949.

Bagwell, Richard. *Ireland under the Tudors.* 3 vols. London, 1885-90.

Baldwin Smith, Lacey. *The Elizabethan Epic.* London, 1966.

Calderon, Pedro Coco, account of, in *Calendar of State Papers (Spanish)*, Vol. IV.

Calendar of State Papers, Domestic Series: Mary and Elizabeth.

Calendar of State Papers, Foreign Series: Elizabeth.

Calendar of State Papers (Holland and Flanders), 1586-8.

Calendar of State Papers (Ireland), 1586-1603.

Calendar of State Papers (Scotland), 1547-1603.

Calendar of State Papers (Spanish), 1580-1603.

Calendar of State Papers (Venetian), 1558-1603.

Camden, William. *Annales . . . Elizabetha.* Edited by T. Hearne. 3 vols. London, 1717.

Chamberlin, Frederick. *The Sayings of Queen Elizabeth.* London, 1923.

Cheyney, E. P. *A History of England, from the Defeat of the Armada to the Death of Elizabeth.* 2 vols. London, 1914.

Commines, Philippe de. *Mémoires.* Translated by A. R. Scoble. 2 vols. London, 1855-6.

Copies de Simancas, Vol. 18: *Archives Générales Royales.* Brussels.

Corbett, Julian S. *Drake and the Tudor Navy.* 2 vols. London, 1898.

Corbett, Julian S. *Papers relating to the Navy during the Spanish War 1585-7*, Vol. XII. Navy Records Society. London, 1898.

Corbett, Julian S. *The Successors of Drake*, London, 1900.

Cottonian MSS.

Cuellar, Francisco de, narrative letter (translated by Frances Partridge), in *Survivors of the Armada* by E. Hardy. London, 1966.

Drummond, Humphrey. *Our Man in Scotland*. London, 1969.

Duro, C. Fernández. *Armada Española*. 9 vols. Madrid, 1877.

Duro, C. Fernández. *La Armada Invencible*. 2 vols. Madrid, 1884-5.

Edwards, Edward. *The Life of Sir Walter Ralegh*. 2 vols. London, 1868.

England, Sylvia L. *The Massacre of Saint Bartholomew*. London, 1938.

Erlanger, Philippe. *St Bartholomew's Night*. Translated by P. O'Brian. London, 1962.

Essen, Leon van der. *Alexandre Farnèse*. 5 vols. Brussels, 1933-7.

Falls, Cyril. *Elizabeth's Irish Wars*. London, 1950.

The Four Masters, Annals of Ireland. Edited by J. O'Donovan. Dublin, 1851.

Fox, John. *Actes and Monuments*. London, 1576.

Fraser, Lady Antonia. *Mary Queen of Scots*. London, 1969.

Froude, James Anthony. *History of England*. London, 1868.

Froude, James Anthony. *English Seamen in the Sixteenth Century*. London, 1895.

Glasgow, Tom, Jr. 'The Shape of Ships that defeated the Spanish Armada' in *Mariner's Mirror*, No. 50, August 1964.

Grierson, Edward. *The Fatal Inheritance*. London, 1969.

Guizot, François. *Histoire de France*. Paris, 1835.

Hardy, Evelyn. *Survivors of the Armada*. London, 1966.

Harleian Miscellany, Vol. I. London, 1808.

Hentzner, Paul. *Travels in England during the Reign of Queen Elizabeth*. Translated by R. Bentley. London, 1894.

Hilton, Ronald. 'The Marriage of Queen Mary and Philip of Spain' in *Papers and Proceedings of the Hampshire Field Club and Archaeological Society*, Vol. XIV, Part 1. 1940.

History of the Spanish Armada . . . for the Invasion and Conquest of England . . . 1588. London, 1759.

Hogg, O. F. G. 'England's War Effort against the Spanish Armada' in *Society for Army Historical Research Journal*, No. 44. March 1966.

Howard, Charles, 1st Earl of Nottingham. 'Relation of Proceedings' in *The Defeat of the Spanish Armada* by J. K. Laughton. Navy Records Society. London, 1894.

Hume, Martin A. S. 'The Visit of Philip II' in *English Historical Review*, Vol. VII. 1892.

Hume, Martin A. S. *Two English Queens and Philip*. London, 1908.

Hume, Martin A. S. Introductions to the *Calendar of Letters and State Papers relating to English Affairs, preserved principally in the Archives of Simancas*, Vols. I-IV.

A Journal of all the Particularities that fell out in the voyage of two Lord Generals . . . [to Cadiz, 1596]. Lambeth Palace MSS., No. 250.

Keightley, Thomas. *History of England*. London, 1839.

Laughton, J. K., editor. *Papers relating to the Defeat of the Spanish Armada*, Vols. I and II. Navy Records Society. London, 1894.

Lewis, Michael. *The Spanish Armada*. London, 1960.

Lewis, Michael. *Armada Guns*. London, 1961.

Loades, D. M. *The Oxford Martyrs*. London, 1971.

Loomie, Albert J. 'An Armada pilot's survey of the English coast-line October 1597' in *Mariner's Mirror*, No. 49. November, 1963.

Machyn, Henry. *Diary 1550-1563*. Edited by John Gough Nicols. London, 1848.

McKee, Alexander. *From Merciless Invaders*. London, 1963.

Mariéjol, Jean H. *Master of the Armada*. Translated by W. B. Wells. London, 1933.

Martin, B. L. Henri. *Histoire de France*. Paris, 1860.

Mattingly, Garrett H. *The Defeat of the Spanish Armada*. London, 1959.

Miller, Amos C. *Sir Henry Killigrew*. London, 1963.

Motley, J. L. *The Rise of the Dutch Republic*. 3 vols. London, 1955.

Motley, J. L. *History of the United Netherlands*. 4 vols. London, 1869.

Mumby, Frank A. *The Girlhood of Queen Elizabeth: A Narrative in Contemporary Letters*. London, 1909.

Naish, G. P. B. 'Documents illustrating the History of the Spanish Armada in *The Naval Miscellany*, Vol. IV. Navy Records Society. London, 1952.

Noble, T. C. *An Historical Essay on the Rise and Fall of the Spanish Armada AD 1588*. London, 1886.

Petrie, Sir Charles. *Philip of Spain*. London, 1961.

Ralegh, Sir Walter. *A Report of the Truth of the Fight about the Isles of Azores*. London, 1591.

Ralegh, Sir Walter. *History of the World*. London, 1614.

Rowse, A. L. *Sir Richard Grenville*. London, 1937.

Rowse, A. L. *Tudor Cornwall*. London, 1941.

Rowse, A. L. *The Expansion of Elizabethan England*. London, 1955.

Rowse, A. L. *Bosworth Field*. London, 1966.

Salisbury MSS.

Sitwell, Edith. *Fanfare for Elizabeth*. London, 1946.

Stephen, Sir James. *Lectures on the History of France*. London, 1851.

Stow, John. *The Annales or Generall Chronicles of England*. London, 1615.

Strachey, Lytton. *Elizabeth and Essex*. London, 1928.

Straker, Ernest. *Wealden Iron*. London, 1931.

Strickland, Agnes. *Life of Mary Queen of Scots*. 2 vols. London, 1837.

Strype, John. *Annals of Queen Elizabeth's Reign.* 4 vols. London, 1725-1731.

Thompson, I. A. A. 'The Armada and administrative reform: the Spanish council of war in the reign of Philip II' in *English Historical Review*, No. 82. October 1967.

Thompson, I. A. A. 'The Appointment of the Duke of Medina Sidonia to the Command of the Spanish Armada' in *Historical Journal*, Vol 12. 1969.

Ubaldino, Petruccio. *A Discourse concerning the Spanish fleete invadinge Englande in the yeare 1588* (translated by Dr Magri-Mahon and Miss Painter and edited by G. P. B. Naish) in *Naval Miscellany*, Vol. IV. Navy Records Society. London, 1952.

Vandenesse, J. de. *Journal des Voyages de Philippe II*, Vol. 4. Brussels, 1882.

Waldman, Milton. *Elizabeth and Leicester.* London, 1946.

Wallace, Willard M. *Sir Walter Ralegh.* London, 1959.

Walsh, William T. *Philip II.* New York, 1937.

Wernham, R. B. 'Queen Elizabeth and the Portugal Expedition of 1589' in *English Historical Review*. No. CCLVIII. January 1951.

White, Henry. *The Massacre of St Bartholomew.* London, 1868.

Wiesener, Louis. *The Youth of Queen Elizabeth 1533-1558.* Translated by Charlotte M. Yonge. London, 1879.

Williams, Neville. *Contraband Cargoes.* London, 1959.

Williams, Neville. *Elizabeth Queen of England.* London, 1967.

Williamson, James A. *Age of Drake.* London, 1946.

Williamson, James A. *Hawkins of Plymouth.* London, 1949.

PICTURE ACKNOWLEDGEMENTS

1. Windsor Castle. Copyright reserved: reproduced by gracious permission of Her Majesty the Queen. 2. Copyright Museo Del Prado, Madrid. Photo: David Manso. 3. Copyright Museo Del Prado, Madrid. Photo: David Manso. 4. Copyright Bibliothèque Nationale, Paris. 5. Photo copyright Thomson Newspapers Ltd. 6. Photo: MAS. 7. Bodorgan, Anglesey. By permission of Lieut.-Col. Sir George Tapps-Gervis-Meyrick. Photo: John Reay. Photo copyright: George Rainbird Ltd. 8. By courtesy of the Plymouth City Art Gallery. 9. National Portrait Gallery, London. 10. National Gallery of Ireland. 11. National Portrait Gallery, London.

Index

254